AF361521

VOLATILE WHITENESS

Race, Cinema, and Europeanization in Spain

Volatile Whiteness

Race, Cinema, and Europeanization in Spain

MARTIN REPINECZ

UNIVERSITY OF TORONTO PRESS
Toronto Buffalo London

© University of Toronto Press 2025
Toronto Buffalo London
utorontopress.com
Printed in the USA

ISBN 978-1-4875-3923-8 (cloth)   ISBN 978-1-4875-3924-5 (EPUB)
                                  ISBN 978-1-4875-3925-2 (PDF)

Toronto Iberic

Library and Archives Canada Cataloguing in Publication

Title: Volatile whiteness : race, cinema, and Europeanization in Spain /
   Martin Repinecz.
Names: Repinecz, Martin, author.
Series: Toronto Iberic.
Description: Series statement: Toronto Iberic | Includes bibliographical references and
   index.
Identifiers: Canadiana (print) 20240502434 | Canadiana (ebook) 20240502701 |
   ISBN 9781487539238 (cloth) | ISBN 9781487539252 (PDF) | ISBN 9781487539245 (EPUB)
Subjects: LCSH: Motion pictures – Spain – History. | LCSH: Race in motion pictures. |
   LCSH: Spain – Race relations.
Classification: LCC PN1993.5.S7 R47 2025 | DDC 791.43094609/045 – dc23

Cover design: Heng Wee Tan

We wish to acknowledge the land on which the University of Toronto Press
operates. This land is the traditional territory of the Wendat, the Anishnaabeg, the
Haudenosaunee, the Métis, and the Mississaugas of the Credit First Nation.

This book has been published with the assistance of the University
of San Diego.

University of Toronto Press acknowledges the financial support of the Government of
Canada, the Canada Council for the Arts, and the Ontario Arts Council, an agency of
the Government of Ontario, for its publishing activities.

Contents

Illustrations

Acknowledgments

This book would not have been possible without support from various entities and individuals. I am especially grateful to my home institution, the University of San Diego, for a variety of travel grants, course releases, and subvention funds that allowed me to have the time and resources to write this book. I am particularly indebted to Deans Noelle Norton and Kristin Moran.

I also express my warmest thanks to the University of Toronto Press, especially my editor, Mark Thompson, whose guidance and support for this project have been tremendously helpful. Likewise, I also thank the entire staff of the Filmoteca Española, especially José Luis Estarrona, Trinidad del Río Sánchez, and Anabel Bueno, who assisted me over a period of several years with viewing films and obtaining access to many of the images printed in this book. Similarly, I thank Bertelsmann Music Group and Warner Chappell Music for granting me permission to print the lyrics of Peret's song "El mig amic." I also thank Hal Leonard LLC for allowing me to reprint the lyrics of Peret's song "El gitano Antón" and the Latin American original on which it is based, "El negro bembón."

I am immensely grateful to friends and colleagues who read earlier drafts of my chapters, including Jeffrey Coleman, Mary Kate Donovan, Rebecca Ingram, Tamara Moya Jorge, Gema Pérez Sánchez, Jonathon Repinecz, and Eva Woods-Peiró, as well the anonymous readers of my manuscript. Their thoughtful feedback enabled me to strengthen this work as much as possible.

I absolutely could not, under any circumstances, have written this book without the steadfast companionship and encouragement of a number of close friends both at USD and in my field. I am indebted in this regard to USD colleagues Peter Mena and Greg Prieto, as well as to my writing group colleagues Dean Albritton, Joanne Britland, Leslie

Harkema, Catalina Iannone, Gaby Miller, Anita Savo, Wan Tang, and Sarah Thomas. There were innumerable moments when I simply did not have the energy, confidence or resilience to keep going. If I somehow managed to pull myself to the finish line, it is largely thanks to them.

Similarly, the intellectual community afforded by TRECE (Taller de Raza, Etnicidad y Ciudadanía en España), a group of scholars who work on critical race studies in Spain, provided me indispensable inspiration and motivation to write this book. I offer my warmest thanks to all those who have joined us in planning or participating in our seminars, conferences, and reading sessions. Although there are perhaps too many to name individually here, your insights have proven critical to this project and to my growth as a scholar more broadly.

I am also grateful to my California-based colleagues Roberta Johnson, Santiago Morales-Rivera, and Maite Zubiaurre who convinced me that this project needed to be a book, and not just an article, after I first presented a piece of it as an invited lecture at UCLA for the Peninsularistas of Southern California Symposium years ago. I also offer my heartfelt gratitude to H. Rosi Song and Benita Sampedro, whose expressions of kindness and support over the years have simply been too numerous to list here.

I will never be able to repay the debt I owe to my PhD advisers from Duke, Stephanie Sieburth and Roberto Dainotto, whose guidance and training profoundly shape all my intellectual endeavours. The same is true of Tabea Linhard, who introduced me to the field of Spanish film studies as an undergraduate in 2004, as well as Justin Crumbaugh, who ignited my curiosity about late-Francoist popular cinema in a graduate seminar he taught at Duke in 2008.

On a personal note, I thank my immediate family, including my parents, Marty and Yolanda Repinecz, my twin brother and academic co-conspirator Jonathon, as well as my partner Bhanu Yerra. There are no words that could adequately express my gratitude for your love.

San Diego, California,
December 2023

VOLATILE WHITENESS

Race, Cinema, and Europeanization in Spain

Introduction

In her 2017 book *Las que se atrevieron* ("The women who dared"), a semifictional memoir about interracial relationships in Spain between the 1960s and 1980s, contemporary Afro-Spanish writer and journalist Lucía Mbomío Rubio describes an instance of racial aggression between kindergarten-aged children at school. When Edjing, a little girl born to a Black[1] father and a white mother in Spain in the mid-1970s, begins to attend kindergarten in 1979, a white girl at the kindergarten named Maribel decides that Edjing does not deserve to eat bread. Maribel tells Edjing that the reason why is: "Por negra" ("Because you're Black";[2] 49). For several days, as bread is passed out to the children during lunch time, Maribel steals Edjing's bread. But Maribel then decides that Edjing should also not be allowed to use silverware, and so begins to systematically hide Edjing's bread *and* her silverware. As a result, "Edjing se vio obligada a comer con las manos 'como una salvaje,' decían todos" ("Edjing was forced to eat with her hands 'like a savage,' everyone said"; 49). Edjing feels pressured to endure this humiliation in silence, and so the behaviour persists until the school cafeteria workers notify the teacher, who in turn, tells Edjing's mother.

This anecdote, which is based on interviews that Mbomío Rubio conducted with real Spanish women who built interracial families during this period, is striking for a number of reasons. How could anti-Black prejudices have become so deeply ingrained in Spanish culture in a year like 1979, when the Black population in Spain was still very small?[3] Where and how would children have absorbed such prejudices in a society that was still overwhelmingly white? And why did Maribel feel that it was her duty to return Edjing to an imagined position of savagery? In short: how could a toddler like Maribel have come to understand Edjing's presence in her classroom as a threat or injury to her own white privilege, or to the racial purity of her community and country?

While there are numerous potential answers to these questions, it is plausible to imagine that one likely source of Maribel's attitudes was mass media. It is revealing, for instance, that a variety of Spanish-born writers of African descent, including not only Mbomío Rubio, but also Desirée Bela-Lobedde, Silvia Albert Sopale, and Rubén H. Bermúdez, have all attested in their works to being ridiculed during their youth by other children at school who referenced images from television, film, advertising, and music as they did so. Albert Sopale, for instance, includes a scene in her 2018 play *No es país para negras* ("No country for Black women") in which white children mock her in the classroom and at recess by singing her lyrics from the "Cola Cao" song, which was written in 1946 and exploits cartoonish, highly stereotyped images of Blacks to advertise a chocolate drink (90–2). In addition to the Cola-Cao song, Mbomío-Rubio and Bermúdez also mention the Conguitos commercials, which date back to the 1960s and also link caricatured Blacks to chocolate, as routine sources of inspiration for childhood teasing (Mbomío Rubio *Hija del camino* 22–3; R. Bermúdez 24). Bela-Lobedde's list of source material for schoolyard taunts includes songs by popular French singer Georgie Dann, whose summer hits of the 1970s and 1980s regularly featured highly stereotyped narratives about Blacks (*Ser mujer negra* 31–41). She also recalls constantly being compared with prevalent images of Blacks from American television of the 1990s, ranging from actors like Will Smith, to NBA stars like Michael Jordan, to rappers and hip-hop musicians (*Minorías* 94).

A notable feature about the above cited works of Bela-Lobedde, Bermúdez, Mbomío Rubio, and Albert-Sopale is that many of them point to the importance of understanding how contemporary racial imaginaries were affected by media culture of earlier decades. Despite the age of advertisements like the "Cola Cao" song or the Conguitos commercials, their widespread circulation in later decades has caused them to remain highly influential in shaping ideas of race in Spain across multiple generations – including that of these writers, who were born in the late 1970s or early 1980s. Mbomío Rubio's text *Las que se atrevieron* goes a step further by inviting us to imagine how the racial imaginaries these cultural materials generated might have impacted not only her own generation, but also the generation of her parents, whose story constitutes the first of her book's six chapters. Through its narratives of widespread ostracism, condemnation, and prejudice against interracial families that formed between the late 1960s and early 1980s, this text underscores the importance of understanding the formation and circulation of racial imaginaries at a time when immigration to Spain was still in its infancy – namely, late Francoism and the first decade of democracy.

Although the "Cola-Cao" song and the Conguitos commercials are among the most frequently referenced examples of how racist images of the past continue to affect Spain's present,[4] these marketing materials were part of a larger domestic media universe that was replete with images of racialized groups such as Blacks, Arabs, and the Roma.[5] As I argue in this book, these images were used to channel and assuage anxieties related to the perceived volatility of Spain's whiteness, which had been imagined as rising and falling at different moments in history. As we will see, anxieties about the fluctuating quality of Spain's whiteness became especially pronounced in popular cinema of the 1960s, 70s, and early 80s, a period that immediately preceded what I call the "era of immigration" in Spain.[6] During late Francoism and the Transition, Spain experienced a range of dramatic social, economic, and political changes that included massive rural-to-urban migration, an economic boom driven by tourism, a pronounced loosening of traditional gender and sexual mores, and of course, a political transition from dictatorship to democracy. In addition, these decades also coincided with the dissolution of Spain's African empire, which occurred between 1956 and 1975, as well as the nation's evolution from a producer of emigration to a destination for migrants from the Global South. These various transformations arguably culminated in Spain's admission to the European Union in 1986, an event that symbolically announced the erosion of Spain's longstanding reputation as an "Africa of Europe." Spain's admission into the EU invited fantasies that the nation had finally, at long last, emerged as a fully-fledged member of a postimperial Global North, while shedding its earlier association with decidedly unmodern qualities like poverty, backwardness, political repression, stubborn colonialism, or intransigent Catholicism.

During the 1960s, 1970s, and 1980s, popular cinema – by which I mean films that appealed to mass domestic audiences – mobilized domestic and transnational discourses of whiteness in order to help Spanish audiences envision their shifting place in the global community. To do so, a variety of film genres like comedy, musical, religious, and *quinqui* (urban crime thriller) films were saturated not only with stereotypical representations of racialized peoples, but also, as we will see throughout the chapters of this book, with white Spanish characters who struggled not to slip backward into a condition of racialized savagery. Hence, even as dominant discourses heralded the nation's Europeanization, popular cinema harboured anxieties that Spain's racial whiteness, a key facet of its ability to claim European belonging, was just as precarious and unstable as ever, and that the nation could degenerate back into an "Africa of Europe" at any moment.

Although many of these genres were long dismissed by cinephiles and academics, popular films of the 1960s to the 1980s were seen in their day by large swathes of the population, especially the working and lower middle classes. Likewise, they continue to circulate amongst contemporary audiences through television programs such as *Cine de barrio* ("Neighbourhood cinema") or *Historia de nuestro cine* ("History of our cinema"), as well as through myriad remakes and innumerable allusions in contemporary media culture. In this way, much of this popular cinema culture has maintained an enduring presence in the national consciousness today. Of particular note in these various genres is the frequency with which Spanish characters cross back and forth over what W.E.B. Du Bois famously theorized as a global colour line separating white people from nonwhite groups (*The Souls of Black Folk* 15). It is also striking that popular cinema's pervasive racial anxieties were coursing through mass film audiences well before the late 1980s or 1990s, the years in which immigration has generally been understood as visibly impacting the Spanish demographic landscape. Although studies of Spanish immigration cinema have largely focused on films from the 1990s forward that depict immigration empathetically,[7] I argue that the abundant depictions of racialized groups in earlier popular cinema primed Spanish audiences' views of these groups, such as Blacks and North Africans, even before they formed large demographic minorities in Spanish society. As a result, I argue that popular cinema of the 1960s to 1980s must be considered an essential precursor to Spain's immigration cinema.

Why Whiteness? Why Spain?

Before delving further into the particulars of this book's methodology, choice of period and corpus, and chapter summaries, we must first consider its effort to contribute to a larger goal of bringing critical race studies, and especially critical whiteness studies, to the study of Spanish culture. Critical whiteness studies aims to unmask what is perhaps the most pernicious and illusive aspect of white supremacy: namely, the normative invisibility of racial whiteness. The hegemonic idea that white bodies are raceless while nonwhite bodies are racially marked pervades nearly every society marked by white/nonwhite racial hierarchies; it has been argued that this allows racial inequalities to persist despite the ostensible disavowal of racism (Bonilla-Silva) or, as the discourse of the "post-racial" holds, to be imagined as a thing of the past altogether (St. Louis; Boulila). Despite the institutionalization of whiteness studies in academia over the last three decades, numerous critics, including some of the field's most prolific practitioners, have long wondered whether the aim of whiteness studies to destroy white supremacy by unveiling and deconstructing its inner workings is an inherently flawed project. The fear has been that whiteness studies can easily be co-opted into an expression of white pride, can be manipulated into buttressing discourses of white victimization or white injury by nonwhites, and can become a fundamentally self-serving vehicle for white people to alleviate their guilt (Wiegman 115–24; Hill 2–7).

It is worth bearing in mind, however, that at its inception, critical whiteness studies was not a project initiated solely by white scholars for white readers. As France Winddance Twine and Charles Gallagher have observed, the evolution of academic whiteness studies can be categorized in three waves, and the first two of these consisted predominantly of works by US African-American theorists. Twine and Gallagher mark the writings of W.E.B. Du Bois, including *The Philadelphia Negro* (1899), *The Souls of Black Folk* (1903), "The Souls of White Folk" (1920), and *Black Reconstruction in America* (1936), as constituting the first wave of whiteness studies. Several of the arguments articulated in Du Bois's works would later be recognized as some of the field's most enduring and deeply examined insights. Among these is his theorization in *The Souls of Black Folk* of a global colour line separating white from non-white peoples (15), as well as his seminal argument in *Black Reconstruction in America* that whiteness functions as a "public and psychological wage" for its beneficiaries (626).

The second wave of whiteness studies, which blossomed in the 1990s, also included many African-American theorists like Toni Morrison and Cheryl Harris, among others. In her foundational text *Playing in the Dark* (1992), Morrison famously contended that "[t]he scholarship that looks into the mind, imagination and behavior of slaves is valuable. But equally valuable is a serious intellectual effort to see what racial ideology does to the mind, imagination and behavior of masters" (1167). Similarly, in "Whiteness as Property," a founding text of critical race theory, Harris maintained that whiteness was construed as a form of property in American law, suggesting that it had evolved "from color to race to status to property as a progression historically rooted in white supremacy" (1714). These African-American thinkers were joined by white scholars such as Richard Dyer, whose influential book *White* focused on how myths of racial whiteness are propagated in transnational visual media, as well as historians such as David Roediger and Matthew Frye Jacobsen, who analysed the consolidation of US whiteness from a wide range of ethnic immigrant roots. A key takeaway from much of this second-wave work was the instability and artificiality of whiteness, whose boundaries shifted over time to include European immigrant groups once understood as nonwhite, such Irish Americans, Jewish Americans, or Italian Americans.[8]

The third wave of whiteness studies, which began in the 2000s, focused significantly on the ways in which whites attempted to "recuperate, reconstitute, and restore white identities and the supremacy of whiteness" in the wake of a number of destabilizing societal transformations, such as deindustrialization, decolonization, and the demise of segregation regimes like Jim Crow in the United States or Apartheid in South Africa (Twine and Gallagher 13). Although some scholars observed a decline in whiteness studies scholarship as the new millennium advanced, a global resurgence of far right and populist political movements in the 2010s has arguably reinvigorated the field's relevance (Kennedy et al. 1–2). Of particular importance to understand this phenomenon is the undeniable power of rhetorics of whiteness to galvanize anti-immigrant sentiment and rekindle imperial nostalgia. A few obvious examples include the election of Donald Trump in the United States in 2016, the electoral breakthrough of Spain's Vox party in 2018, and Brexit in 2020 – but a complete list of right-wing populist victories during this decade would undoubtedly be much longer.[9]

Despite its origins in US and anglophone cultural studies, critical whiteness studies has, over time, adopted an increasingly transnational purview, as its analytical frameworks have been applied to a variety of contexts ranging from Latin America, to Asia, Africa, and throughout Europe.[10] Even so, as numerous scholars have observed, the field has struggled to overcome its reputation as attuned primarily to the realities of the US and English-speaking countries (López 9; Persánch 4). In Spanish cultural studies, the impact of critical race or critical whiteness studies has been noticeable in the last two decades, although much work remains to be done. For instance, recent years have witnessed an increasing degree of scholarly attention afforded to the representation of racial minorities in hegemonic Spanish culture, as well as to cultural production created by racialized Spaniards.[11] With the exception of Silvia Bermúdez's study *Rocking the Boat*, whose purview begins in the 1980s, nearly all academic literature that addresses immigration and the voices of racialized Spaniards has focused its attention on a post-1990 period, as the 1990s is the decade that is most often understood as initiating what we might call the "era of immigration" in Spain. Likewise, studies of Spanish racial identities, including whiteness studies, in pre-immigration periods have also emerged in recent years.[12] Even so, the period I call "Europeanization," which includes the late-Franco era and first decade of democracy, has thus far received limited attention in any study of race in Spain. Similarly, studies that examine the popular culture of late Francoism and the Transition have also dedicated scant attention to issues of race or whiteness.[13]

In analysing Spain, this book begins from the premise that Western modernity, which is racialized as white by and within a hegemonic Global North, is "translated" and "readapted" by various cultures around the world (Bonnett 70). Yet this book also assumes, following Neda Maghbouleh, that for some groups, "whiteness can be intermittently granted and revoked" (5). Arguing against a "unidirectional story" of how various ethnicities or nationalities crossed the colour line from nonwhite to white, Maghbouleh argues that some groups' relationship to whiteness is shaped by a "racial hinge" – that is, their whiteness can be marked by a certain back-and-forth pattern of acquisition and loss – and they can even be seen as occupying whiteness and non-whiteness in different ways at the same time (4–5). The present book draws on this argument to suggest that the story of racial whiteness in Spain is similarly not unidirectional. On the contrary, as popular cinema of 1960s to the 1980s illustrates, Spanish viewers understood their journey towards whiteness as being marked by a jarring combination of both forward and backward movement, and even as they imagined themselves as becoming whiter, deep-seated anxieties about slipping backwards across the colour line remained embedded in the national consciousness. In this way, as the title of this book suggests, Spain's journey towards whiteness was – and, in my view, remains – marked by a certain turbulence and volatility, rather than by a straightforward metamorphosis from "Africa of Europe" to "Global North."

Indeed, it is possible to argue that Spanish whiteness has been volatile since its inception. Perhaps the oldest manifestation of an idea of racial whiteness in Spain can be found in the idea of *casticismo*, the notion of a distinctively Iberian ethnoracial heritage that has informed many articulations of Spanish racial identity from the early modern era onward. As Christiane Stallaert writes, the concept of *casticismo* evolved in conjunction with the gradual process of religious homogenization of the Iberian Peninsula that occurred throughout the Middle Ages. In particular, she notes, while a *castizo* identity was always regarded as mixed due to the various histories of conquest and settlement that marked early Iberian history, the advance of the so-called Christian *Reconquista* ("Reconquest") caused the term to gradually be defined as the exclusion of Moorish and Jewish blood (20–2). Towards the end of the *Reconquista*, various disciplinary mechanisms, such as blood purity laws, the Inquisition, and religious expulsions, were instituted to punish or remove those who could not prove their "pure" Christian, *castizo* heritage. George Mariscal has interpreted the ethnoreligious stratification of early modern Spain as a kind of "racial formation" that predated Europe's conquest of the New World (9). This argument refutes the oft-repeated critical assumption that "a modern conception of race does not occur until the rise of Europe and the arrival of Europeans in the Americas" (Omi and Winant, qtd. in Mariscal 9).

From the sixteenth century onward, Spain's *castizo* identity became inextricably intertwined with its emergence as a global imperial power. On one level, imperial Spain's extensive participation in the transnational projects of Indigenous dispossession and the African slave trade played a pivotal role in shaping what W.E.B. Du Bois would later refer to as a global colour line predicated on worldwide white domination. Yet, on another level, even at the height of its imperial trajectory, Spain's belonging on the white side of the colour line was considered circumspect by other European powers. This is most tellingly manifest in the myth of the Black Legend, which first surfaced in the sixteenth century as rumours of Spanish brutality in the New World generated a European perception of Spain as barbaric and fanatical. These discourses maintained a strong foothold in both domestic and transnational cultural imaginaries of Spain in subsequent eras. As Susan Martin-Márquez has pointed out, "From the start the Black Legend was a racialized concept," as it enabled other European powers such as Britain, which was eager to pave the way for its own colonial endeavours, to interpret Spaniards' presumably exceptional cruelty in the Americas as a byproduct of the savagery they had inherited from their racial mixture with Moors (*Disorientations* 40–1). Barbara Fuchs echoes this assertion, noting that the idea of Spain as "black" served to highlight simultaneously Spain's perceived moral depravity, as well as its racial associations "with Islam, with Africa, with dark peoples" (117).

The central contradiction of the Black Legend, in which Spain's historical role as a global colonial power contrasted with its status as an "Africa of Europe," was perhaps most apparent during periods of colonial loss. As Baltasar Fra-Molinero has argued, the Spanish-American War of 1898, in which Spain was forced to cede its last remaining colonies in Asia and the Americas to the United States, "increased [Spain's] sense of inadequacy as a 'white' European country;" consequently, the feelings of imperial loss and melancholia that this war generated were widely perceived as a "crisis of whiteness" (148). María deGuzmán has corroborated this idea by attesting that depictions of Spain in US media of the time often portrayed the country as closer to the colonized world than to that of the colonizers (xxix). The dubious nature of Spain's whiteness is especially apparent in two American political cartoons that depict Spain in the context of the Spanish-American War. In the first, which was published in the 9 July 1898 issue of the satirical magazine *Judge*, Spain is represented as a murderous, uncivilized ape – an animal long used as a symbol to connote Black inferiority – with blood on its hands (figure 0.1). The blood refers to the sensationalist although unsubstantiated popular theory from the period that Spanish military forces were responsible for the explosion of an American ship called the U.S.S. Maine, in which more than 260 US crew members and officers were killed. In the second cartoon, which was published in the 27 April 1898 issue of the humour magazine *Puck*, Spain is portrayed as a weakened, forlorn king, with visibly North African features, whose backwards-pointing sword bears the inscription "400 years of misrule" (figure 0.2). The boat is sailing away from an island, where a tall, proud Uncle Sam clasps the hand of a Black woman bearing a Cuban flag. The image plainly declares that dark-skinned races of the colonies cannot survive without white salvation and protection; thus, the racialized Spanish colonizer, at once European and not, must be expelled.

Although these cartoons were created by and for viewers based in the United States, their depiction of Spain as more akin to Black or Arab countries than to American whiteness echoed paranoias that were also prevalent in Spain, where turn-of-the-century intellectuals wondered whether the "elementos 'orientales' de la sangre española" ("'Oriental' elements of Spanish blood") were to blame for the nation's imperial decline (Álvarez Junco 456). Indeed, although the conquest of the New World had given Spain a claim to belonging in global whiteness, images such as these political cartoons implied that, precisely at a time when European imperialism in Africa was expanding, Spain's historical racial contamination by various heritages deemed inferior, whether Jewish, Islamic, Roma or African, meant that it could not be imagined as on par with other so-called white countries.

Significantly, however, in the ensuing decades, Spain would attempt to reassert its belonging in global whiteness by developing an African empire that could symbolically replace the one it lost in the Americas and Asia. The African empire would emerge from a smattering of territories across the African continent that Spain had acquired over the eighteenth, nineteenth and early twentieth centuries. These included: present-day Equatorial Guinea, which Spain obtained from Portugal under the terms of the Treaty of El Pardo in 1778; present-day Ifni, which was ceded to Spain by Morocco in 1860; present-day Western Sahara, which it obtained in 1884 as a consequence of the Conference of Berlin; and the Moroccan Protectorate, which was acquired through a treaty signed with France in 1912. Although most of these territories had been

Figure 0.1. "The Spanish Brute Adds Mutilation to Murder." *Judge* magazine, 9 July 1898.

Figure 0.2. Illustration from *Puck* magazine, 27 April 1898.

acquired before 1898, Spain's efforts to develop a significant colonial infrastructure remained limited until the early twentieth century, when the "crisis of whiteness" provoked by the so-called disaster of 1898 created a need for a new empire (Fra-Molinero 148). Yet, as I argue in chapter 2, the loss of the later African empire, which occurred between 1956 and 1975, also produced a "crisis of whiteness" because it destabilized the Franco regime's intertwined promises of upward economic mobility and becoming European. Despite the regime's concerted efforts to suppress information about decolonization during these years through *materia reservada* (classified information) laws and relentless media censorship, anxieties that the loss of the African empire would trigger a loss of whiteness nonetheless permeate popular cinema of the era. As we will see, a number of films attempted to "whiten" the nation's reputation by absolving it of both the horrors of colonial violence and the embarrassment of colonial loss.

The volatility of Spain's imperial identity, which rose and fell in the Americas, Asia, and Africa across different moments in history, accentuated the volatility of its whiteness, which shifted back and forth across an imaginary colour line depending on the time and position from which one viewed it. The shapeshifting quality of Spain's whiteness acquires a further layer of complexity when we consider the close association of Spanish national identity with Roma culture from the eighteenth century onward (Charnon Deutsch 50–4, Fra-Molinero 149–52). The acceleration of European tourism to Spain during the eighteenth and nineteenth centuries led to a proliferation of art, music, and literature produced about Spain that accentuated its presumably romantic and exotic features; more often than not, such works were set in Andalusia, a region whose conspicuous Islamic heritage and large Roma populations stood out to foreigners as emblematic of Spain's essential difference. As Charnon-Deutsch has observed, the stereotypical figure of the Andalusian Gypsy woman emerged as a dominant symbol of Spain abroad and signalled a conflation in the European popular imaginary of Andalusian, Roma, and Spanish national identities (Charnon Deutsch 11).

Over time, the figure of the mythical Andalusian Gypsy, as well as its connotations of racial exoticism or distinctiveness, would also become pervasive in domestic popular culture. This is demonstrated by the omnipresence of the "Gypsy woman" trope in a wide range of theatrical, literary, cinematic, and musical cultural production of the twentieth century. These cultural forms epitomized the nation's ambivalent, fluctuating and precarious whiteness. In her landmark study of folkloric musical cinema from the 1940s and 50s, Eva Woods Peiró has argued that this genre's central figure of the "screen Gypsy" served to perform Spanish modernity by projecting a stable, coherent vision of the nation's racial identity. Specifically, she argues, folkloric musicals of this period created "symbolic frontiers" that enabled Spain to distinguish its dominant race from "internal ethnic others," such as the Roma, "who were seen as more closely related to Arabs than to northern Spaniards and Europeans" (3). Because the "screen Gypsy" character was usually played by *paya* (non-Roma) actors and was often assimilated to the dominant society via marriage by the end of the film, these films also simultaneously narrated a whitening of Spanish identity. As a result, Spanish racial identity in these films emerged as simultaneously "whitewashed and racialized" (2).

When Franco came to power after the wake of the Spanish Civil War, he sought to capitalize on the vision of Spanish racial identity as a fusion or blend of various racial heritages, including its African, Moorish, and Roma elements, because he "believed that racial strength was based on mixture and hybridity ... not the domination of one pure race over all mixed ones" (Goode 1). Franco's celebration of Spain's racial fusion was intimately related to his ambitions for colonial expansion. As Woods-Peiró observes, Franco imagined himself as carrying on the torch of the Catholic Monarchs, "restoring Spain to its golden days of global empire" by portraying the nation as "the racially fused imperialist contender in capitalist modernity" (16). Franco's preference for the idea of Spanish racial fusion or hybridity proved useful, as this notion enabled Spain to distinguish its racial discourses from those of Nazi Germany and thus claim that racism had never gained a foothold in Spain (Goode 1–3). A similar mythology about Spain's uniquely anti-racist orientation undergirded the Franco regime's justifications for maintaining imperial control over its various African territories during the 1950s and 1960s despite a global tendency towards decolonization (Nerín 12; Stucki 129). The idea that Spain had never been racist, either at home or in its empire, thus became an entrenched pillar of Francoist ideology, as it served to promote the idea that Spain was not only different but also superior to the rest of Europe and the United States.

By the 1960s, however, these ideologically rigid conceptions of Spanish "difference" had begun to weaken and were gradually giving way to a new discourse of Spain's Europeanization. The Stabilization Plan of 1959 was a key trigger of this shift, as it aimed to integrate the country into global capitalism by liberalizing Spanish markets and attracting foreign investment. It also played a key role in igniting Spain's tourism boom of the 1960s and 1970s, for which the "Spain Is Different" tourism campaign aimed to perform "modernity *a la española*" by commodifying the nation's culture and folklore (Crumbaugh, *Destination Dictatorship* 4). Increased contact between Spaniards and other Europeans also occurred through emigration to Northern Europe, as about three million Spaniards emigrated to Northern European countries France, Belgium, Switzerland, or Germany between 1959 and 1974 (Richardson 68).

The myth of becoming European, however, was often punctured by difficult realities. In addition to being marked by both internal and international mass migrations, which included the nation's evolution into a receiver of immigration, the period between the 1960s and the 1980s was also characterized by prolonged spikes in unemployment, uncertainty about social change and the loss of Francoism, decaying standards of living on urban peripheries, and the general economic fallout of the global petroleum crisis of 1973. As I will demonstrate, the turbulent social and economic conditions of this period triggered historically rooted Black Legend anxieties that the nation's imaginary journey towards Europeanization might be derailed at any moment and might slip backwards into a state of degeneracy and primitiveness.

During late Francoism, anxieties about the loss of whiteness were palpable not only in relation to the loss of the African empire, but perhaps even more acutely as a result of Spanish emigration to Northern Europe. This reality, which was both an economic necessity and a source of anxiety to the Franco regime, highlighted working-class Spaniards' subaltern position in European host countries where, as various texts from the era demonstrate, Spaniards were often perceived as racialized within their host societies (see chapter 1). In the wake of the global petroleum crisis of 1973, apprehensions about emigration became enmeshed with anxieties that Spain was being humiliated by Arab countries, the perceived villains of the crisis (see chapter 4). After the Transition, as immigration to Spain began to accelerate, a feeling of dread quickly emerged that an already struggling nation would soon be overrun by racially "inferior" groups. That paranoias about an invasion of racialized immigrants can be traced back to popular culture of the late 1970s is striking in itself, given that actual immigration during those years was still minimal (see chapter 4). Anxieties about Roma encroachment on mainstream Spanish society can be traced back even earlier, as massive rural-to-urban migrations triggered fears of Roma racial contagion on mainstream Spanish society from the 1960s onwards (see chapter 3).

By portraying emigration, colonial loss, immigration, and Roma contamination as symptomatic manifestations of the perennial Black Legend, popular cinema of late Francoism and the Transition channeled Spanish aspirations of achieving European belonging as well as its fears of forever remaining an "Africa of Europe." Through their frequent depictions of Spaniards as traversing the boundaries of whiteness, such as the white/Black, white/Roma, or white/Arab colour lines, these films simultaneously accentuated Spaniards' ability to acquire whiteness, as well as their fears of losing it even after gaining it. Spanish fears of the volatility of whiteness during this period were symptomatic of a deeper colonial memory, given that the Black Legend itself constituted a loss of whiteness despite early modern Spain's historical role in establishing a global colour line.

Why Popular Cinema?

In a memorable scene of *El negro que tenía el alma blanca* ("The Black man with a white soul," dir. Hugo del Carril, 1951), Emma (María Rosa Salgado), a young white woman who aspires to become a dancer, has a bone-chilling nightmare: she dreams that she becomes Black. As she sleeps, she imagines herself in a mysterious dreamscape, surrounded by scantily clad Black men playing drums. Amidst the cobwebs, skulls, and dead animals hanging from the trees, two masked men dance around her and wrap a chain around her body; they slowly lead her towards another Black man standing on a platform. It is Peter Wald, an Afro-Cuban singer with whom she has been paired to dance in real life, but who, in her dream, has transformed into an ominous monster. With her wide-open eyes, flowy nightgown, and wavy locks of brown hair, she bears a marked resemblance to Dorothy approaching the Wizard of Oz as she advances towards the sinister Wald. Cross-cutting between close-ups of Emma's face and those of cackling Black men build tension towards the scene's climax, in which Emma, a paragon of white femininity, suddenly reappears on the screen in full blackface. Her image then briefly doubles to show her white self looking on in horror at her Black self (figure 0.3). After she faints, she is led to an altar, where extreme-close-ups of a dagger imply that she is about to be sacrificed in a cannibalistic ritual. A scream punctuates the scene, and Emma wakes up safely in her bedroom – and still safely white.

Although the film's campy portrayal of racist tropes such as Black hypersexuality and cannibalism was far from original, this scene is striking because it represents one of Spanish cinema's common strategies for channeling anxieties about the loss of whiteness – namely, the nightmare sequence in which a white character imagines being overpowered or killed by a racialized character. This trope appears in several other films. A similar example can be found in Luis García Berlanga's classic film *Bienvenido, Mr. Marshall* ("Welcome, Mr. Marshall," 1953) in a sequence in which the character Don Luis,

Figure 0.3. A still from Emma's nightmare in *El negro que tenía el alma blanca* (dir. Hugo del Carril, 1951).

who is strongly reminiscent of Don Quixote, dreams that he has discovered the Americas but is thrown into a boiling cauldron by natives after landing ashore. Yet another example occurs in *Un beso en el puerto* ("A kiss at the port," dir. Ramón Torrado, 1965), when the ultra-famous singer and actor Manolo Escobar dreams that he has found himself in a highly stereotypical Gypsy encampment and must wrestle with a demonic Gypsy man who tries to stab him. Fears of the loss of whiteness also underpin graphic rape sequences that depict white women being assaulted by racialized men, a pattern that emerges in films like *Encrucijada para una monja* ("A nun at the crossroads," dir. Julio Buchs, 1967), *Esa mujer* (dir. Mario Camus, 1969), or the horror film *La noche de los brujos* ("The night of the sorcerers," dir. Armando de Ossorio, 1974).

As these examples illustrate, popular cinema offers a rich archive for thinking about how mass media in Spain both articulated and fuelled apprehensions about the instability of Spain's whiteness throughout the twentieth century, especially in the decades that marked the period of Europeanization. Consequently, this book centres its analysis on commercial genres and films of the so-called Viejo Cine Español

("Old Spanish Cinema," or VCE), a term often used to describe popular genres of late Francoism and their democratic-era successors, rather than on films that belonged to the Nuevo Cine Español ("New Spanish Cinema," or NCE), a body of state-funded art cinema that whose production was incentivized primarily to be shown in foreign art festivals (Triana Toribio, *Spanish National Cinema* 71–7). VCE was consumed far more extensively by domestic audiences than NCE during these years; as a result, it can offer a better understanding of how recurring tendencies, patterns, and tropes reached large audiences across gender, class, and geographical boundaries. In this way, the book aims to contribute to an increasingly rich bibliography on popular film genres from the period, such as studies of comedy (Marsh, Crumbaugh, Huerta Floriano and Pérez Morán), religious film (J. Pérez), *quinqui* cinema (Whittaker, González del Pozo), child musicals (Hogan), as well as comparative approaches (Lázaro Reboll and Willis). Although most of these studies focus on individual genres, subgenres, or cycles, the present book takes a comparative approach, as it is interested in exploring how a popular imaginary of race emerged across multiple genres.

The popular film genres I focus on in this book, comedy, musicals, religious and *quinqui* films, did not all share the same audiences. Some genres, like the *macho ibérico* comedy, catered primarily to working-class men, especially those who had recently migrated from the country to the city.[14] Others, such as religious movies, especially those that revolved around nuns, seemed to appeal especially to female audiences (J. Pérez, *Confessional Cinema* 120). The gendering of audiences is similarly noticeable in films that appealed to younger viewers. Marisol, for instance, was known in her era as an idol for young girls, while *quinqui* films were known to have strong viewer base of adolescent boys. At the same time, reconstructing the audiences of these films is not always an easy task. One major challenge is that box office records were not collected in Spain until 1965, which makes it difficult both to measure the success of films made before this year, and also to compare their success to films made later. The most useful approach to this problem has been proposed by Valeria Camporesi, who traced the number of weeks that films from this era were shown in the Madrid theatre in which they debuted as a way of measuring their popularity (119–26). Yet even this approach is only a rough one, as it does not capture how films performed in smaller cities or rural areas, or how well they were received as they travelled away from the high prestige theatres to lower prestige ones. Even after box office records were systematically collected from 1965 onward, they were often deliberately tampered with, and did not include the *cine de barrio* (neighbourhood cinema) circuit, where films could be shown in continuous session even after they had been removed from the release or re-release circuit (Gómez-Sierra 96). Although *cines de barrio*, a crucial site of popular cinema consumption, were common in Spain throughout much of the twentieth century, they declined from the late 1960s onward due to the advent of television, yet remained relevant until at least until the early 1980s, as Mery Cuesta attests in her analysis of *quinqui* cinema (96).

The arrival of television, of course, not only affected *cines de barrio*, but cinema viewership overall. Box office statistics paint a bleak picture of the effect of television on domestic film consumption: after reaching a high point of 123 million spectators in 1968, viewership of domestic films in theatres declined every year after 1969, dropping to 78 million in 1975 and 35 million in 1979 (Camporesi 76). Yet television also offered new opportunities for a rebirth of Spanish film viewership, as many Spanish films from earlier periods were routinely rebroadcast on television from the 1970s forward and tended to attract large audiences. Domestic film viewership on TV benefitted from the establishment of screen quotas in 1983, according to which at least 20 per cent of films broadcast on *Televisión Española* were required to be Spanish; this number jumped to 25 per cent in 1987 (Camporesi 93–4). Camporesi's analysis further demonstrates that Spanish films shown on television received comparable viewership to foreign ones and also that audiences throughout the 1980s showed a particular interest in domestic genre films from earlier eras, such as Franco-era comedies, musicals, and religious films (94). In the 1980s, the afterlife of these older film genres and cycles was similarly extended by the advent of VHS technology, which was accompanied by a flourishing of video rental and direct-to-video industries. A case in point is a director like Mariano Ozores, who, thanks to the direct-to-video market, was able to continue making Francoism-style slapstick comedies until the early 1990s despite the strict quality standards instituted by the Miró law in 1983 (Ikaz 180).

From the mid-1990s onward, the enduring popularity of late-Francoist and early-democratic popular cinema would be further nourished by television programs such as *Cine de barrio* and *Historia de nuestro cine*, which have been broadcast on channels operated by *Televisión Española* since 1995 and 2015, respectively. As Duncan Wheeler has observed, in 2011, five of the top seven domestic films watched on Spanish television were – still! – popular comedies, musicals, and religious films of the Franco era, which reached audiences precisely through programs like *Cine de barrio* (142). Furthermore, he notes, a great deal of older popular cinema has achieved a cult status among younger viewers, as "hipsters in the Malasaña area of Madrid or El Raval in Barcelona can be seen wearing T-shirts of Paco Martínez Soria … alongside the names of some of his iconic film titles: *Abuelo, Made in Spain*, and *La ciudad no es para mí* (155). For Wheeler, it is precisely the familiarity and predictability of popular cinema's "lifelong actors" that foments this cinema's lasting appeal to transgenerational audiences (153). After all, the characters played by actors like Martínez Soria, Alfredo Landa, Gracita Morales, Concha Velasco, Tony Leblanc, and a host of others "frequently maintain continuity albeit under radically different circumstances and across different media" (153). In recent years, even elite circles of the Spanish film establishment have re-evaluated the legacy of much of this cinema. This is demonstrated by the designation of Mariano Ozores, whose extensive oeuvre of slapstick comedies was long regarded as epitomizing the aesthetic poverty of Spanish popular cinema, as the winner of a lifetime achievement *Goya de Honor* in 2016.

However, little scholarship has posited the question of what effects Spanish popular film culture of the 1960s to 1980s might have on contemporary Spain's racialized communities. In light of the relationship between media images and racial exclusion outlined by Afro-Spanish writers like Mbomío Rubio, Bela-Lobedde, Bermúdez, or Albert-Sopale, I argue that it is important to approach these films *not only* from the perspective of what meanings they might have had for their for their original viewers or why they might be beloved by their contemporary fans. Although those are certainly questions that this book engages, I argue that we must *also* ask how these films might have shaped Spaniards' views of racialized communities in their original era, and how they might continue to do so today. In other words, in this book, I ask to what extent a great deal of popular film culture may be part of a problem described by Afro-Spanish writer Franscisco Zamora Loboch in *Cómo ser negro y no morir en Aravaca* ("How to be Black and not die in Aravaca"). In this essay, which was written in 1994, Zamora Loboch establishes a link between what he sarcastically calls "humor negro" ("Black humour") – that is, the abundance of anti-Black proverbs, refrains, and punchlines that have saturated Spanish literature and culture since early modern times – and contemporary outbursts of racism and xenophobia (39). Noting that "una de las grandes medicinas que tiene el hombre blanco para curar su eterno estado depresivo es reírse del negro" ("One of the great medicines the white man uses to cure his eternal depression is laughing at Blacks"), he contends that the omnipresence of anti-Black humour in Spanish culture contributed to the entrenched racism that set the stage for the murder of Dominican migrant Lucrecia Pérez Matos, an event now recognized as democratic Spain's first racial hate crime (48). Although his essay focuses on anti-Blackness in particular, its insights are equally applicable to prejudice focused on other racial groups who are regularly mocked in Spanish culture, including Arabs, Asians, the Roma, and their descendants.

The deleterious effects of seemingly banal everyday racism in popular culture are also underscored by Paloma Chen, a Chinese-Spanish poet who won the National Prize for Live Poetry in 2020. In her poem "Toda la vida" ("All our lives"), Chen critiques commonly used defences used to excuse racist expressions or tropes in Spanish popular culture, including statements such as: *"Pero es que son expresiones de toda la vida / Es que hemos dicho esto toda la vida"* (*"But those are expressions we've used all our lives / We've said this our whole lives"*) (lines 9–10, original emphasis). In response to these justifications, Chen writes: "Pues la palabra ha sido un privilegio toda la vida … / y toda la vida hemos bebido agua no potable … / y toda la vida hemos tragado, pero no digerido" ("Well, the word has been a privilege all our lives … / and all our lives we have drunk undrinkable water … / and all our lives we have swallowed, but not digested;" lines 13–20). Although Chen's poem centres on the racist impact of language, its verses are equally applicable to film images, including many of those studied in this book, which might feel nostalgic, comforting, uplifting, or hilarious to some viewers, while simultaneously striking others as a form of "undrinkable water" (line 17).

With this context in mind, the chapters of this book aim to excavate a variety of Spanish popular cinema's engagements with racial imaginaries during the 1960s to 1980s. Chapter 1 examines one of the most emblematic varieties of late-Francoist cinema: namely, the *macho ibérico* comedy, in which actors like Paco Martínez Soria, José Luis López Vázquez, Manolo Escobar, or Alfredo Landa played working-class Spanish everymen navigating their way through a country transformed by tourism, economic development, and migration.[15] This genre served simultaneously as an instrument of governmentality through which the regime could promote the upward mobility narratives of tourism and *desarollismo* (Crumbaugh, *Destination Dictatorship* 10) and as a kind of "social therapy" through which working-class emigrants from rural areas could adjust to urban life (García de León 41). As we will see, however, popular comedy's efforts to trumpet narratives of upward mobility while assuaging the anxieties of rural emigrants were inseparable from a racial iconography of whitening. This is most evident in the genre's deployment of the *sueca* trope – that is, the bombshell, bikini-clad Northern European female tourist who supposedly flooded Spain's beaches during the tourism boom. As I argue in this chapter, the *macho ibérico*'s sexual pursuit of *suecas*, which several scholars have identified as allegorically suggestive of Spain's desire for Europeanization, was offset by its abundant racial denigration of Blacks, despite the very limited presence of actual Black people in Spain at the time. The representation of the Spanish *macho ibérico* as caught between opposing poles of the *sueca*'s whiteness and the inferiority of Blackness epitomized the nation's desire to rid itself of the "Africa of Europe" stereotype and ascend into global white belonging.

Chapter 2 explores how popular cinema of various genres channeled anxieties about the loss of Spain's imperial identity, which, as mentioned earlier, occurred between 1956 and 1975. Despite the regime's official efforts to limit or silence the public discussion of African decolonization, the chapter examines how late-Francoist popular cinema addressed decolonization obliquely through a "missionary imaginary" inherited from early Francoist missionary films. This missionary imaginary was perpetuated and reworked during late Francoism in a variety of ways, such as through the Afro-Cuban actor René Muñoz's feminine Black male characters, through the star image of the child prodigy Marisol, or through the recurring trope of the Black rapist in films about Africa. Starting from Richard Dyer's observation that "The white male spirit achieves and maintains empire; the white female soul is associated with its demise," the chapter argues that these disparate cinematic threads, whose protagonists were either women or feminized men, sought to defend Spain's waning African empire by personifying it with characteristics of white femininity, such as benevolence, innocence and vulnerability (184). By contrast, it shows, decolonization movements were demonized as the embodiment of Black masculine savagery, which would invariably be unleashed if imperialism were to end. At the same time, the chapter also argues that as decolonization progressed in the real world and became increasingly seen as inevitable, popular cinema portrayed the loss of the empire as a painful yet necessary step towards Europeanization rather than an unthinkable affront to Spain's imperial essence.

Chapter 3 examines how popular cinema's representations of the Roma evolved between late Francoism and the Transition. Specifically, it examines how the long-entrenched image of what Woods-Peiró has termed the "screen Gypsy" – that is, the singing and dancing "Gypsy woman" from Andalusia – became entangled with and eventually gave way to the figure of the *quinqui*, the racially ambiguous, young male delinquent of urban peripheries. Although this shift is most pronounced in the *quinqui* film cycle of the late 1970s and 1980s, the embroilment of the musical Gypsy and urban *quinqui* stereotypes can be traced as far back as the 1960s and is evident in the *macho ibérico* musicals that starred Manolo Escobar and Peret. Given that the *quinqui* trope emerged as a consequence of massive rural to urban migrations, the chapter argues that the tension between the musical Gypsy and the urban *quinqui* epitomized the contradictory myths and anxieties surrounding Spain's Roma communities during this period. On one hand, the fantasy of colourful, folkloric Gypsies served the regime's interest by providing fodder for the "Spain Is Different" tourist campaign; on the other, fears of Roma encroachment on society became prevalent as urban peripheries became increasingly populated with Roma migrants and their racially mixed descendants. By analysing the star images of Escobar, who was *payo*, Peret, who was Roma, and Ángel Fernández Franco, a *payo* who displayed Roma influences in *quinqui* films, the chapter argues that the *quinqui* trope channeled Black Legend anxieties that Spain's Roma racial heritage might derail its upward ascent into global whiteness.

Finally, chapter 4 examines the afterlife of the *macho ibérico* comedy during the democratic era. The films analysed in this chapter, which include comedies made by the ultra-prolific director Mariano Ozores and his imitators during the first decade of democracy, were long dismissed by critics as backward-looking embers of Francoist nostalgia. Even so, many of these *comedias ozoristas*, as they have been called in Spanish, commanded tremendous audiences despite the overall decline in film viewership during the 1970s and 1980s, and have remained well known to audiences in subsequent generations. These films also live on through their successors in the contemporary cinematic landscape, which include two blockbuster franchises directed by Santiago Segura: *Torrente* (five films, 1998–2014) and *Padre no hay más que uno* (four films, 2019–24).[16] Unlike the optimistic tone of late-Francoist popular comedies, the democratic *destape* comedy was marked by a fear of downward economic mobility sparked by the global oil crisis of the 1970s, a sharp drop in emigration and tourism, a rise in unemployment and crime, social paranoias about an imminent invasion of foreigners, and the uncertainties generated by the loss of Francoism. Although the racism of past and present *comedias ozoristas* is often disguised by distancing mechanisms such as nostalgia, irony, and humour, I argue that their dangerous potential comes into focus when we consider the use of similar comedic formulas by Vox, contemporary Spain's most prominent far right party. Specifically, I argue that the resemblance between the apolitical racial humour of comedy films and the overtly political racial humour of Vox accentuates the ability of humour to soften the edges of racist political discourse, thus priming audiences to be more receptive to racist political agendas.

Although these chapters collectively examine an ample range of genres and films, the sheer volume of popular cinema produced during these years, coupled with the relative paucity of comparative cross-generic scholarship about it, makes any attempt to be exhaustive impossible. The book focuses primarily on films that were made to appeal primarily to Spanish audiences, and which were thus distributed and consumed principally (albeit not exclusively) within Spain's borders. Consequently, other genres that were produced or co-produced in Spain, but which were designed to appeal to transnational audiences, such as horror or the Western, are occasionally examined but are not the book's main focus. Likewise, this book focuses on the representations of racial groups that surfaced most frequently in popular films of the period – namely, Blacks, Arabs and the Roma. Although it includes periodic references to the depiction of other groups, such as Native Americans or Asians, these latter groups surface more sporadically in the corpus of films examined here. Finally, although the book makes periodic reference to the engagement of race in arthouse, *auteur*, or socially engaged films, it invites other scholars to pursue a more sustained examination of that topic.

The films I analyse in this book were generally not known for their aesthetic innovation. Even so, they used a variety of formal features to construct a white gaze upon nonwhite bodies. The nightmare sequence and its corollary, the rape sequence, which I mentioned earlier, are only two examples from this broader array of features that reveal a white gaze. A number of other examples will surface frequently throughout my analyses. One of the most prominent is the point of view shot: in these films, racialized bodies are most often shown through the gaze of fictional white protagonists. The point of view shot can come in the form of a long shot, which allows the racialized body to be admired for its muscularity, exoticism, or hypersexuality, as well as in the form of close-ups or medium shots, which can be used to objectify parts of the body such as breasts, muscles, bottoms, etc. On many occasions, the point of view shot is complemented by a low angle, which visually magnifies the racialized subject and therefore contributes to their portrayal as deviant, ominous, or sensational.

Close-ups and medium shots are also often used to spectacularize the faces of racialized characters, especially by emphasizing their aberrant sexuality, their arrogance, or their propensity to violence. This pattern occurs with the African ambassador in *Los económicamente débiles* ("The economically weak," dir. Pedro Lazaga, 1960; see chapter 1), the African rebels in *Encrucijada para una monja* (see chapter 2), and the African royal family in *Es peligroso casarse a los 60* ("It's dangerous to get married at age 60," dir. Mariano Ozores, 1981; see chapter 4). Other times, close-ups and medium shots serve to neutralize the perceived threat of the racialized body by framing the faces of white and racialized characters together. This pattern occurs in *macho ibérico* comedies that depict hypermasculine Spanish men kissing racialized women (see chapter 1), or in close-ups that highlight interracial friendships, such as the one shared by 1960s child star Marisol with her Black sidekick, who was played by Equatorial Guinean actress Joëlle Rivero (see chapter 2). Even so, close-ups and medium shots that depict interracial closeness, whether sexual or platonic, still accentuate power dynamics by showing one person to be taller than the other, by showing one character as physically overpowering the other, or by using facial expressions to portray one as more intelligent.

Yet even as these films work to construct a white gaze, they also underscore the volatility of the Spanish viewer's whiteness in a variety of ways. Although the above tactics generally work to suture the viewer to the perspective of white Spanish characters, those characters are often also portrayed as possessing a whiteness that is unstable, precarious, or easily lost, which equally calls into question the stability of the viewer's own whiteness. As all four chapters demonstrate, interracial contact was an especially common source of anxiety about the purity of whiteness in the cinema of those years, as sexual attraction between white and racialized characters was most often stigmatized as degenerate yet nonetheless portrayed as omnipresent and inevitable. Many films, especially *macho ibérico* comedies, implied a link between the supposed hypersexuality of groups like Blacks, Arabs, or the Roma and that of white Spaniards, whose mixed racial heritage was often imagined as endowing them with an abnormally voracious sexual appetite. Anxieties about the supposed contamination of interracial sexual contact are especially notable in the contrast between the abundant portrayals of interracial sexuality and the scarce depictions of visibly interracial children, even in films that deal with children born of interracial unions like *Encrucijada para una monja* and *Esa mujer* (see chapter 2). Likewise, jokes about racial transformation, whether they occurred in dialogue or through the comical use of stereotypical costumes or blackface makeup, simultaneously revealed aspirations about becoming white as well as anxieties about the fragility of whiteness. In some films, especially *quinqui* ones, the racial boundary that traditionally separated Roma and *payo* Spaniards becomes so porous that it is almost indistinguishable, and this was portrayed as a terrifying symptom of Roma encroachment on *payo* society (see chapter 3).

The instability of the white gaze that these films construct underscores the multiplicity of meanings and interpretations that all films can invite. This book takes as a given that both racial stereotypes and the popular film narratives that deploy them can harbour a wide variety of emotional investments for audiences that comprised many different identities and experiences, such as those shaped by gender, class, age, geography, and, of course, race. A number of contemporary Spain's racialized writers have emphasized the complex range of emotional work that film and other forms of popular culture can perform, especially for marginalized audiences. We might recall, for example, Francisco Zamora Loboch's investment in the popular Western novel, which he describes in his poem "Estefanía" (1999) and which I have analysed elsewhere, due to its ability to make oppressive realities look fictitious and therefore subject to revision ("Don Quijote in Africa"). We might also consider the unnamed child narrator of *L'últim patriarca* ("The last patriarch"), a 2008 novel by Moroccan-Catalan writer Najat El Hachmi, who is drawn to the film *The Poltergeist* (dir. Tobe Hooper, 1982) because she imagines her turbulent home life to be a frightening parallel universe like the one depicted in the film (176–80). We might also think of Taiwanese-Spanish writer and musician Chenta Tsai Tseng, whose autobiographical text *Arroz Tres Delicias* ("Rice three delights") describes a young child re-enacting scenes from *Snow White and the Seven Dwarves* (dir. William Cottrell et al., 1937). As Tsai Tseng explains, the child's attachment to the film emerges from their perception of a parallelism between Snow White's escape from a hunter's pursuit and their own desire to escape the harsh realities of their childhood (28).

While these examples illustrate the possibility of individuals and communities to interpret popular culture against the grain, it is fundamental to excavate and understand the hegemonic yet understudied racial imaginaries that popular cinema of the 1960s to the 1980s constructed, disseminated, and reinforced. Although it is widely accepted that audiences can use mass culture as a tool of survival or to nourish politically subversive ideas, this book focuses on the racial messages of popular cinema in an effort to counter the deeply embedded legacy of the denial of racism in Spain. The urgency of this task becomes especially clear when we consider that popular cinema's abundant trafficking in racial tropes and imagery has largely gone unacknowledged until now, even though this prolific body of cinema has been widely consumed by large audiences both in the era of its production and today. A lack of attentiveness to popular cinema's hegemonic racial imaginaries is dangerous not only because it perpetuates the false myth that Spain is free of racism, but also because it tacitly reaffirms that myth's equally false corollary – that racism in Spain only emerged as a consequence of immigration but was never present before. This book aims to dispel both of these myths.

Chapter 1

The Wages of Whiteness in Late-Francoist Comedies

One of the best remembered popular comedy films of late Francoism, Pedro Lazaga's *Vente a Alemania, Pepe* ("Come to Germany, Pepe," 1971), narrates the comical misadventures of Pepe (Alfredo Landa), a working-class Spaniard who moves away from his economically depressed hometown in rural Spain to a bustling German metropolis. This film was released at a time when large numbers of working-class and rural Spaniards were migrating to Northern European countries such as Germany, France, and Switzerland to escape unemployment during the so-called development years of late Francoism. *Vente* is one of relatively few films of the era to directly represent the travails of Spaniards in Northern Europe, given that popular cinema's dominant messaging about freewheeling beach resorts and newfound economic prosperity did not easily cohere with the actuality that many Spaniards could not find work in their home country.[1] Even so, given that in the 1960s and 1970s, about three million Spaniards emigrated to Northern Europe (Richardson 68) and another three million were internally displaced within Spain (Riquer i Permanyer 263), the audiences of *Vente* would have recognized a resemblance between many of Pepe's predicaments and their own lived reality. For instance, many viewers would have probably understood that, like the fictional Pepe, who travels to Germany without a prearranged work contract, myriad Spaniards emigrated to Germany clandestinely in defiance of the Francoist government's efforts to regulate their movement – about one in three, in fact (Muñoz Sánchez 30).

Other aspects of Pepe's situation in Germany, however, are not realistic at all; instead, they are the product of the popular comedy film's whimsical conventions. When, at one point, Pepe is hired as a model for a razor company, he must stand in a store window display for hours on end, wearing only underwear, so that passers-by can gawk at his short frame, chubby physique, receding hairline, and thick, black body hair. Pepe's embarrassment is further magnified because he must share the display with a younger, taller, fitter, blonde-haired German man with perfectly hairless, milk-white skin. At first, Pepe's humiliation is quickly transformed into a source of pride, given that the mostly female onlookers are more titillated by the stocky, hairy Pepe than the pale German hunk. However, this pride reverts to humiliation when Pepe spots his possessive Spanish fiancée, who has travelled to Germany unannounced, staring at him in shock amongst the onlookers.

This scene encapsulates what was perhaps the most predictable joke of late-Francoist popular comedy: namely, the idea that a *macho ibérico*, or stereotypically Spanish everyman, could become a desirable sex object to *suecas*, the mythically attractive and liberated women of Northern Europe. As several scholars have noted, Landa's undressed body was a central part of this joke: his bowed legs invariably invited ridicule when bared (Pavlović 82, Fouz-Hernández and Martínez-Expósito 11) and his old-fashioned, white underwear made him look "anything but sexually desirable" (J. Pérez, *Fashion* 108). Even so, the *macho ibérico / sueca* narrative suggested that Spanish masculinity, despite its obvious inadequacies, was desirable and upwardly mobile, a reflection of Spain's attractiveness as a tourist destination and its increasing economic prosperity in the 1960s and 1970s. The highly formulaic films that deployed this narrative were known by a variety of names, such as *la comedia sexy*, *la comedia celtibérica*, or even simply *landismo*, given the frequency with which they starred Alfredo Landa or other actors with similar physical features. Despite their lack of aesthetic or narrative finesse, it is easy to imagine how such films could have been not only amusing, but also cathartic and even empowering to the film's working- and lower-middle class viewership. For, as Justin Crumbaugh has argued, popular comedy's idealization of the *macho ibérico* as an embodiment of national virility suggested that Spain's perceived backwardness could be transformed into a profitable commodity and sign of modernity (*Destination Dictatorship* 100–3). Such a logic, Crumbaugh notes, mirrored the larger "Spain Is Different" marketing campaign, which aimed to capitalize on Spain's presumably unique folklore and culture in an effort to attract European tourists during the tourism boom (68).

Yet, as I will demonstrate in this chapter, popular comedy's humorous representation of the power dynamics between Spain and other areas of the world imagined to be more modern, including not only Northern European countries such as Germany, but also English-speaking countries such as Britain and the United States, was thoroughly intertwined with a visual iconography of race. *Vente a Alemania, Pepe* is a case in

point: this film's effort to spectacularize the phenotypical dispari-
ties between Pepe and his German counterpart, such as their differences in height, body type, hair colour, and body hair, was a frequent
visual strategy in popular comedy films of the period.[2] Regardless of
whether the *macho ibérico* was an emigrant chasing German women, a
beachgoer pursuing libertine foreign tourists, or a rural bumpkin surrounded by urban hippies, Spaniards were frequently portrayed not
only as *less modern* than Northern Europeans or English-speakers, but
also as *less white* than them. Throughout the genre, the visual contrast
between Spaniards and Anglo-Europeans strongly suggests that these
two groups represent what Richard Dyer has termed as differing "gra-
dations of whiteness" (12). Such visual patterns assume that Spaniards
embody an off-whiteness or ethnic whiteness that contrasts with the
"Nordic" or pure whiteness of *suecas* and Americans. This was tellingly
emphasized not only by the obvious physical contrasts between the
body of Landa and those of Northern European men, but also by the
recurring portrayal of the *macho ibérico* as barely able (or altogether unable) to control his sexuality. Indeed, the hilarious attraction of *suecas*
to the *macho ibérico* despite his physical mediocrity was imagined to be
precisely a consequence of what Fouz-Hernández and Martínez-Exposito
have called "offshore readings of Spanish masculinity," which, they
argue, "tend to emphasize elements of difference and otherness along
racial and broadly defined cultural lines" (3).

   However, the racialized imaginary of late-Francoist comedies was not
only limited to distinguishing degrees of whiteness among Spaniards,
Northern Europeans, and Americans. Rather, many films of the genre also
featured highly stereotypical representations of racial groups deemed inferior to Spaniards on the global racial hierarchy, including Arabs, Native
Americans, Asians, and, most prominently of all, Blacks. Although such
stereotypes do not surface in *Vente a Alemania, Pepe*, they appear with in-
sistence throughout the genre. In a multi-year study of over two hundred
popular Spanish films produced from 1966 to 1975,[3] a team of researchers headed by Miguel Ángel Huerta Floriano and Ernesto Pérez Morán
enumerate a plethora of popular comedies that deployed transnationally
recognizable, stereotypical humour about these nonwhite groups in an
effort to "mock all things foreign and, by contrast, glorify all things Hispanic" (*El cine popular del tardofranquismo*, location 5993). Although Huerta
Floriano and Pérez Morán note that all foreigners were subject to stereotyping in these comedies, the frequency and negativity that characterizes
their depiction of supposedly inferior races is striking.

A paradigmatic example of Black racial caricature in late-Francoist
comedy can be found in another emigration-themed film, *París bien*

vale una moza ("Paris is well worth a girl," dir. Pedro Lazaga, 1972), in which Landa's character plays a struggling emigrant in France. After scrounging up a paid gig as a wrestler, he is nicknamed "El Oso de los Pirineos" ("The Bear of the Pyrenees") and must fight an African muscleman named "el Gorila de Camerún" ("The Gorilla of Cameroon") in a match that the Spaniard miraculously wins, despite his clear physical disadvantage. This film's narrative formula of an underdog white man obtaining victory over a racialized enemy mirrors the earlier film *Los económicamente débiles* ("The economically weak," dir. Pedro Lazaga, 1960), a film about a ragtag soccer team that manages to raise its regional classification despite the efforts of various racialized antagonists to derail its ascent. Yet another example emerges in *Las que tienen que servir* ("Women who have to serve," dir. José María Forqué, 1967), a comedy about Spanish women who work as housekeepers for American military personnel at Torrejón Air Base. In this film, a hypermasculine African-American man relentlessly beats his Spanish wife, but Alfredo Landa's *macho ibérico* character successfully co-opts the Black man's resentment against American whites to his own advantage. Likewise, in *Una vez al año ser hippy no hace daño* ("Once a year it doesn't hurt to be a hippie," dir. Javier Aguirre, 1969), a hippie-inspired anthem called "Los negros con las suecas" ("Black men with European women") extols interracial sex while reinforcing coarse anti-Black stereotypes. Spanish paranoias about interracial sex reappear in *El alma se serena* ("The soul settles down," dir. José Luis Sáenz de Heredia, 1970) and *Ligue story* ("Lust story," dir. Alfonso Paso, 1972). In these films, sex between Spanish men and Black women oscillates between constituting an inconceivable form of degeneration and offering an opportunity to recover the lost glory of Spain's colonial past. All of these films were commercial successes, having reached between one and three million viewers during their theatre runs.[4] Notably, in almost all of these films, the Black characters around whom the racial comedy revolves are nameless, and the actors who played them were overwhelmingly absent in the credits.

These widely consumed comedies aimed to teach their large domestic audiences that Spain was moving upward not only economically, but also racially. Drawing on W.E.B. Du Bois' interrelated ideas of a global colour line and of whiteness as a wage, this chapter will argue that the late-Francoist comedy film's abundant use of racial caricature was a counterpoint to its idealized portrayals of Anglo-European whiteness. In particular, these comedies suggested that development-era Spain was freeing itself from the "blackness" or "Africanness" associated with the Black Legend, a long-entrenched imaginary of Spain's backwardness, primitiveness, and colonial failure, and moving closer to the desirable whiteness of the Anglo-European world. By imagining late Franco-era Spain as being racially whitened, these comedies represented Spain as reversing a long trajectory of colonial decline. They also sought to compensate for the failures of late-Francoism's development project, given the particular hardships that rural and working classes faced as they emigrated by the millions within Spain and beyond. This chapter will argue that late-Francoist cinema's narratives of racial uplift aimed to reverse the racialization of geographically displaced Spanish labourers. According to this imaginary, which surfaces in a number of literary, autobiographical, and filmic references from the period, working-class Spaniards were often seen as closer to being Black than white.

In what follows, we will first review the ideas of a global colour line and of whiteness as a wage – both of which have proven foundational to the critical whiteness studies bibliography – and consider their applicability to late-Francoist Spain. We will subsequently consider two categories of case studies of popular comedy films from the period. Although neither category is exhaustive, each intends to identify recurring representational patterns of racial caricature, which undoubtedly also appear in other films not studied here. The first category, in which I examine *Los económicamente débiles*, *Las que tienen que servir*, and *París bien vale una moza*, comprises comedies that portrayed Spanish men as becoming whiter by expelling or vanquishing their "inner African." The second group, in which I analyse *Una vez al año ser hippy no hace daño*, *El alma se serena*, and *Ligue Story*, comprises films that imagined the consequences of Spanish men having sex across the Black / white colour line in a reversal of the *macho ibérico* / *sueca* narrative. In both groups of films, racial caricature, especially of Blacks, served to counteract the feelings of exploitation and inferiority that many displaced Spanish labourers experienced by showing that Spain's off-whiteness was on the verge of catching up with Anglo-European modernity. At the same time, however, both groups of comedies portrayed Spain as retaining a distinctive, deracialized off-whiteness that could serve as a commodity on the world stage. According to these films, Spain was indeed "different" from Europe – but perhaps not *too* different.

The Wages of (Off-)Whiteness: Race and Migration in Development-Era Spain

In the 1960s, numerous social and economic changes were underway in Spain, such as the tourism boom, increased urbanization, shifting gender mores, and a marked increase in ownership of television sets, automobiles, and other appliances. These changes were symptomatic of the rapid integration of Spain's economy into global capitalism, which produced a monumental increase in wealth and prosperity for average Spaniards between 1960 and 1975.[5] The seeming dream-come-true of Spain's ability to approach the modernity and well-being of other Western European countries fuelled the popularity of comedy films, whose narratives of *machos ibéricos* chasing *suecas* delighted millions of Spanish viewers. Importantly, this genre maintained its popularity with audiences over the 1960, 1970s, and even the early '80s despite the precipitous decline in cinema viewership that began in the late 1960s due to the advent of television.[6] Although Annabel Martín has compellingly argued that "regime-friendly films … did little to unravel the deep social and personal dissatisfaction looming underneath the supposedly upward times of economic progress" (57), it is also true, as María García de León has argued, that this upbeat genre served as a kind of "social therapy" for its viewers (41). For García de León, the therapeutic function of humour about *paletos* ("rural bumpkins") enabled newly urbanized rural immigrants, who formed the brunt of the genre's viewership, to laugh at their rural origins and identify more deeply with their new urban surroundings.

The popular comedy's effort to help Spaniards imagine themselves as becoming free from their rural roots overlapped with its portrayal of Spain as dissociating itself from the Black Legend, a longstanding imaginary that linked Spain's perceived cultural backwardness to its racial inferiority. The genre's function as a vehicle of Black Legend anxieties stemmed from its effort to mediate between audiences' demand for comic relief, on one hand, and the ideological concerns of the late-Franco regime, on the other. Despite its upbeat rhetoric about development and upward mobility, the late-Franco regime feared being perceived as an anachronism in an increasingly democratic and postcolonial Western Europe. While the economic boom offered Francoism the ability to claim credit for Spaniards' increased prosperity, the advent of television, tourism, and emigration threatened the regime's ideological hegemony by giving its subjects increased access to the world beyond Spain's borders, especially of nearby Western European democracies. Emigration to Northern Europe was a particularly double-sided issue: while it offered much needed remittances and curbed domestic unemployment, it also fomented a perception of Spaniards as low-wage labourers (Fernández Asperilla, "La emigración" 68–9) and created opportunities for anti-Francoist mobilization (Fernández Asperilla, "El asociacionismo" 149–50). Furthermore, as I explain in greater depth in chapter 2, the regime of the 1960s struggled to balance its investment in maintaining its colonial presence in Africa with the global trend towards decolonization. All of these factors intensified the regime's anxieties that Spain, quite simply, was behind the rest of the world, and was struggling to catch up.

The popular cinema industry was required to reinforce, or at least not blatantly contradict, the regime's ideological prerogatives. As Duncan Wheeler has observed, "there can be no doubt that filmmakers' prime intention was to make a living: they were hardly likely to overtly bite the hands that feed, and they were at least passively complicit" with the dictatorship's authoritarian values (147). Due to the popular comedy's role as a vehicle for promoting development-era promises of upward economic mobility, this genre constituted a convenient medium to put a positive spin on the regime's concerns about its geopolitical stature. To this end, popular comedies appropriated the iconography of race, especially a Black / white colour line, to dramatize the idea that Spain was moving upward on the global hierarchy of nations through its narratives of Spain's racial whitening.

Yet, in late-Francoist comedy films, the insistent appearance of a Black / white colour line indexed not only the regime's anxieties about its international image, but also rural and working-class Spaniards' anxieties about their mass displacement during the 1960s and 1970s. As a consequence of mass migrations, Spain's major cities grew tremendously, but the population of rural Spain was halved, and would continue to dwindle in subsequent periods (Riquer i Permanyer 262–3). The depopulation of rural areas was accelerated not only by internal migration within Spain, but also by emigration to Northern Europe. After all, most of those who emigrated abroad returned to Spain after a few years, but overwhelmingly settled in urban areas rather than their rural hometowns (Fernández Asperilla, "La emigración" 68). Due to this mass internal and international displacement, a variety of literary, filmic, and autobiographical sources from the 1960s and 1970s indicate that emigrant Spaniards were often portrayed as "Black," even though they were obviously not racially Black. The figurative "blackening" of emigrant Spaniards served simultaneously to highlight their economic desperation and their perceived racial inferiority.

One notable text in which impoverished rural emigrants are described as "Black" is Luis Martín Santos' classic novel *Tiempo de silencio* ("Time of silence," 1962), whose narrative is set in the late 1940s. Specifically, migrants who live in a shantytown on the outskirts of Madrid are racialized in this manner (46). One of the novel's principal secondary characters, known by the nickname El Muecas ("Funny face"), is an inhabitant of the shanty town, and is called a "Príncipe negro y dignatario" ("Black prince and dignitary") by the narrator because he imagines himself as superior to the other migrants (46). At one point, El Muecas muses to himself that the ramshackle neighbourhood's newest arrivals, who hail from "el lejano país del hambre" ("the faraway country of hunger"), are little more than "infra-hombres" ("subhumans") who belong to a "raza inferior" ("inferior race") (45). Indeed, in an expression that is itself strongly reminiscent of Du Bois, El Muecas considers the upper-middle classes, who live far away in the city centre, and the impoverished shanty-town residents to be "situados a uno y otro lado de la barrera del color" ("situated on different sides of the colour line") (46). He even surmises that the world's economically powerful peoples, whom he and other rural emigrants had no choice but to serve, "habían de ser blancos, rubios y con los ojos alucinantemente azules" ("had to be white, blonde, and with amazingly blue eyes") (46). As Nathan Richardson observes, the novel's use of a Black / white racial spectrum to describe Spanish class differences reflected an increasingly prominent globalization of labour in which the world's supposedly white, "developed" countries exploited racialized "underdeveloped" regions (224).

The Black / white racial dichotomy similarly emerges in numerous other late-Francoist representations of internal Spanish migrations. For instance, we might recall the social realist film *La piel quemada* ("Burnt skin," dir. Josep María Forn, 1967), which narrates the tribulations of an Andalusian labourer named José who emigrates to the Costa Brava. This film compares Andalusians to Blacks by featuring two back-to-back music and dance sequences that are performed for Northern European tourists at a beachfront club. The first number is announced as a "danza ritual africana" ("African dance ritual") and shows a scantily clad, Black female dancer performing a fast-paced, decidedly erotic dance while accompanied by vigorous drums. The second sequence is a flamenco performance in which José, the Andalusian migrant protagonist, jumps on stage with professional musicians to show off his impressive dance skills to the delight of onlookers. By juxtaposing these two dance sequences, the film comments on the self-exoticizing thrust of Spain's tourist industry, in which Andalusian folklore, like the African dance that immediately precedes it, was commodified as a racialized, pornographic spectacle for tourist consumption.

Southern emigrants in Catalonia are also compared with Blacks in the experimental short, animated film *Blanc i negre* ("Black and white," dir. Jan Baca and Toni Garriga, 1974). This anti-Francoist, underground film of eleven minutes portrays Black labourers as being kidnapped from a jungle, put to work in factories, forced to perform their music and culture, segregated in residential ghettoes, and, ultimately, exterminated after one of them sleeps with the white boss's wife. The film's visual style is strongly reminiscent of American blackface, given that its Black characters are portrayed with oversized red lips that stand out amongst their otherwise undifferentiated facial features. As Xose Antonio Prieto Souto has commented, this narrative of Black exploitation was an allegory for the experiences of southern migrants in Catalonia, who, the film suggests, experienced a similar degree of abuse and exploitation as Black peoples around the world (296). Prieto Souto also notes that this animated short film was one of the ten most highly sought-after films distributed by Central del Curt, an alternative Catalan film distribution company, during the period 1976–9 (295).

Importantly, the racialization of Spanish labourers was not merely a cinematic or literary trope. Rather, autobiographical testimonies of Spanish emigration to Northern Europe also assert that their class-based exploitation was filtered with decidedly racial undertones. One such example is the first-person narrative *Moi, la bonne* ("I, the maid," 1975), which was written by Maria Arondo, a Spanish woman who worked as a domestic in France in the 1960s. As Rocío Negrete Peña has noted, Arondo's development of a socially conscious voice in this text is based on her awareness of occupying a different class and racial position with respect to her French employers (206). Arondo writes, for instance, that she and other Spanish women workers shared "un fort sentiment d'infériorité" ("a strong feeling of inferiority") with respect to their French employers, who often overworked, mistreated, and humiliated them (38). According to Arondo, the prevalent attitude among French households that employed Spanish women was that "plus on est jeune et plus on est étrangèr, plus on a des chances de travailler dur" ("the younger and more foreign we are, the more chances we have to work harder") (22); she also writes that "pour ceux-là, on est d'une race inférieure" ("To them, we were an inferior race") (117). Her assertions are further evidenced by the emergence of the "Conchita" stereotype of Spanish women houseworkers in numerous forms of French popular culture during the 1960s. As Bruno Tur notes, this stereotype superimposed long-established French caricatures of Spanish women, who had been portrayed since the nineteenth century as Andalusian "femmes fatales," with newer forms of ridicule, such as the idea that Spanish women were unable to master the French language, follow French customs, or adapt to the modernity that characterized French ways of life (75–8).

Spanish emigrants in Germany also reported numerous instances of racially inflected xenophobia. This is especially evident in a testimonial

novel entitled *Vida de un emigrante español* ("Life of a Spanish emigrant")
by Víctor Canicio, who worked in Germany during the 1960s and later
became a writer. In this autobiographical novel, Canicio portrays German
workers as giving the protagonist, Pedro, the nickname "Negrín" ("little Black man"), noting that they introduced him to friends and family who would come by the workshop as "el negro" ("the Black guy")
(76). Pedro stipulates that "Me llamaban el negro por el color del pelo
y porque debía tener todavía la piel tostada por el sol" ("The called me
Black because of the colour of my hair and because I must have still
had my skin darkened by the sun") (76). Furthermore, the text indicates
that this moniker was more than just a rhetorical flourish, given that
various forms of discrimination were widely practised against Spaniards in Germany. To name but a few examples, Canicio's protagonist
notes that German workers earned double the amount that he did for
performing the same labour (77), that romantic or sexual relationships
between Spaniards and Germans were frowned upon and might result
in violence (79, 136–7), and that Spanish schoolchildren were often ignored and allowed to fall behind by German teachers (129). He also
notes that the economic crisis of 1973 exacerbated German xenophobia
towards Spaniards, as migrants "[became] the target of violent attacks
and event homicides due to the rise of unemployment in Germany"
(González-Allende 141). Canicio's account of German xenophobia towards Spaniards is echoed in the documentary *El tren de la memoria*
("The train of memory," dir. Marta Arribas and Ana Pérez, 2005). In this
film, elder Spaniards recall their experience of emigration to Germany
during their youth, and mention a plethora of instances in which they
were treated like "gente sucia" ("dirty people"), "como las ovejas"
("like sheep"), "lo mismo que los judíos" ("the same as the Jews"), or
even "como los indios" ("like Indians").

The frequent comparisons between Spanish labourers and "Blacks"
or other presumably inferior races in cultural production of the 1960s
and 1970s accentuate a marked dissonance between late-Francoism's
cheerful promises of prosperity and the hard realities of economic
abuse and social exclusion experienced by many Spanish migrants,
both within Spain and abroad. The disjuncture between Francoism's
fictions and the lived realities of many of its subjects is crucial to help
us understand why popular comedy films so often resorted to racial
imagery to portray Spain as crossing a global colour line from Black to
white. These films offered their viewers something that W.E.B. Du Bois
once referred to as the "public and psychological wage" of whiteness
(*Black Reconstruction* 626). This concept suggests that belonging in racial
whiteness offers a certain form of compensation, whether material or

nonmaterial, to those who are recognized as belonging to it, and which is denied to those of other races. In the Spanish case, the "wage" of whiteness was primarily psychological in nature. In addition to its therapeutic function of helping audiences adjust to urban life, popular comedies also offered relief to their viewers by reminding them that they did not occupy the lowest position on the global stage, even though they often felt like they did. Instead, these comedies suggested, Spaniards were much closer to Anglo-European whiteness than to inferior races such as Blacks. At the same time, by promoting the idea that Spaniards could craft their own, nationally distinct brand of off-whiteness, popular comedies reinforced the messaging of the "Spain Is Different" campaign, which portrayed Spanish culture as possessing the right balance of exoticism and comfortable familiarity to attract European tourism while still remaining within the purview of European whiteness.

The function of racial caricature in late-Francoist popular comedies becomes especially clear when we analyse an analogous process of white racial formation in the United States. In *The Wages of Whiteness*, a text that draws heavily on Du Bois' thought, David Roediger argues that the formation of a white American working-class identity was inseparable from the practice of blackface minstrelsy – a widespread performance genre of anti-Black caricature that was primarily enacted by white artists for white audiences. For Roediger, minstrelsy specifically demonstrated that "Blackness could be made permanently to embody the preindustrial past" that white workers, many of whom were struggling to adapt to demands of industrialization, simultaneously "scorned and missed" (97). At the same time, blackface minstrelsy was full of ambiguities, such as its portrayal of transgressive sexual acts and fantasies, including interracial ones. "Although blackface provided a mask behind which erotic longings could find expression," Roediger writes, "the shows [made] it uncertain how far the audience was meant to empathize with – and how far it was meant to recoil from – the sexual freedoms portrayed" (120). Over time, he writes, blackface played an important role in leading European immigrant groups whose whiteness was considered suspect or questionable, such as the Irish, to align themselves with a mainstream, anti-Black, white working-class identity in order to raise their status in American society and thereby profit from the wages of whiteness (137).

Despite being based on a different cultural and historical context, the analyses of Du Bois and Roediger can help us to understand why narratives of racial whitening surfaced frequently in late-Francoist popular comedy cinema. Their arguments make clear that racial caricature during Francoism also epitomized, following Roediger, the "preindustrial past" associated with the rural world that so many Spaniards left behind, and which they also simultaneously "scorned and missed" (97). Racial humour thus provided not only the therapeutic function of enabling displaced labourers to laugh at their rural origins, but also an equally therapeutic function of contrasting their upward mobility with the immobility of racially inferior groups. Some comedies accomplished this by suggesting that Spanish men could harness their astuteness, cleverness, or their survival instinct to vanquish an African rival who usually embodied an even more exaggerated primitiveness than rural Spanish characters. Other comedies offered spectacles of interracial sexuality as an ideologically ambivalent "mask behind which erotic longings could find expression" (120). Given their thematic focus on men's sexual repression, late-Francoist comedies exploited depictions of interracial sexuality, which allowed viewers to indulge in a thrilling but temporary fantasy of losing whiteness while also reassuring them that the sexual conquest of racial others could help Spaniards re-establish their lost supremacy and masculinity at the global level. In both cases, popular comedies implied that Spaniards could improve their position on the global colour line while retaining a nationally specific brand of whiteness that could serve as a competitive advantage in a global, capitalist market.

Racial Transformation Comedies: Overcoming the "Inner African"

A recurring trope in late-Francoist comedies is the idea that Spaniards, especially working-class men of rural origins, could shed their "Africanness" and ascend into European whiteness by outsmarting racial others who possessed greater social stature or physical prowess. In this way, the films call attention to Richard Dyer's observation that "the white spirit could both master and transcend the white body, while the non-white soul was a prey to the promptings and fallibilities of the body" (23). In addition, these comedies portray racial and masculine power as deeply intertwined, given that Spanish men's "Africanness" is associated with emasculation while the assertion of whiteness entails a recovery of virility. Finally, by portraying Spanish men as *earning* their whiteness through their cleverness, these films imagine whiteness as a kind of wage – a just recompense for the suffering, displacement, and toil that many Spanish workers were experiencing during the development years.

An early example of the racial transformation motif can be found in the soccer-themed comedy *Los ecónomicamente débiles* ("The economically weak," dir. Pedro Lazaga, 1960), a precursor to the *landista* comedy.[7] This film, which recounts how a ragtag, local soccer team called Casamata, F.C. dramatically improves its performance, reinforces its upward mobility narrative by portraying working-class Spaniards as recovering supremacy over several racialized groups. The first such instance occurs in an early scene, in which the team's newly appointed coach, Pepe (Antonio Ozores), who is dismayed by the players' ineptitude during practice, tells a Black player to pass the ball to his teammate Pichurri, a working-class Spaniard. When the ball flies over Pichurri's head, Pepe asks Pichurri sarcastically, "¿Por qué no has ido a por ese balón? ¿No me vas a salir ahora con que tienes prejuicios raciales?" ("Why didn't you go for that ball? Don't tell me you have racial prejudices!") Pichurri, however, responds by pointing to a large hole in his boot that prevents him from running or kicking properly. Although most of the scene is filmed in long shot from an omniscient high angle, Pichurri's response is accompanied by two extreme close-ups that accentuate his big toe protruding from his tattered boot. These shots underscore a presumably outrageous scenario in which a Black man can afford decent shoes while a Spaniard cannot. Furthermore, by establishing a correlation between the team's deficiency and the presence of Blackness, this scene suggests that the team's improvement will require a kind of whitening, an expulsion, in other words, of its "Africanness."

Later in the film, Pepe, who dreams of leaving the Casamata to coach a professional soccer team, decides to apply to a prestigious coaching school. To do so, he must take a three-part entrance exam that includes a written portion, an oral portion, and a demonstration of soccer technique alongside numerous other test-takers, most of whom are foreign. However, Pepe's severe underperformance with respect to his foreign counterparts reiterates the training scene's theme that Spain needed to recover its lost supremacy over other races. For instance, during the scene of the written exam, Pepe is physically surrounded by foreigners: seated in front of him is someone who looks European but doesn't speak Spanish; behind him is an Argentine; and sharing the row with him are a Chinese man and a Black man. A series of uncomfortable dialogues follows in which Pepe and the other test-takers speak to each other in hushed tones in an attempt to cheat on the test; although these dialogues are filmed in medium shot from a variety of perspectives, Pepe is always near the centre of the frame and close-ups on his face mark the centrality of his point of view. The humour of the scene derives from Pepe's ability to mock foreign accents and languages. In one dialogue, he pretends to understand the European's language but clearly does not. In another, he responds to a question from the Argentine by reproducing a grossly exaggerated Argentine accent.

Pepe's status anxieties come most palpably into relief when he asks his Chinese neighbour for help during the test. "Eh, Mao," Pepe says in a mocking Chinese accent, "¿quieles soplalme soble el tluco de la diagonal?" ("Eh Mao, wanna help me out with the question about the Brazilian diagonal?"). The Chinese neighbour offers him a note, but it is of no use because it is written in Chinese. The scene's intent is clear: by suggesting that Pepe fails the test while caricatured foreigners are successful, it bluntly implies that Spain was falling behind nations that, according to a properly ordered racial and imperial hierarchy, it should be ahead of. Yet, Pepe's portrayal as being able to imitate both an Argentine and a Chinese accent – however badly – foreshadows the film's larger message: Spaniards, through their craftiness and adaptability, will indeed manage to trounce their foreign competitors and rise to a new level of global power.

Spain's efforts to reaffirm its global and racial supremacy finally come to fruition in a subplot that revolves around the film's most glaring racial caricature: namely, its depiction of an arrogant female ambassador from Cachalandia, a fictional African country that has just obtained independence. Her presence in the film serves as a catalyst of comical mayhem. Although she intends to receive beauty treatments at an upscale women's salon where Timoteo, one of the soccer players, works as a stylist, her visit coincides with Timoteo's effort to smuggle his male teammates into the salon to enjoy various relaxation treatments. This sets up a whimsical situation in which the male soccer players must escape the salon without being seen by the African ambassador.

The ambassador's role as a caricature of Blackness is emphasized by several visual elements. The first is point of view: in the first sequence in which she appears, the ambassador and the director of the salon appear small at the end of a hallway while Pepe, who is hiding behind a wall, watches them approach in the foreground of the shot. Yet even from a distance, it is conspicuously evident that the African ambassador has two large bones protruding from her hair. The bones in her hair feature prominently in every subsequent shot in which she appears, thus marking her as closer to a cartoon than to a realistic character (see figure 1.1). The stereotypical depiction of Africans with bones in the hair or nose, was, of course, widely circulated transnationally, especially in comic strips, cartoons, and advertisements of the twentieth century, and was often used to accentuate the association of Blackness with cannibalism. Although she is framed from Pepe's point of view in this introductory sequence and in subsequent others, there is, notably, no sequence in which her point of view as a character is revealed. Instead, her condescending attitude, which becomes evident when she claims that she has

Figure 1.1. The fictional African ambassador in *Los económicamente débiles* (dir. Pedro Lazaga, 1960).

seen better salons elsewhere, marks her not only as comical, but as a threat to the racial and gendered hierarchies defended by Francoism. Like the previous scenes of the Casamata's practice and Pepe's test, the ambassador's presence in the film suggests that Spain had to find a way to recover its deserved supremacy over nonwhite races, who, it is implied, must be returned to their properly inferior status.

The male soccer players' attempt to escape the salon unnoticed is also saturated in various tropes of racial caricature. Pretending to be a newly hired hairdresser, Pepe leads the African ambassador to a styling chair and proceeds to cut the bones out of her hair. He then uses the bones to disguise Pichurri, another male player who is hidden elsewhere in the salon, as the ambassador. After weaving the bones into Pichurri's hair, he paint's Pichurri's face black using a face mask. Shortly after, Timoteo sends all the salon's staff and clientele into a frenzy by feigning to have seen a mouse. During the ensuing fracas, Pepe and Paco escape with Pichurri, who is now dressed in blackface and drag. At the same time, Pepe and Paco are themselves dressed in pseudo-Arab attire, pretending to be the ambassador's bodyguards.

Although the sight of a working-class Spanish man, like Pichurri, wearing not only blackface but also drag was undoubtedly meant to elicit laughter from the film's audiences, it also serves to re-establish the destabilized racial and gender hierarchies. Specifically, Pichurri's outrageous costume calls attention to what he *is* by showing what he *is not*. Despite his disguise, it is clear that he is neither Black nor a woman; therefore, paradoxically, his preposterous apparel reaffirms his white masculinity. The same is true of Pepe and Paco, whose pseudo-Arab costumes accentuate their Spanishness. By marking distance between these characters and the film's assortment of racial others – especially the African ambassador, who embodies the antithesis of the Franco regime's values – the film portrays them as regaining the whiteness and masculinity that they were previously lacking throughout the film. Furthermore, given that their costumes represent overlapping mockery of Black Africans and Arabs, their racial ascent signals Spain's ability to overcome the Black Legend, according to which Spain's Islamic and African heritage was imagined to be the root of its backwardness. Finally, the Spaniards' use of racial and gender cross-dressing as a part of a scheme to save Timoteo's job reveals the film's link between the idea of Spaniards' cleverness and working-class prosperity. According to the film, it is precisely the intelligence of Spaniards that enables them not only to survive economically, but also to earn a higher place on the global spectrum of masculinity and whiteness. This message is reinforced by the cross-dressing scene that occurs just before the final sequence, in which the Casamata team achieves a higher regional classification by winning an upset victory over a neighbouring team.

As a precursor to the *landista* comedy, *Los económicamente débiles* foreshadowed the greater intensity and frequency with which popular films of the later 1960s and 1970s would combine the themes of economic uplift and racial whitening. A case in point is *Las que tienen que servir* ("Women who have to serve," dir. José María Forqué, 1967), which also recycles the narrative formula of Spanish men outsmarting racial others. More specifically, this film, which reworks the *sueca* formula to comically depict relationships between Spaniards and Americans who live near the American military base at Torrejón de Ardóz, imagines working-class Spaniards as breaking out of their ambivalent location on the racial spectrum of Blackness and whiteness. The film narrates how two Spanish women, Juana (Concha Velasco) and Francisca (Amparo Soler Leal), work as housekeepers in the luxurious, futuristic home of an American military couple, Mr and Mrs Stevens. Despite their constant proximity to American affluence, the housekeepers are dating two buffoonish, working-class Spaniards: the unambitious driver Antonio (Alfredo Landa) and the rustic egg-seller Lorenzo (Manolo Gómez Bur). Conflict arises when two dashing, muscular Americans named Nathan and Spencer begin courting the women, thus inflaming Antonio and Lorenzo's sense of national and masculine pride. Predictably, however, Juana and Francisca ultimately reconcile with their Spanish partners by the film's end. Although the film draws much humour from the idea that Spaniards could look and feel out of place in their own country, it nonetheless assuages its viewers' anxieties of backwardness by heavily ridiculing the African Americans who belong to Torrejón's American community. This humour serves to remind Spanish viewers that they were not inferior to *all* Americans, and that they, unlike Blacks, could improve their standing by asserting their white identity.

The film's first portrayal of American Blackness as problematic occurs in its opening credit sequence, which depicts a baseball game being played near Torrejón de Ardoz. Although most of the baseball game is filmed through long shots or extreme long shots, the interspersing of several medium shots that focus on Black players highlights not only the cultural foreignness of the game, but also the racial foreignness of Black Americans in Spain. As the sequence ends, the camera reveals a traffic sign written in English while a male voiceover sarcastically announces, "Como es evidente, estamos en España" ("As you can see, we're in Spain"). By linking the quintessentially American sport of baseball to racial Blackness and to the existence of an English-speaking community in Spain, this opening sequence articulates both anxiety about Spain's contamination by foreign cultures as well as a desire to participate in Anglophone modernity – a contradiction that emerges in countless late-Francoist comedies.

The tension between a desirable modernity imported from abroad and the presence of unwanted, dark-skinned foreigners is manifest again in the representation of the Stevens' next-door neighbours, a married couple that consists of an African-American man and an older Spanish woman named Lola. Given that this film debuted in 1967, the same year in which the US Supreme Court overturned anti-miscegenation laws in the landmark Loving vs. Virginia case, the film's representation of a binational, biracial marriage could at first seem like a progressive embrace of the American civil rights movement, which many Spaniards of the day were watching with great interest.[8] However, the film's constant denigration of the couple precludes any such interpretation. In the scene that introduces the neighbours, the unnamed Black man is shown pretending to cut the hedges on his expansive, luxurious property as an excuse to gaze at Juana and Francisca, who are playing cards next door in the Stevens' backyard. As he looks over the fence, the viewer would expect a sequence in which the two women would be shown from the Black man's point of view. Instead, however, the camera immediately discards the Black man's gaze by showing Juana and Francisca's dialogue as a shot-reverse shot in medium close-up that is punctuated by close-ups of their cards. In this way, the camera shows Juana and Francisca as they see each other, rather than suturing the viewer to the Black man's point of view. Tellingly, the camera's efforts to privilege the point of view of Spanish characters while erasing the Black neighbour's perspective is further emphasized when the two women, who are initially oblivious to his presence, turn towards him upon hearing a commotion. A point-of-view shot from Juana and Francisca's perspective shows Lola berating her husband and beating him with a fly swatter on the other side of the fence; as a result, the two younger women erupt in derisive laughter aimed at both of them. In doing so, the camera directs viewers to look at the Black man from Juana and Francisca's perspective, but not the other way around. This is further emphasized by the subsequent dialogue, in which the Black man disappears from the frame altogether. Lola, still located on the other side of the fence and shown from the women's point of view, defends herself as "una señora americana" ("an American lady"), but Juana and Francisca remind her that they are aware of her immoral past, ridiculing her as a "pilingui," a slang word for prostitute.

By foregrounding the gaze of Juana and Francisca while erasing the perspective of the Black man, this sequence offers a categorical judgement of the interracial couple's relationship. Specifically, it portrays this relationship as founded on the hypersexuality and aggressive behaviours of two degenerate individuals, while construing Juana and Francisca as unsullied by the Black man's perverse gaze. These disparaging connotations are reinforced in several subsequent scenes, in which the Black man is shown constantly chasing after and beating Lola while the sound of pseudo-African drums plays in the background. According to the various scenes that depict the dysfunctional interracial couple, Lola and her husband might be an appropriate match for each other, but any decent Spanish woman should avoid marrying a Black man because of his uncontrollable temper and libido.

By suggesting that Spaniards should look up to white Americans while looking down on African Americans, the opening credit scene and the various scenes involving the interracial couple imply that Spaniards could imagine themselves as occupying an intermediate place on the United States' Black/white racial hierarchy. However, in the film's climactic scene, the working-class male characters, Antonio and Lorenzo, symbolically reassert their supremacy over white Americans by cleverly exploiting American racial tensions. At this point in the film, Juana and Francisca have broken up with their Spanish boyfriends in order to entertain their American suitors, Nathan and Spencer, more seriously. On the evening of Mr Stevens' birthday party, Antonio and Lorenzo show up at the Stevens' house to reclaim Juana and Francisca's affection; however, their physically intimidating American rivals aggressively ask them to leave. To console themselves, Antonio and Lorenzo drink copious amounts of wine and return to the party uninvited, entering the Stevens' house through a window. Predictably, the American admirers make short work of the Spanish intruders: they are able not only to beat them up, but also lift them, spin them around, and throw them unceremoniously out the window. But the Spaniards don't give up: after landing in the yard, Antonio notices Mr Stevens' Black neighbour sitting outside, and enlists his help in the brawl. As the Black neighbour enters the house, a long shot frames his full body, contrasting his large, muscular physique with the shorter, thinner frames of the other male characters (see figure 1.2). Throughout the sequence, the long shots that accentuate the Black man's formidable body are punctuated by medium close-ups that reveal his impassively violent facial expression, which remains unflinching as he easily knocks the Americans unconscious. After dispensing with Nathan and Spencer, the neighbour turns his aggressive gaze to Lorenzo, the puniest Spaniard in the room, as if to attack him, but Antonio stops him from doing so by declaring, "Ser amigo" ("He friend") while patting him on the chest. Once again shown in medium close-up with the much shorter Antonio in front of him, the Black man's face finally breaks into a vapid smile, the first and only change in expression he shows in the whole film. Notably, the nameless Black man never speaks a word in this sequence or throughout the film, which compounds his dehumanization.

The film's appropriation of American race relations highlights the Spaniards' ability to claim parity with American whites by asserting their superiority over Blacks. In the climactic fight scene, Antonio's ability to so easily manipulate the Black neighbour into beating up the white Americans suggests that Antonio not only presumes Blacks' innate propensity to violence, but also that he knows how to exploit Black-American frustration with white-American racism. At the same time, by portraying the Black man as a nameless, voiceless brute who is unable to tell the difference between a Spaniard and a white American, the film reinforces the stereotype of Black stupidity while underscoring Spaniards' racial whiteness. Consequently, although Antonio and the Black man share a resentment towards white Americans, the film's indulgence in anti-Black caricature precludes the possibility of imagining any kind of meaningful alliance between Spaniards and African Americans. Instead, the film implies that working-class Spaniards should feel humiliated by their subservient status to white Americans, and

Figure 1.2. An African-American muscleman in *Las que tienen que servir* (dir. José María Forqué, 1967).

by extension to several other nationalities, given the ongoing context of Northern European emigration, because this situation located them closer to Blacks than to white Europeans on the global racial spectrum. By using their ingenuity to vanquish their own "Blackness," the film suggests, Spaniards could demonstrate their belonging in a racially white Anglo-European modernity.

A third film that exemplifies the narrative formula of the *macho ibérico* who outsmarts a Black rival can be found in Pedro Lazaga's 1972 film, *París bien vale una moza* ("Paris is well worth a girl"). Like *Los económicamente débiles* and *Las que tienen que servir*, *París* portrays late-Francoist Spain as having suffered a racial humiliation that must be overcome through a national reassertion of white masculinity. In this film, Don Rafael, a wealthy landowner of rural Spain, sends the struggling peasant Juan (Alfredo Landa) to Paris in search of Don Rafael's estranged daughter. After several setbacks, it is revealed that Rafael's daughter has long since passed away. However, during his adventures, Juan coincidentally meets Rafael's granddaughter, Sophie (Concha Velasco), and marries her with Rafael's blessing by the end of the film. Although

Juan's journey to France is framed as a personal errand for a rich *señorito*, the film's narrative strongly resembles the then-ongoing reality of Spanish emigration to Northern Europe. After all, much of the story focuses on the protagonist's desperate efforts to find work in France, a country that, in real life, served as a major destination for Spanish labourers of the period.

The film's circuitous depiction of emigration accentuates the regime's anxiety about how the exodus of Spanish labourers would promote an image of Spain as backward or inferior within Europe. As in other films, these anxieties surface through the film's engagement with racial caricature. As soon as Juan arrives in Paris, he is robbed and left penniless before he even leaves the station. The Parisian police chief, in a generous effort to help Juan recover, sets him up with a paid gig as a wrestler. Juan is given the nickname of "El Oso de los Pirineos" ("The Bear of the Pyrenees") and is asked to participate in a rigged match against "El Gorila de Camerún" ("The Gorilla of Cameroon") in which the "gorilla" will pretend to defeat Juan soundly without actually hurting him. Clad only in the skimpiest of briefs, the two men's bodies are marked by a series of racialized contrasts that invert those we see in *Vente a Alemania, Pepe*. We will recall, for a moment, that in *Vente*, Landa's character is portrayed as physically inferior to a strapping, white German; by contrast, in *París*, Landa's short stature, mediocre physique, and higher pitched voice portray him as hopelessly feminized and thus mismatched against his much taller, outrageously muscular, darker-skinned opponent. Similarly, in a sequence that is strongly reminiscent of *Las que tienen que servir*, "el Gorila" easily lifts Juan up over his head, spins him around several times, and hurls him on the floor of the ring. The camera sensationalizes the fight by interspersing medium close-ups with medium and long shots, thus alternating between Juan's exaggerated facial expressions and the spectacle of his thrashing.

By whimsically reinventing a David and Goliath narrative, the fight scene between "el Oso de los Pirineos" and "el Gorila de Camerún" is clearly intended to suggest a competition between Spanish and African masculinities. Because the fighters' names bluntly evoke the well-worn refrain about Spanish backwardness, "Africa begins at the Pyrenees," we may read the fight scene as a metaphorical battle of Spanish masculinity to defeat its own perceived backwardness, that is, its "inner African." By dramatizing the idea of Spain as the "Africa" of Europe – a stereotype largely fabricated by Northern European countries, including France – the scene articulates Spain's desire to achieve the European whiteness to which France already belongs. The internal nature of the *macho ibérico*'s battle against his own racial origins becomes apparent

Figure 1.3. A boxing match in *París bien vale una moza* (dir. Pedro Lazaga, 1972).

as the scene progresses. According to the plan, which is explained to the competitors before the match begins, "el Gorila" must pull Juan's ear to let Juan know when to concede defeat. However, the problem is that Juan has a tick: having his ear pulled triggers the childhood memory of overly zealous nuns disciplining him in school. Consequently, whenever anyone pulls his ear, he loses control of himself and flies into a rage. Predictably, when the "Gorila," on the verge of victory, pulls Juan's ear, Juan instantly manages to push his much larger rival out of the ring, overwhelming him with punches and kicks (see figure 1.3). Juan then leaps out of the ring into the crowd, intent on continuing to batter his rival among the audience. What was supposed to be a highly controlled, rigged match degenerates into an all-out brawl.

This scene's portrayal of Juan's victory against the "Gorila de Camerún" hinges on a specific emotional trigger; namely, his memory of the militant religiosity of early Francoism, which is symbolized by nuns pulling his ear. In this way, the scene underscores a conflicted memory of early Francoism during the later decades of the dictatorship. Given that the regime of the 1960s and 1970s aimed to exploit the trappings of Spain's cultural difference to perform the nation's modernity, it understood that the militantly National-Catholic rhetoric that marked its early years, especially during the immediate post-Civil-War period, contradicted the tourist-friendly image it sought to construct. By conflating stereotypes of Spain as hyperreligious and racially African, the scene directly references entrenched Black Legend discourses that had long been portrayed as indicators of Spanish backwardness. At the same time, however, Juan's ability to channel the traumas of his childhood as energy to drive his miraculous comeback underscores his capacity to transcend the Black Legend and defeat his "inner African."

In sum, while the three comedies discussed above initially highlight their Spanish male protagonists' proximity to racial Blackness, they also portray these protagonists as expelling or overcoming their Africanness in a variety of ways. In each film, working-class Spanish men manage to cross the global colour line, thus distancing themselves from the Black Legend while recovering a previously lost power associated with masculinity and whiteness. Similarly, in all three films, the protagonists use their cleverness and ingenuity to transform the tropes of racial backwardness, such as blackface, Black hypermasculinity, or Spanish religious fanaticism, into emblems of Spain's racial and masculine power. The films thus underscore Spaniards' ability to harness their experience of abasement, exploitation, and hardship to improve their nation's geopolitical standing. In this way, the films depict Spain's belonging in global whiteness as fair compensation for a longsuffering populace that deserved to be granted its rightful place on the world stage.

From *suecas* to *negras*: The Pleasures and Perils of Interracial Sex

In addition to the expulsion of the "inner African," another recurring racial motif in late-Francoist comedies is their preoccupation with interracial sex. The example studied above, *Las que tienen que servir*, stands out among these films by depicting a relationship between a Spanish woman and a Black man; it was much more frequent for popular comedies to depict interracial sex as a consequence of Spanish men's uncontainable lust for women deemed racially inferior. Like the *sueca* narrative that it inverted, the *macho ibérico*'s desire for miscegenation was symptomatic of the comedy genre's eroticization of all foreign women, who were generally perceived as more sexually liberated than Spanish women of the time. However, although the *sueca* emblematized Spain's yearning to belong in Anglo-European modernity, the symbolism of interracial sex, especially between Spanish men and Black women, harboured a range of ambivalent, contradictory meanings. While it was often construed as a titillating fantasy of a temporary loss or contamination of whiteness, it also allegorized Spain's upward mobility by suggesting that Spanish men could sexually "conquer" other races.

The multiple meanings of interracial sex derived from conflicting discourses that were prevalent during Spain's development era. On one hand, a deeply rooted imaginary held that Spaniards had historically welcomed racial mixing in the Americas, given the reality of *mestizaje* between Spaniards and Indigenous peoples. This idea was especially promoted by the Franco regime through the discourse of Hispanotropicalism, a theory that emphasized the benevolence of Spanish imperialism to justify the regime's reluctance to grant independence to its African colonies during the 1950s and 1960s (Nerín 12; Stucki 129). According to this logic, Spaniards' historical proclivity towards interracial sex, which in the past had enabled them to help inferior peoples reach their full potential, was emblematic of the nation's unique imperial legacy, and thus was also indicative of its whiteness. In late-Francoist comedies, the myth of the Spanish empire's embrace of interracial sex was sometimes construed as an indicator of its modernity, as it offered a convenient point of comparison to the United States, where controversies around interracial relationships were hotly contested during the civil rights movement.

Needless to say, the Hispanotropicalist myth of Spanish tolerance towards interracial sex was strongly contradicted by Francoist policies in its African colonies and by prevalent anti-miscegenation attitudes in the metropole. As Gustau Nerín notes, in the Spanish Guinean colony, interracial sex between Spanish women and Guinean men was heavily stigmatized and was severely punished, given the dominant European stereotype of Black men as brutal predators of white women (90–3). Similarly, while evidence indicates that sex between Spanish men and Guinean women was tacitly tolerated in the Guinean colony to varying degrees throughout the nineteenth and twentieth centuries, the Franco regime attempted to curtail it by imposing a strict sexual morality code in which Spanish settlers, who were overwhelmingly male, could be fined or repatriated for having extramarital relations with Guinean women[9] (113–14). The anti-miscegenation mentality that governed sexual norms in the Guinean colony under Francoism was also dominant in development-era Spain, despite the Hispanotropicalist myth. This is especially apparent in late-Francoist comedy's representation of 1960s youth counterculture, especially hippie culture, which was seen as symptomatic of an Anglophone cultural invasion and was ridiculed for its excessively permissive attitude towards sexual perversions like homosexuality and interracial sex. As we saw in the introduction, the prevalence of anti-miscegenation sentiment in Spain during this period is further documented in Lucía Mbomío Rubio's 2017 book, *Las que se atrevieron* ("The women who dared"). In this text, Mbomío Rubio recounts the experiences of multiple white, Spanish women who formed interracial relationships with Black men, especially with Guinean students or exiles, during late Francoism and the Transition. All the women whose stories are included in the collection recount how their relationships garnered suspicion, condemnation, and ostracism within their majority white communities.

The contradictory meanings of interracial sex, which included its use as a metaphor of Spain's upward mobility or as a path to regaining its lost imperial splendor as well as its role as a thrilling fantasy of a transgressive act that was extremely stigmatized in real life, can be traced in several popular comedies of the 1960s and 1970s. One film that attempted to harness the idea of interracial sex as an indicator of Spain's belonging in global modernity is *Una vez al año ser hippy no hace daño* ("Once a year it doesn't hurt to be a hippie," dir. Javier Aguirre, 1969). This film narrates how a struggling group of provincial, travelling musicians must update their outdated, folkloric musical style to cater to the cosmopolitan environment of Torremolinos, a newly constructed beach resort. Drawing on a widespread imaginary in which displaced Spanish labourers were imagined as closer to racial Blackness than whiteness, this film explicitly imagines Spaniards as "Blacks" who are chasing after white *suecas* and compares their right to do so to ongoing racial struggles abroad, most notably, the US civil rights movement.

The film begins by portraying the musical trio, whose members include Lisarda (Concha Velasco), Ricardo (Alfredo Landa) and Silvestre (Manolo Gómez Bur), as trapped in a cycle of performing antiquated kitsch for rural and small-town audiences. In the opening scene, the trio perform a 1940s hit called "Mi casita de papel" ("My little house of paper") as an Alps-themed yodel number, complete with matching costumes and pseudo-yodeling, in a Spanish town nestled in the mountains. The visibly bored audience does not even applaud when the group finishes; instead, they begin dancing immediately when a rock-and-roll recording is played. Soon thereafter, we see the trio in another town performing a Cuba-themed song, "Frenesí tropical" ("Tropical frenzy"), in which all three musicians, including the men, are dressed in frilly, midriff-baring outfits, and singing a rhythmical song about a "negra linda" ("pretty Black woman") and a "negro loco" ("crazy Black man"). Although the audience is initially sceptical, they react with enthusiasm when Lisarda accelerates her hip shaking.

Like several of the comedies we have studied, these two opening performances imply that Spain's geopolitical position is caught between the racialized poles of whiteness (the Alps) and Blackness (Cuba). While the unsuccessful Alps number underscores Spain's unfulfilled aspiration to achieve the whiteness of Northern Europe, the Cuba-themed song about Black lovers, which is applauded for its extravagant sexuality but not for its musical style, calls attention to Spain's anxieties about its racial standing and its colonial past. Given Spain's past colonial relations with Cuba and, in particular, the "crisis of whiteness" that the loss of this colony triggered for Spain in 1898, the caricatured depiction of Cuba accentuates both Spain's nostalgia for a past where its racial and cultural supremacy was undisputed as well as its anxiety about its uncertain global standing during the development era (Fra-Molinero 148). Thus, these two performances establish a foundational premise for the film: namely, that the group's acquisition of a more modern, Anglo-European musical vocabulary allegorizes not only the regime's desire to participate in modernity, but also its aspiration to revive Spanish colonial power through its assertion of belonging to European whiteness.

As the film develops, the trio meets Johnny, a Spaniard who joins the group as a fourth member to teach them new musical genres. The foursome's first effort at a hippie anthem, "Los negros con las suecas" ("The Black men with Swedish women"), portrays the beach of Torremolinos as an antiracist utopia through lines such as: "Los negros a las suecas perseguirán, / las suecas a los negros divertirán, / todos juntos y unidos se abrazarán" ("The Black men will chase the Swedish women, / the Swedish women will amuse the Black men, / everyone will embrace each other in unity"). The lyrics also feature several references to the then-ongoing American civil rights movement, such as: "No existirá el color ni lucha antirracial" ("There will be no colour nor antiracist struggle"), "La playa es un hogar sin discriminación" ("The beach is a home with no discrimination"), and "No se puede jugar con la segregación" ("No one should play with segregation"). As the group sings, a montage shows fast-forwarded shots of Black men and *suecas* chasing each other up and down the beach. At one point, a Black man takes a break from chasing *suecas* and sits on the sand, rubbing conspicuously white-coloured sunscreen all over his body. Shortly thereafter, the Black men are replaced by Alfredo Landa who, wearing an animal outfit with horns on his head, pursues a group of *suecas* in their stead. At the end of the song, we see several shots of white women and men running together and holding hands.

Despite its antiracist lyrics, this sequence only shows Black men at the beginning of the song; by its end, the beach is populated only by white people. Pointedly, the montage implies that the Black men do not disappear, but rather, that they are gradually whitened to the point that they become indistinguishable from other beachgoers. The first stage of their whitening occurs when one of the Black men stops chasing *suecas* to rub the white sunscreen on his skin. Recalling Richard Dyer's observation that tanning became a ubiquitous marker of whiteness in global twentieth-century visual culture because it "displays white people's right to be various," this image is the first indicator that the Black man is about to undergo a process of whitening (49–50). The second stage occurs when the Black man is substituted by a horned Landa in an animal costume. Although Landa's skin is not Black, his animal costume suggests that, as a Spaniard, he shares the Black man's racialized hypersexuality. The next phase in the progression, in which Landa's animal suit disappears and in which the all-white beachgoers revel in harmonic unison, constitutes a full achievement of whiteness – one where the racial difference between Blacks, Spaniards and *suecas* has been negated, and all are equally white.

This scene explicitly draws a comparison between the *macho ibérico's* desire to pursue *suecas*, on one hand, and the major victories of the American civil rights movement, such as desegregation and the legalization of interracial marriage, on the other. As in other films, the scene's initial equation of Spanishness to Blackness fails to produce a meaningful solidarity between the two. Rather, the scene portrays interracial sex as a path to the erasure of racial difference and, therefore, as a path to upward mobility. It suggests, in other words, that by traversing the colour line sexually, Spaniards will be able to traverse the colour line themselves. By intertwining the *macho ibérico's* erasure of his Blackness with civil rights discourse and hippie protest culture, the scene commodifies these movements' allure as emblems of global modernity while emptying them of their ideologically threatening political content. Instead, both movements are portrayed as consonant with late-Francoism's effort to portray Spaniards as transcending the "Africa of Europe" stereotype. Importantly, however, the depiction of Alfredo Landa as a sex-crazed animal self-consciously alludes to the regime's strategy of selling Spain's exoticism as a commodity. For although Landa is replaced by racially unmarked whites in the sequence, the whole film, like the entire corpus of *landismo* cinema, revolves around the premise of Landa's irrepressible sexuality as a source of infinite jokes. Thus, the sequence establishes parity between Spaniards and *suecas* not only by erasing Spaniards' "Blackness," but also by underscoring the artificiality of Landa's "difference."

While *Una vez al año* portrays interracial sex between "Black" Spaniards and white *suecas* as a path to upward mobility, other comedies draw on entrenched anti-miscegenation prejudices to depict interracial sex as a titillating fantasy, but one which is ultimately beneath the dignity of Spanish men. This is the case with *El alma se serena* ("The soul becomes serene," dir. José Luis Saenz de Heredia, 1970), a film that promotes Spain's ability to profit from a commodified, deracialized "Africanness" while condemning interracial sex between Spaniards and Blacks as an inconceivable moral low. This film narrates the story of a small-town woman, Chelín (Concha Velasco), who attempts to wean her childhood crush, Manolo (Alfredo Landa), off his dissolute, urban lifestyle so he will marry her. Over the course of the film, Chelín's rural origins are repeatedly depicted as a form of "Africanness," an idea that parallels development-era Spain's efforts to transform its own status as an "Africa" of Europe into a competitive advantage on the world stage. However, Chelín's attempts to woo the hedonistic Manolo culminate in her dramatic intervention to prevent him from engaging in racial miscegenation with Black women. Consequently, the film's positive depiction of Chelín's figurative "Africanness" contrasts sharply with the embodied Africanness of Black women, which must be denigrated to illuminate Spain's belonging in European whiteness.

The idea that Spain can profit from its historical portrayal as an "Africa" of Europe surfaces when Manolo and his pleasure-seeking companion Bernabé (José Sacristán) decide to take the naive, provincial Chelín to a hippie orgy. Chelín, who stands out because of her rustic demeanor, is befuddled when several hippies around her order unusual cocktails such as "astronauta muy seco" ("very dry astronaut"), "descapotable con petardo" ("convertible with firecracker"), and "vietnamita doble" ("double Vietnamese"). However, her companions look on in shock when she orders a "congoleño con mochila" ("Congolese with backpack"), a regional oddity that no one other than the waiter has ever heard of. Downing the drink in one gulp, Chelín is transformed into a hippie who seeks to overcome her "complejo de paleta" ("bumpkin complex"): she quickly changes clothes, interrupts the band, and belts out a traditional tune in a modern pop style, declaring coarsely that "¡las de provincias... sabemos hacerlo como la que más!" ("We girls from the provinces can do it just as well as anyone else!") The next morning, Chelín wakes up as her normal self, embarrassed, and hung over.

Chelín's circular transformation from rural prude to hippie hedonist and back again is a telling metaphor for late-Francoist Spain's desire to portray its own metamorphosis from backwardness to modernity. While the hippies' drinks glorify Western capitalism by referencing consumer status symbols ("convertible") or anti-Communist crusades such as the Cold War space race ("astronaut") and the Vietnam War ("double Vietnamese"), Chelín's "Congolese" cocktail draws on the stereotype of African backwardness in order to reinforce her status as a rural outsider. By extension, her drink also underscores Spain's status as a "Congo" within Europe. The fact that this drink catalyses her sudden transformation into a pop singer who defends rural sexual prowess mirrors the regime's goal of turning Spain's "Africanness" into a competitive advantage.

However, the film later stipulates that any capitalist exploitation of Spanish exoticism must be accompanied by a clear affirmation of Spanish racial whiteness. Roughly halfway through the film, Bernabé brings two Black African women to his house, hoping that he and his friend, Manolo, will be able to seduce them. Dressed in a pseudo-African costume, he invites Manolo to play drums with him while they watch the women dance, a strategy which Bernabé hopes will serve to "calentar el horno" ("heat up the oven"). The scene spectacularizes the women's Blackness through a dizzying concatenation of camera angles that accentuate the frenetic movement of their hair and bare feet, as well as their revealing attire. When Chelín, who is cooking upstairs, discovers what the men are up to, she becomes enraged, and declares that Manolo must "¡dejar de ser un degenerado que se refocila en el lodo arrastrado por un gurrumino sin escrúpulos!" ("stop being a degenerate who plays in the mud while being dragged by a coward with no morals!"). She also screams that the only meal Manolo deserves is "¡que [le] frían las negras un explorador!" ("for the Black women to fry [him] an explorer!"). (See figure 1.4.)

In this climactic scene, Chelín's strident reaction to Manolo's fraternization with African women marks a key juncture in the film. For shortly after Chelín's outburst, Manolo reconciles with her and agrees to get married; the plot then veers towards Chelín's machinations to maintain his sexual interest as his wife. Thus, Chelín's intervention is a turning point in which Manolo's downward moral trajectory is diverted away from the low point of racial miscegenation and back towards the goal of marriage with a Spanish woman. Unlike the symbolic Africanness of Chelín's "Congolese" drink, which is presented as a sign of Spain's capacity for modernization, the function of embodied Africanness in this scene is one of abjection: Black skin, including the desire for it, is portrayed as external and inferior to Spanishness. For Chelín, sex between Spaniards and Blacks is a problem precisely because it brings Spain, long racialized as an Africa of Europe, too close to that which it yearns not to be. This becomes especially conspicuous when we consider that the Black women in this scene are clearly an inversion of the

Figure 1.4. Pseudo-African costumes and music in *El alma se serena* (dir. José Luis Saenz de Heredia, 1970).

sueca stereotype. Like *suecas*, they are foreign and beautiful; yet their spectacular, racialized primitiveness marks the exact opposite of the *sueca*'s white modernity.

Chelín's remarks during her angry eruption are especially revealing of her desire to separate Africanness from Spanishness. For example, her reference to miscegenation as "refocilarse en el lodo" ("playing in the mud") conjures the image of a white-skinned person sullied or contaminated by dark mud. Similarly, her insinuation that Manolo must rid himself of Bernabé's "mud" suggests a need to wash racial contamination off the national body. Chelín further calls attention to need to improve Spain's racial stature by calling Manolo a "degenerado" ("degenerate") a term that connotes deterioration, and Bernabé a "gurrumino" ("coward"), an epithet that connotes weakness and effeminacy. These insults indicate her perception that sex with Black women will degrade Spain's already tenuous racial stature. She reiterates this idea by sarcastically wishing that the women "frían…un explorador" ("fry an explorer") for Manolo. With this comment, she implies that the men's perverse sexual "exploration," which she likens to the explorations of early modern colonizers, may result in the cannibalization of the Spanish race altogether. However, despite portraying Manolo and Bernabé as emasculated by their perverse desires, her statements ultimately reinforce Spain's belonging on the white side of the racial line. After all, her reference to past Spanish colonizers is ultimately a call to restore a destabilized racial order in which Spain, formerly at the vanguard of European imperialism, established itself as unquestionably superior to, and distinct from, inferior races such as Blacks.

The opposing meanings exemplified in *Una vez al año …* and *El alma …*, in which interracial sex is respectively figured as a metaphor for the nation's upward mobility and as an indicator of racial and moral degeneration, are paradoxically intertwined with each other in *Ligue story* ("Lust story," dir. Alfonso Paso, 1972). This film narrates the comical entanglements of several Spaniards, including both men and women, who try to solve their love problems by posting and responding to personal dating advertisements in the newspaper. One of the characters, a *macho ibérico* named Agustín (Cassen), unwittingly establishes correspondence with a deceitful hippie named Mari Sole, who is scheming with several of her friends to entrap and humiliate an earnest relationship-seeker as a practical joke. The film's association of interracial sex with hippies mirrors the ambivalent attitudes towards youth countercultures of the 1960s displayed in other films, in which hippies were simultaneously constructed as foreign, immoral degenerates, but also as emblematic of a global, white modernity distinguished by its permissive attitudes.

After establishing contact via the newspaper dating ads, Agustín and Mari Sole begin a tryst that culminates in a night of drunken sexual debauchery with the local community of hippies. Mari Sole first takes Agustín to a hotel bar, where she displays her sexual unrestraint by kissing a Black man in front of him – an action that delights the repressed Agustín. However, when her friends surreptitiously drug Agustín's drink, he behaves so erratically and aggressively towards other women that he is removed from the bar. Mari Sole and her friends then take Agustín to a costume party that is being held in the back yard of a large mansion. This party is presented as a *macho ibérico*'s utopian fantasy: it is primarily attended by scantily clad women of diverse nationalities, including not only Northern European *suecas*, but also Asian, Latin American and African women, all of whom are dressed in skimpy, yet campy costumes that include shepherds' hats, Native American feathered headbands, Mexican sombreros, hula skirts, and the like. It is also attended by several overtly effeminate men dressed in women's costumes, a detail which bluntly implies that the party is full of homosexual men. In this way, the film portrays homosexuality and interracial sexuality as overlapping perversions of global modernity, a link that would become especially pronounced in post-Transition popular comedies (see chapter 4).

The party's most conspicuously caricatured attendee is an aggressive Black woman with a masculine demeanor. Dressed in a pirate costume, she beats or slaps anyone whose behaviour she disapproves of. As happens in several other films, she is first shown in a long shot that reflects the point of view of Agustín and several Spanish companions; visually, she occupies the centre of the frame, a position of power that she refuses to cede even as various Spaniards attempt to displace her from it. When Agustín sees her, he is instantly titillated, declaring: "Morena tiene que ser la tierra para ser buena, y ¡la mujer para el hombre también debe ser morena!" ("Soil must be dark to be fertile, and the woman must also be dark for the man!") Despite Agustín's overture, the Black woman violently pushes him away, ejecting him from the frame while she remains at the centre. Watching the scene from the sidelines, Mari Sole approaches the Black woman in an attempt to defend Augustín, but the woman pushes her to the ground, also ejecting her from the frame. Agustín, infuriated, hits the Black woman twice, but fails to knock her over or even cause her to budge. He then lectures her that he had no choice but to be physically aggressive with her because "Los españoles, cuando insultan a una mujer en nuestra presencia, nos jugamos la vida si es preciso, porque la mujer es hija, la mujer es esposa, la mujer es madre, y ¡madre no hay más que una!" ("When a woman is insulted in our presence, we Spaniards risk our lives if we have to because women are daughters, women are wives, women are mothers, and everyone only has one mother!") As he speaks, the camera slowly zooms in on the two characters and places Agustín in the centre of the frame. When he finishes his monologue, the Black woman takes him aside and pulls him into a long, passionate kiss.

Agustín's tirade, in which he physically strikes a Black woman while lecturing her about the sanctity of women, is particularly revealing. For Agustín, the woman's Blackness masculinizes her, and in doing so, renders her closer to the stereotypes of Black musclemen that surface in *Las que tienen que servir* or *París bien vale una moza* than to a white Spanish woman like Mari Sole. Consequently, Agustín's *macho ibérico* sexuality becomes the corrective through which the Black woman's deviant gender performance can be domesticated and feminized. According to this logic, it is precisely by beating her and yelling at her that he accomplishes the task of feminizing her, given that, after his tirade, she voluntarily submits to his masculine power, as it is she, not he, who initiates their kiss. The idea that their kiss constitutes a taming of the Black woman is especially emphasized by a long take in which Agustín physically leans over the woman as she sinks backwards into his arms, thus re-establishing his dominance over her. In this way, Agustín's masculinity is portrayed as a corrective to a social order that hippies – who incarnate a range of moral problems, including foreign contamination, promiscuity, and homosexuality – have destabilized. The next scene further emphasizes this point: upon witnessing the confrontation between Agustín and the Black woman, women of various nationalities are aroused by his performance of virility and line up for a chance to kiss him, too. A close-up focuses on Agustín's face as he kisses several women representing various caricatured origins, one by one. After he kisses each woman, he announces the area of the world she represents: "¡Europa! ¡África! ¡América! ¡Oceanía!" At the end, however, an Asian man turns up in the line to kiss him, but Agustín sends him away, telling him, "¡A comerte un flan!" ("Go jump in the lake!").

The implications of the scene are both obvious and self-contradictory. On one hand, the *macho ibérico*'s unbridled sexuality, which can conquer or subdue women from all over the world, emblematizes late-Francoist Spain's ability to return the nation to its earlier stature as an imperial power. However, as in other films, the consequences of interracial sex in *Ligue story* are portrayed as morally ambivalent. We must recall, of course, that Agustín has been duped into attending this party by Mari Sole, a disingenuous hippie who isn't really interested in dating him at all. Similarly, Agustín's sexual antics only occur because he is drunk and has been drugged by hippies; furthermore, he comes dangerously close to kissing another man. In addition, shortly after the orgy, the police arrive to break up the party, and the film concludes by showing Agustín locked up in jail for his unruly behaviour. Once again, interracial sexuality is shown to be a thrilling spectacle that invites fantasies of imperial resurgence and masculine power, but one whose thrill derives precisely from its status as a threat to the very forms of power it is imagined to reinforce.

Whether they portrayed interracial sex as a threat to Spanish male supremacy or as reaffirming of it, popular comedy films such as *Una vez al año ser hippy no hace daño, El alma se serena,* and *Ligue story* all emphasize Spain's belonging on the white side of the colour line. In some of these films, Spanish male protagonists are portrayed as maintaining their virility, dominance, and power by avoiding interracial sex, while in other films, interracial sex enables them to prove themselves as the deserving heirs of Spain's colonial legacy. Although these comedies drew on contradictory discourses such as the myth of *mestizaje*, Francoism's antipathy towards miscegenation, and even US civil rights, they all invited their working-class viewers to envision their nation as transcending the Black Legend by imagining it as superior to degenerate races, of whom Blacks were considered the epitome. In doing so, popular comedies about interracial sex offered consolation to Spanish viewers whose lives had been destabilized by rapid social and economic change, and who were frustrated by what they perceived as their lowly position on the world stage.

Conclusion

In this chapter, we have seen how a variety of popular comedy films from the late-Francoist era exploited several formulas of racial caricature to portray Spain as belonging in global whiteness. In these films, the development-era regime's promises of upward economic mobility were interwoven with their depiction of Spain as ascending into Anglo-European whiteness and as distancing itself from various racial groups imagined as inferior. In this way, popular comedies of the era offered whiteness as a psychological wage to their working-class viewers, many of whom were frustrated by the disparity between late-Francoism's promises of prosperity and the hard realities of emigration. Specifically, these comedies offered relief to their audiences by teaching them that they were not as low on the global racial hierarchy as they thought. Rather, the logic went, the regime's development project would free them of the Black Legend, an entrenched discourse that associated Spain's supposed primitiveness with its racial inferiority, and return Spaniards back to the "white" side of the global colour line while still enabling them to exploit a deracialized version of Spain's "difference" as a national marketing strategy. Although the expression "lavarle la cara al país" ("washing the country's face") is often associated with post-Franco Spain's efforts to scrub the unflattering traces of dictatorship from the nation's global image, this phrase could also be used to describe the later years of Francoism, when the regime was deeply invested in "washing the nation's face" of its perennial status as a racialized other of Europe. Consequently, popular cinema of late Francoism played a crucial role in articulating and implementing a national vision of Spain's white, European identity, a vision that would continue to play an important role in the democratic era.

Chapter 2

Imperial Death: White Femininity and the Missionary Imaginary

In an early scene of *Misión blanca* ("White mission," dir. Juan de Orduña, 1946), an elder Spanish missionary priest named Father Suárez introduces the newly arrived Father Mauricio to a Catholic mission in Spanish Guinea. While reassuring him about the rewards of missionary life, Father Suárez also highlights its dangers, such as disease and rebellious natives. At one point, a small monkey approaches Father Mauricio and enthusiastically demands his affection. The monkey, Father Suárez explains, is familiar to the mission, and is always excited by new arrivals because it is looking for its master, who died three years earlier. However, the monkey soon loses interest in Father Mauricio and wanders to a nearby tombstone, where its master is buried. Father Mauricio is deeply moved by the story.

Childish, loyal, and simple-minded, the monkey allegorizes the Black Africans the missionaries aim to evangelize. Like the monkey looking for its master, the analogy suggests, Africans are yearning to be reunited with the true god they otherwise will not know and need missionaries to bring them closer to that deity. In the late 1940s and 1950s, missionary films like *Misión blanca* portrayed Spanish missionaries as selfless, dedicated heroes who put themselves in harm's way to improve the lives of inferior peoples like Africans, whose dim intellect and primitive mores render them closer to apes than to Europeans. Such films became in vogue in Francoist Spain because they offered the regime a way to distance itself from its Fascist origins and portray itself as a bulwark of Christian values. At the same time, these films' imperialist orientation emblematized the Franco regime's promises of returning the impoverished, war-torn Spain of the 1940s to an earlier era of global power.

Although missionary cinema declined after the 1950s, it left a lasting imprint on popular cinema of the late-Franco era. Specifically, it gave rise to what I term a "missionary imaginary" – that is, a cinematic iconography that portrayed imperial Spain as sacrificing itself to rescue racialized peoples – that persisted in popular cinema until at least the 1970s. This imaginary, which surfaced in both religious and secular genres, fashioned a self-exculpatory narrative about colonialism that coincided with the loss of Spain's African colonies between 1959 and 1975. Like neighbouring Portugal, Spain was a latecomer to decolonization, which had been happening around the globe since the end of the Second World War. Despite pressure from the United Nations, Franco's government resisted decolonizing its African possessions in Morocco, Guinea, Ifni, and the Sahara, but gradually softened its position to avoid becoming an international pariah. Although the regime heavily suppressed dissident perspectives on decolonization through censorship and *materia reservada* (classified information) laws, popular cinema offered a comforting, nostalgic mythology about the end of the empire. A particular feature of this mythology was the feminization of late imperial Spain. In films of this period, Spain's civilizing mission was imagined to radiate feminine qualities like maternity, innocence, gentleness, and vulnerability, which were envisioned as ameliorating or healing the barbaric tendencies of its colonized subjects.

The missionary imaginary of late Francoism was transmitted through several genres, including religious, musical, and even horror films, and evolved significantly over the course of the 1960s and 1970s. In the early 1960s, cinema glorified and defended Spain's imperial legacy by promoting a "Hispanotropicalist" view of empire, emphasizing Spain's uniquely benevolent imperial mission, which was seen as morally superior to the empires of other European powers (Nerin 12, Stucki 129). Films of these years celebrated the ability of the Spanish empire to subjugate inferior races, especially Blacks, who were portrayed on screen as feminized and whitened by Spain's civilizing light. By the late 1960s and 1970s, however, many films abandoned the idea that the Spanish empire was different from or superior to other European empires. Instead, during these later years, filmic portrayals of the empire emphasized Spain's commonalities with other European powers such as Britain, France, and Belgium, which were also facing the disintegration of their empires at that time. Consequently, the image of the domesticated, feminine Black subject of the early 1960s was substituted in the later 1960s by the trope of the Black male rapist of innocent white women. By personifying European empires as feminized victims and Africa as a hypermasculine rapist, this latter cinematic formula portrayed Spain as free of culpability for both the humiliation of imperial loss and the various humanitarian disasters that emerged from it.

Furthermore, by erasing the distinctions between Spain and Europe that were central to Hispanotropicalism, the Black rapist trope also signalled Spain's full assimilation into a white, postimperial Europe.

The next section will first review some historical context about Spain's African empire, especially its collapse during the 1960s and 1970s, and will theorize its association with white femininity in film. Popular cinema's shifting strategies in coming to terms with Spain's loss of empire are then uncovered by examining a range of case studies that span several genres, such as religious films, musical comedies, melodramas, and horror. As we will see, by associating late imperial Spain with archetypal characteristics of white femininity, such as selfless maternity, innocent girlhood, or vulnerability to sexual aggression, these films contributed to a larger erasure of colonial memory in the post-Franco era. By whitening and feminizing late imperial Spain, these films buttressed the larger narrative of Spain's integration into a global modernity that imagined itself as not only racially white, but morally white, as well.

Screening Imperial Loss: A Brief Overview

To better understand the relationship between decolonization and popular film during late Francoism, a review of Spain's colonial experience in Africa is necessary. Although Spain acquired its various colonies in North and Sub-Saharan Africa over a span of more than two centuries,[1] it only exerted sustained efforts to develop a colonial infrastructure in these territories in the early decades of the twentieth century. Spain's interest in exploiting previously marginalized African colonies was an effort to mitigate the humiliation of the Spanish-American War of 1898, after which Spain had been forced to cede its long-held possessions in Cuba, Puerto Rico, and Philippines to the United States. The development of an African empire was thus an attempt to replace a much older global empire that had once spanned Asia and the Americas.

Significantly, the value of Spain's African empire was often more symbolic than economic in nature. Of the various African colonies, present-day Equatorial Guinea proved the most economically profitable to Spain during the colonial period due to its primary exports of timber, cacao, and coffee; the North African colonies, by contrast, were "poor areas, where colonial action had been late and weak," and consequently did not provide a significant economic benefit to Spain until the discovery of phosphate reserves in the Sahara colony in the mid-1960s (Pardo Sanz, "Política descolonizadora" 84). Although African imperialism was despised by much of Spain's populace during the early decades of the twentieth century,[2] opposition to it was thoroughly silenced upon the ascent to power of General Francisco Franco in 1939, whose government promised to return the nation to the imperial splendor of yesteryear. The symbolism of African colonialism was especially important to Franco, given that he and several of his ministers, including his long-time second-in-command, Luis Carrero Blanco, who served as Minister Undersecretary of the Presidency from 1941–73, had built their military reputations by serving in North Africa (Pardo Sanz, "Política descolonizadora" 84). In an effort to exploit the African empire's potent symbolism in the years after the Civil War, a wide variety of Francoist media and publications touted the regime's ambitions of expanding its colonial dominions to include all of Morocco, Gibraltar, Oran, and parts of present-day Nigeria, and Gabon, among other areas (Martin Márquez, *Disorientations* 249–50).

After the Second World War, the defeat of the Axis powers left Franco's government isolated on the world stage. Forced to abandon its expansionist plans, the regime nonetheless hoped to retain control over its remaining African colonies as long as possible. To do so, it replaced its talk of expansion with a rhetoric of Christian paternalism and sacrifice, a discourse that was especially promulgated through government-sponsored missionary films. Throughout the late 1940s and 1950s, missionary films such as *Misión blanca, La manigua sin Dios* ("The godless swamp," dir. Arturo Ruiz-Castillo, 1949), *La mies es mucha* ("The harvest is great," dir. José Luis Saenz de Heredia, 1949), *Balarrasa* (*Reckless*, dir. José Antonio Nieves Conde, 1951), and *Una cruz en el infierno* (*Flame over Vietnam*, dir. José María Elorrieta, 1954), among others, extolled the virtues of the evangelizing spirit that presumably motivated Spain's imperial endeavours. Although almost all of these films featured white male protagonists, they propagated a vision of masculinity that was "anti-militaristic" and therefore "feminised" (Labanyi, "Internalisations" 30). Brad Epps has further argued that colonial films of this period propagated a "masculine mystique" by constructing their male characters as enigmatic and self-abnegating (42). The feminized masculinity of missionary heroes accentuated the altruistic, self-sacrificing qualities of Spanish colonialism, while distinguishing it from the racism and greed of other European empires. Similarly, the genre lauded Spain for playing a maternal role to a large family of colonized and formerly colonized nations, in which contemporary African colonialism was seen as a continuation of Spain's eternal colonial mission.

Missionary cinema's effort to romanticize and glorify Spain's role in Africa by associating it with qualities such as sacrifice or altruism calls attention to the way in which cinema became a critical tool for popularizing Hispanotropicalism, a Francoist theory of Spanish impe-rialism. As scholars like Gustau Nerín and Andreas Stucki have argued, Hispanotropicalist discourse was concocted roughly around the 1950s, the same period as missionary cinema's heyday, in order to present a fic-tion of the Spanish colonial project as antiracist and benign, thus distin-guishing it from other European empires (Nerín 12, Stucki 9). Drawing on both foreign discourses such as Portuguese Lusotropicalism and the homegrown rhetorics of *Hispanidad* and Regenerationism,[3] Hispano-tropicalism suggested that Spain's past and present imperial legacies in Asia, the Americas, and Africa were characterized by qualities such as: "the complete absence of racist attitudes, the innate African vocation of Spanish people, the missionary tendency of the Hispanic nation, the lack of economic exploitation of colonial territories, and the presence of *mestizaje*" (Nerín 12). This vision guided much of Spain's efforts to hold on to its empire in the 1950s and 1960s despite the rapid disintegration of European empires all over the world during those years.

Hispanotropicalism's vision of Spanish colonialism as kinder, less racist, or more benign than other European empires was aspirational at best, and generally outright false. Obviously, the claim that Spanish colonialism was driven only by spiritual concerns and not by economic ones is easily debunked in view of the Spanish private sector's heavy involvement in Guinea's timber, cacao, and coffee industries, in Spain's concerted efforts to exploit the Sahara colony's phosphate reserves from the 1960s forward, and in the desire to of some Spanish ministers like Carrero Blanco to resist decolonization in order to protect Spanish economic interests in its African colonies (Álvarez Chillida, "El proceso" 71–2). Likewise, the notion that racism was absent from Spanish co-lonialism in Africa does not withstand even the slightest historical scrutiny. As Nerín has shown, all aspects of life in the Guinean colony were governed by a rigid system of racial segregation that permeated neighbourhoods, businesses and public services (48–9); similarly, se-vere restrictions were imposed on interracial sexual relationships, espe-cially between Black men and white women, because of the dominant myths about African hypersexuality (80–93). These numerous forms of racial segregation also disprove the claim that Spanish colonialism in Africa encouraged *mestizaje* or interracial mixing. On the contrary, as we will see later on in the chapter, the stigmatization of interracial sexu-ality, which was inseparable from the fear of white women giving birth to Black children, proliferated from the colonies to metropolitan Spain itself by way of popular cinema, which insistently reinforced the notion that unions between Black men and white women could only result from rape and that their offspring would be objects of shame.

Although Hispanotropicalist discourse, which emphasized Spain's role as a benevolent colonizer, was arguably always undergirded by discourses of femininity, in the 1960s, as Stucki has argued, this imperial rhetoric took an even more overtly "feminine turn" (4). Following the model of the larger Portuguese empire, Spain's defences of its African colonial presence accentuated the metropole's efforts to improve the lives of colonized women in Africa, which was a consequence of women's expanding roles in European societies during this period. A prominent example of Spanish imperialism's "women-centered," yet *not feminist*" orientation during this period was the increased educational activities promoted by government-sponsored women's organizations, such as Portugal's Mocidade Portuguesa Feminina ("Portuguese Female Youth") or Spain's Sección Femenina ("Female Section") in the African colonies during the 1960s and 1970s (4, original emphasis). Yet despite these organizations' ostensible efforts to improve African women's lives, they essentially promoted the idea that European women should teach African women to adhere to a better form of traditional gender roles. According to this logic, African women needed to learn that they should not be treated as chattel or servants by African men but should still perform the domestic household role and "maintain sociopolitical stability, both in the family and the empire" (11). Offering a particularly compelling summary of the so-called feminine turn of late Iberian colonialism, Stucki writes: "In this Iberian version of uplifting African women, we find white women trying to save black and brown women from black and brown men – and from themselves" (12).

Spain's portrayal of itself as intending to improve the lives of colonized women during the later years of its African empire is thoroughly punctured by Joanna Allan's analysis of women's resistance against colonial and patriarchal oppression during the same period. As Allan demonstrates, both casual and violent forms of racism were omnipresent in colonial Guinea's religious missionary institutions, despite the rosy portrayal of them in Hispanotropicalist discourse and in missionary cinema. For instance, Allan's compelling oral historical research illustrates that although Spanish nuns in colonial Guinea who worked at schools, clinics, or other institutions referred to themselves as "white angels for the black girls" (77), in practice, the nuns used a range of techniques to enforce obedience and submission of Guinean women and girls, such as force feeding, whippings for speaking African languages, and numerous other forms of child abuse (68–71). Schools for girls run by the Sección Femenina were also highly repressive, as numerous tactics were used to teach Guinean women and girls to follow rigidly gendered customs of propriety, hospitality, and sexual conduct

(85–6). Furthermore, by controlling access to scholarships for Guinean women to study in Spain and to employment opportunities upon their return to Guinea, the Sección Femenina was able to use these opportunities as tools of subjugation: such prizes were generally awarded to women seen as loyal to the colonial administration while women perceived as too rebellious or promiscuous were bypassed (87–8).

Perhaps unsurprisingly, the Franco regime's efforts to frame its imperial ambitions as an expression of Christian charity or as evidence of a desire to improve women's lives did little to stem the growing tide of anti-imperial sentiment, both in the international arena and in the colonies themselves. Almost immediately after Spain was admitted to the United Nations in 1955, the UN began pressuring it to relinquish control over its African colonies. In particular, the surprise loss of the Moroccan protectorate in 1956, less than a year after UN admission, motivated Franco's government to tighten its grip on its remaining colonies even further. Consequently, it borrowed stall tactics from the playbook of other European empires by granting the remaining colonies a change in status to "province" in 1958–9 and "autonomy" in 1963–4. The main goal of these distinctions was to justify Spain's dubious claim to the United Nations that it no longer had any colonies, but only overseas territories that had been fully integrated into the metropolis. Although these nominal status changes were intended to postpone decolonization, they ended up having unforeseen effects. For instance, in Spanish Guinea, the declaration of provincial status by the colonial government in 1959, which was carried out without any consultation of the Black population, generated resentment among anticolonial activists, thus accelerating the consolidation of nationalist organizations such as MONALIGE (National Movement for the Liberation of Equatorial Guinea) and IPGE (Popular Idea of Equatorial Guinea) (Álvarez Chillida, "El proceso" 73–5; Campos Serrano 100).

Furthermore, the nominal changes of the African colonies' relationship with their colonial metropole were symptomatic of internal factionalism within the Franco regime. The best-known example was the long-running spat between Carrero Blanco, who vociferously favoured maintaining Spain's colonial control over its African territories, and Fernando María Castiella, the Minister of Foreign Affairs from 1957 to 1969, who strongly advocated for decolonization. Yet the aims of both men were essentially neocolonial: while Carrero Blanco supported colonialism to protect Spanish economic interests, Castiella opposed it to avoid ostracism at the UN and to gain leverage for Spanish claims over Gibraltar (Álvarez Chillida, "El proceso" 71–2). Furthermore, Castiella also hoped that Spain would maintain influence over the former colonies after independence (72). In this way, despite their disagreement over decolonization, both ministers were, at heart, hoping to empower Spain to hold on to different versions of its waning imperial stature.

The "feminine turn" that marked Spanish imperial discourse at the same time as the empire itself was being weakened by both internal and external pressures reflects a broader tendency in the representation of European imperial cultures identified by Richard Dyer. For Dyer, the demise of European empires was often personified through a lens of white femininity to reflect the "doubt and uncertainty" that was increasingly engulfing previously celebrated white masculine values, such as "expansiveness, enterprise, courage and control," which had once legitimized imperial conquest (184). The intimate relationship of imperial decline with a "feminine turn" is evident in Spanish popular cinema: while earlier missionary films such as *Misión blanca* had focused primarily on the feminized masculinity of male protagonists, in the 1960s and 1970s, films that addressed imperial themes increasingly prioritized female protagonists and relationships. One example is the hagiographic genre, a corpus of films that narrated the lives of Catholic saints. As Jorge Pérez has demonstrated, this genre, which became the missionary genre's most obvious heir in the development era, played a critical, albeit indirect role in defending Spain's imperial legacy by idealizing saints – especially, but not exclusively, white women saints like Teresa of Avila or Rosa of Lima – as embodiments as the ideology of *Hispanidad* (*Confessional Cinema* 54–9). There were, of course, variations on this pattern. For instance, *Fray Escoba* ("Father Broom," dir. Ramón Torrado, 1961), the most popular saint film of the decade, did not eulogize a white woman saint, but portrayed its Black male protagonist, St Martin de Porres, as whitened and feminized by Spain, the maternal imperial nation. This point was further reinforced by *Fray Escoba*'s two sequels, the missionary melodrama *Cristo negro* ("Black Christ," 1963) and the religious western *Bienvenido, Padre Murray* ("Welcome, Father Murray," 1964), which were also directed by Torrado and starred the Afro-Cuban actor René Muñoz.

The feminization of imperialism can also be observed in secular genres of the era, such as musical comedies that starred the child prodigy Marisol. Despite their family-friendly narratives, Marisol musicals like *Tómbola* ("The raffle," dir. Luis Lucia, 1962), *Marisol rumbo a Río* ("Marisol Goes to Rio, dir. Fernando Palacios, 1963), and *Las cuatro bodas de Marisol* ("Marisol's four weddings," dir. Luis Lucia, 1967) addressed the African empire in a variety of ways, such as by giving Marisol a Black female sidekick, who was played by Equatorial Guinean actress Jöelle Rivero, or by portraying Marisol herself as a missionary nun in Africa.

These Marisol films especially advanced the idea of a "feminine turn" in the Spanish empire by portraying Marisol as a salvific figure to a Black girl, as in *Tómbola* and *Marisol rumbo a Río*, or by showcasing the altruistic work of missionary nuns, as in *Las cuatro bodas*.

As decolonization movements advanced, popular cinema continued to feminize Spain's African empire, but its representation of colonial subjects, especially Black Africans, no longer portrayed them as the loyal, obedient, or domesticated characters once played by René Muñoz or Joëlle Rivero. Instead, from the late 1960s onward, Black Africans were increasingly villainized as hypersexual aggressors against innocent white women. In films like the missionary melodrama *Encrucijada para una monja* ("A nun at the crossroads," dir. Julio Buchs, 1967), the musical melodrama *Esa mujer* ("That woman," dir. Mario Camus, 1969), and the erotic horror film *La noche de los brujos* (*Night of the sorcerers*, dir. Armando de Ossorio, 1974), imperial loss is allegorized through the trope of white women protagonists being raped by Black African men. By establishing an analogy between decolonization and rape, these latter films underscored how imperial loss enabled Spain to experience a shared trauma with other postimperial European nations – an idea that simultaneously released the nation from guilt and brought Spain's own full whiteness and Europeanness into relief.

Whether it portrayed colonized Africans as the empire's acquiescent disciples or as its destructive rebels, popular cinema's construction of Spanish colonialism as embodying a benevolent femininity had an especially important role in shaping audiences' views of decolonization during the 1960s and 1970s. After all, the Franco regime adamantly refused to sponsor films that expressed empathy for anticolonial movements. This condemned the anticolonial film projects of School of Barcelona directors Joaquím Jordá and Jacinto Estevá to remain forever unfinished due to a lack of financing (Elena, *La llamada* 188). Similarly, the screening of foreign anticolonial films was also blocked by Francoist censorship. A key example is the Italian film *Battle of Algiers* (dir. Gillo Pontecorvo, 1966), which garnered tremendous international success throughout the later 1960s for its portrayal of anticolonial resistance in Algeria, but did not debut in Spain until 1978, when the transition to democracy was well underway (Lara 36). As a result of the regime's censorship, Francoist myths about the end of the empire in popular cinema reached large and diverse audiences of multiple genres and remained virtually uncontested by opposition cinema.

In the 1970s, Francoism's efforts to suppress critical perspectives on colonialism were compounded by the enactment of *materia reservada* (classified information) laws, which censored information about the postcolonial disasters that arose from the haphazard decolonization processes of Spain's African colonies. For instance, all press coverage of Equatorial Guinea, which quickly descended into a bloody dictatorship after achieving independence in 1968, was forbidden from 1971 to 1976 (Schlumpf 290). A similar law was enacted between 1972 and 1974 regarding Western Sahara, a colony whose botched decolonization process has led it to remain embroiled in an unresolved battle for independence from Morocco to this day (López García 74). The silences created around decolonization and its aftermath during the later years of Francoism contributed to a generalized lack of awareness about Spain's colonial legacies in Africa that persists in the present (Pardo Sanz "La décolonisation" 182, Muñoz Martínez 130). For this reason, the task of disinterring and exposing Francoist cinema's fictions about Spain's relationship with its empire is even more urgent today.

The remainder of this chapter is divided into three sections. The first explores the domestication of Black masculinity in Ramón Torrado's trilogy of religious films that starred René Muñoz: *Fray Escoba*, *Cristo negro*, and *Bienvenido, Padre Murray*. The second examines the representation of the empire through the symbol of girlhood in three Marisol films: *Tómbola*, *Marisol rumbo a Río*, and *Las cuatro bodas de Marisol*. The third analyses the trope of the Black rapist in *Encrucijada para una monja*, *Esa mujer*, and *La noche de los brujos*. These various case studies will demonstrate not only the personification of the empire in terms of white femininity, but also the evolution of cinema's imperial mythologies as decolonization advanced. Specifically, these case studies will illuminate how, in the wake of inevitable imperial collapse, Hispanotropicalist defences of the Spanish empire's superiority eventually yielded to the idea that letting go of the empire would enhance Spain's path towards Europeanization.

An Imperial Miracle: René Muñoz and the Feminization of Black Masculinity

Perhaps the late-Francoist film genre that most overtly amplified the missionary imaginary of the 1940s and 1950s was the hagiographic film, or saint movie. As Pérez has argued, a number of 1960s saint movies, including *Rosa de Lima* (dir. José María Elorrieta, 1961), *Fray Escoba* (dir. Ramón Torrado, 1961), and *Teresa de Jesús* (dir. Juan de Orduña, 1962), echoed missionary cinema's goal of defending Spanish imperialism by portraying their protagonists as crusaders of Spanishness both at home and in the Americas (*Confessional Cinema* 54–9). Yet *Fray Escoba* stands out among other saint movies as especially significant for several reasons. For one, according to Valeria Camporesi's analysis, it was the most commercially successful Spanish film of 1960–1 and arguably the most popular saint film of the decade (123–4). Secondly, *Fray Escoba* ruptured a long-established industry practice by centring its narrative around a Black character, St Martin de Porres, who was also played by a Black actor, the Cuban-born René Muñoz. Prior to that point – and in many subsequent films, too – racialized characters in fiction films were played by white Spanish actors in dark make-up or were simply uncredited extras.[4] Muñoz's performance as the mild, self-abnegating St Martin was so successful that it generated two spin-off films directed by Torrado that also showcased Muñoz's saintly aura: the missionary melodrama *Cristo negro* (1963) and the religious Western *Bienvenido, Padre Murray* (1964). Furthermore, the tremendous success of *Fray Escoba* throughout the Spanish-speaking world permanently shaped the rest of Muñoz's career, as he reprised the role of St Martin and similar religious roles in many Latin American television programs between the 1960s and the 1990s.

Muñoz's embodiment of saintliness was contingent on his performance of femininity, a characteristic that diverged from the assumed hypermasculinity of Black men, which was an essential feature of Spanish and European colonial discourse (Nerín 90–3). Unlike the cartoonish, highly caricatured Black men that often surfaced in comedies (see chapter 1) or in advertisements like those of Cola-Cao or Conguitos, Muñoz's's screen presence was defined by a number of markedly feminine features, such as his large eyes, narrow face, soft tenor voice, and slender physique (see figure 2.1). These features allowed his characters to radiate feminine qualities like compassion, tenderness, sadness, or awe – a far cry from the stupidity or brutishness that characterized most other Black men in Spanish cinema. In this way, Muñoz's feminine aura located him closer to what Labanyi has called the "feminised" masculinity of white missionary stars of the 1940s and 1950s ("Internalisations" 30). Furthermore, as a Black actor, Muñoz conveyed a realistic authenticity that a white actor in blackface, like Hugo del Carril in the 1951 version of *El negro que tenía el alma blanca* ("The Black man with a white soul"), could not. *Fray Escoba*'s producers clearly understood that this film would be best served by casting a real Black actor rather than a white actor in dark make-up. Unlike other Franco-era films in which Black characters appeared, it was especially important for *Fray Escoba* to feel as authentic as possible, given that the film's release in December 1961 was timed to exploit the worldwide attention generated by the Vatican's real-life canonization of Martin de Porres in May 1962. The need for realism likely factored in the decision of *Fray*

Figure 2.1. René Muñoz in *Fray Escoba* (dir. Ramón Torrado, 1961).

Escoba's producers to replace the established white actor Ángel Aranda, who was originally slated to play the role of St Martin, with the inexperienced Muñoz, whom they randomly spotted walking down Madrid's Gran Vía in the early 1960s (Muñoz, "A San Martín de Porres yo le debo mucho.")

Muñoz's performance of a feminized Black masculinity in his films with Torrado was not only a commercially successful formula for the Spanish film industry, but also a convenient ideological opportunity for the Franco regime to defend the preservation of its African empire. This becomes especially clear when we consider how the second film, *Cristo negro*, aimed to recreate the commercial success of *Fray Escoba* by transplanting Muñoz's saintly screen persona from seventeenth-century Lima to the Guinean colony of the early 1960s. These latter years, as we will recall, were marked by growing tensions around the Guinean colony's status, as the granting of provincial status in 1959 sparked resentment among the native populace and triggered anticolonial resistance movements (Álvarez Chillida, "El proceso" 73–5). *Cristo negro*'s direct depiction of African anticolonial resistance movements gaining traction in a Spanish colony was highly unusual in Francoist cinema of the time, given that decolonization was usually represented only obliquely, such as through allegories or foreign settings. The third film of the trilogy, *Bienvenido, Padre Murray*, was a commercial flop, but is of interest to our analysis because it added an unusual twist to missionary and imperial themes by framing them within the Western genre. By glorifying Spanish imperialism across diverse geographical, historical, and generic contexts at a time when Spain struggling to hold on to its empire, the Muñoz-Torrado trilogy implied that Spanish imperialism of the present was just as morally laudable and necessary as that of the past. Muñoz's performances of submissiveness and devotion, in other words his feminized Black masculinity, conveyed an eloquent defence of imperialism by underscoring Spain's spectacular ability to subjugate and neutralize the perceived excesses of undomesticated Black masculinities.

The ideological ambitions of the trilogy become clear when we consider how the multiple intertextual linkages between the three films aimed to graft characteristics of the hagiographic genre, to which only *Fray Escoba* strictly belonged, to the other films, *Cristo negro* and *Bienvenido, Padre Murray*, thus endowing them with a "saintly" quality despite not being saint films. As Pamela Grace has argued, a central convention of hagiographic films like *Fray Escoba* is their use of "miracle-time," that is, their normalization of an imaginary realm of time and space in which miracles, apparitions, and divine interventions are not only possible, but commonplace (5–6). Indeed, as in any hagiographic film, miraculous occurrences are abundant in *Fray Escoba*, which frequently depicts St Martin as healing the sick, levitating, having conversations with Christ, and possessing impossible knowledge, among other unnatural feats. Yet the otherworldly "miracle-time" of *Fray Escoba*'s filmic universe accentuates the foundational "miracle" that makes all the other miracles in this film possible: namely, the Spanish empire's ability to transform Black men from hypermasculine savages into docile, obedient saints.

Muñoz's miraculous femininity in *Fray Escoba* is especially emphasized by the contrast between St Martin's submissive, self-effacing demeanour and the primitive savagery of all other Black men who appear in the film. While St Martin is repeatedly depicted in close-ups that emphasize his watery eyes and trembling voice, his masochistic endurance of taunts and insults, or his performance of extreme deference to his superiors, the other Black men in the film are portrayed as inclined to criminality and lacking in intelligence. This pattern becomes especially clear in a scene in which an aging St Martin clandestinely visits slave quarters in colonial Lima to bring food to its residents. As the slaves joyously accept the loaves of bread and other gifts that St Martin has brought them, one male slave remains apart from the rest with a downcast look. St Martin approaches him and asks him if he will return what he has stolen. The slave, shocked at St Martin's miraculous knowledge of his crime, admits to his infraction and agrees to return the stolen item. In this scene, it is important to notice the different effects that the lighting has on the two characters (see figure 2.2). The depiction of the slave follows a pattern identified by Pérez, in which racist lighting practices made racialized characters look sweaty, shiny, or dirty (*Confessional Cinema* 43–9). Facing away from the light source, the slave's face is so shadowy that it is difficult to distinguish his features other than his forehead, which is marked by a bright white shine. By contrast, the front of St Martin's face and head is completely illuminated, making it seem as though St Martin's light is being reflected on the slave. Thus, while Pérez's argument is accurate in the case of the slave, the partial luminosity of St Martin's face indicates that the connotations that lighting could evoke were variable, even for racialized characters. In this scene, the illumination of St Martin's face, which, as usual, is exceptionally sweet and gentle, calls attention to the supernatural quality of his feminine saintliness, which intersects with his miraculous knowledge of the slave's theft. His otherworldly traits, including his being whitened and feminized by Spanish imperialism, stand in stark contrast to the decidedly un-miraculous Black slave, whose shadowy face and propensity to crime jointly call attention to the natural inferiority of uncolonized Black masculinity.

In addition to the juxtaposition of St Martin's saintly demeanour with the coarseness and ignorance of other Black men, *Fray Escoba* also spectacularizes the femininity of its protagonist by emphasizing his efforts to *lower* his social standing, a narrative that inverted the dominant rhetoric of upward mobility promoted in other films of the era, such as comedy (see chapter 1). For instance, upon admission to religious life, St Martin insists on occupying the monastery's lowliest post, that of broom sweeper, despite the efforts of several other characters to pressure him to aim higher. Similarly, St Martin laterconsiders selling himself as a slave to pay off the monastery's debts, reasoning aloud to a fellow friar that "Los otros son esclavos, y yo no soy más que ellos" ("The others are slaves, and I am no more than them.") According to the film, St Martin's propensity for self-abnegation, which dramatically inverts the narratives of economic ascent associated with development-era rhetoric, softens the hardened racism of his detractors. As such, his self-effacing femininity paradoxically paves the way for his

Figure 2.2. St Martin (René Muñoz) speaks to a slave in *Fray Escoba* (dir. Ramón Torrado, 1961).

ascent, as he ultimately becomes the Dominican monastery's first Black monk and one of the first Black saints of Latin America, while never uttering a single rebellious word and certainly without sparking the kind of social unrest that was being seen in the United States or in various African countries at the time.

The other films of the trilogy, *Cristo negro* and *Bienvenido, Padre Murray*, aimed to transplant the miraculous aura of Muñoz's femininity to different periods and imperial contexts. *Cristo negro*, which is set in colonial Guinea, portrays Muñoz's character, Mikoa, an African adolescent who assists the white missionary clergy, as only partially feminized, as he is caught between the feminizing, whitening influence of Spanish imperialism and the corrosive, aggressive hypermasculinity that was imagined as innate to Black African men. Specifically, Mikoa's feminine demeanour is repeatedly punctured by internal conflict, as he continually struggles to suppress feelings of anticolonial resentment and hatred due to his bitterness towards Charles, the white man who killed his father. Yet despite this inner conflict, Mikoa nonetheless remains markedly different from the film's other Black men: while Mikoa is gentle, intelligent, and kind-hearted, the others are ignorant, belligerent, prone to drunkenness, and usually semi-nude. *Cristo negro* further marks Mikoa as different from other Black men by explicitly recalling Muñoz's role as St Martin: in two scenes, Mikoa is shown praying fervently to a statue of St Martin, in whose honour he was baptized with the Christian name "Martín."

The tortured quality of Mikoa's femininity in *Cristo negro* unfolds throughout the film. The tension becomes especially acute in the film's two parallel depictions of attempted rape, which occur in almost immediate succession within the diegesis. In the first scene, while a lively, traditional African celebration is occurring near the mission, a drunk Guinean attempts to rape Sister Alicia, the ever cheerful, virtuous, white Spanish missionary nun; however, his attempt is foiled by another Guinean who hears the commotion and rescues her in the nick of time. In the second scene, Charles, the white man who killed Mikoa's father years ago, accosts a Guinean woman named Dina but is intercepted by the protagonist, Mikoa. When Charles accidentally falls backward, Mikoa has an opportunity to stab him and avenge his father's death; however, he cannot bring himself to do so because of his Christian beliefs. As Susan Martin-Márquez has argued, both scenes of attempted interracial rape stigmatize interracial desire by "associating desire for racial Others with depravity" ("De Cristo negro..." 64). Yet these scenes also stage a battle between the excesses of Black masculinity and the whitening, feminizing powers of Spanish imperialism. In both scenes, the civilizing mission of Spanish imperialism emerges as temporarily victorious, as Sister Alicia is saved from sexual assault, and Mikoa chooses to stay true to his Christian values. Even so, *Cristo negro*'s portrayal of a tumultuous collision between feminine civilization and masculine racial barbarity foreshadows not only the film's end, in which the mission will be burned to the ground by anticolonial rebels, but also films of the later 1960s and 1970s, in which the trope of the Black rapist emerges as a demonizing caricature of anticolonial movements.

The struggle between Mikoa's loyalty to the mission of the Spanish imperial project and the innate savagery attributed to Black men in general becomes especially apparent in his gruesome martyrdom at the end of the film. In the film's final sequence, as Mikoa runs through the blazing mission, he stumbles unexpectedly upon the dead bodies of Spanish missionaries, including Sister Alicia, whom the rebels have killed. However, a different fate awaits Mikoa: instead of merely killing him, the rebels make a drawn-out spectacle of his death. When they see Mikoa trying to save the mission, they drag him away by his arms, tie him to a cross, and shoot him to death once he is bound and helpless, leaving his body visible to passers-by. As Martin-Márquez has argued, the conversion of Mikoa into a literal "Black Christ" figure in this final sequence serves to "neutralize the irresistible and threatening attraction of the racial Other," a theme which surfaces earlier in the film when Mikoa expresses desire for a white woman ("De Cristo negro..." 66). Yet it also serves to accentuate the presence of "miracle-time" in this otherwise non-hagiographic film: Mikoa's ability to overcome his innate propensity to bloodlust is ultimately portrayed as a kind of "miracle" that distinguishes him from the film's other Africans, and thus endows his transformation into a "Black Chrïst" with a triumphant quality despite the destruction of the mission. By showcasing the power of Spanish imperialism to help a Black adolescent overcome his desire for revenge and evolve into a saintly martyr, the film's final crucifixion scene exudes a miraculous aura whose ultimate purpose is to extol the imperial mission as awe-inspiring.

Muñoz would produce yet another religious character in *Bienvenido, Padre Murray*, a religious Western film that flopped in theatres and was panned by critics for being an uninspiring "Fray Escoba in the West" (Vergara, qtd. in Castro de Paz). Its failure is perhaps best explained by the incoherence between Muñoz's religious persona and the rugged masculinity expected of Western film protagonists. Despite its poor commercial performance, this film is interesting because it inverts the missionary imaginary's racial dynamics and frames them in a Western setting: in this film, a Black priest must rescue a lawless white town near the US / Mexico border from corruption, vice, and, above all, virulent racism. Indeed, the latter quality is made evident in the film's opening scene, which depicts an angry white mob breaking into a jail and lynching a Black man named Jerome for a theft which, as we later learn, he did not commit. In the film's main plot, which occurs several years after the opening lynching, the white townspeople, who have spent twenty years with no priest or minister, are thrilled to learn that the bishop is sending them a new priest, but are dismayed when they discover that Muñoz's character, Father Murray, is Black. Like St Martin in *Fray Escoba*, Father Murray masochistically endures all manner of taunts, insults, and humiliations at the hands of the white townspeople, and even narrowly escapes an attempt to lynch him. Also, like *Fray Escoba*, this religious Western is peppered with incidents that can only be described as miraculous, such as a shootout scene where Father Murray stands at close range to two shooters, but none of their multiple bullets ever hits him. At the end of the film, after Father Murray has helped unmask an embezzlement scheme orchestrated by the town's corrupt leaders, he reveals his true motivation for coming to the town: to clear the name of his father, Jerome, the Black man who was lynched in the opening scene.

By portraying a Black priest who ministers to racist American whites, this film expands and complements the Hispanotropicalist arguments of the cycles' previous two installments. If *Fray Escoba* and *Cristo negro* invited contemporary African colonialism to be compared with the early modern American empire, *Bienvenido, Padre Murray* clearly sought to contrast the benevolence and moral rectitude of the Spanish empire, personified by Father Murray, with the degradation and depravity of the United States, riven by racial conflicts during the 1960s. Since viewers would have undoubtedly recognized Father Murray's character as a proxy of St Martin in *Fray Escoba*, the film essentially imagines that St Martin, the domesticated Black son of the Spanish empire, might serve as a kind of "missionary" to the savage world of civil-rights-era United States, where spectacles of racist violence committed by whites against Blacks, including lynchings, were being watched closely in Spain.[5] The film's glorification of Hispanic imperialism as an antidote to American racism is further buttressed by the close alliance that forms between Father Murray's character and a devoutly Catholic Mexican character named García, who rescues Father Murray from several crises, including an attempted lynching. Significantly, the alliance between these characters is based not only on their shared allegiance to Catholicism, but also on their darker skin tones; for, as García observes repeatedly, they both are "tostados" ("toasted") in comparison with the white majority.

At the same time, the effort of *Bienvenido, Padre Murray* to condemn American racism must be taken with a grain of salt. After all, its opening scene, which depicts how an angry mob lynches an innocent Black man, bears an uncanny resemblance to the final scene of *Cristo negro*, which also depicts mob justice committed against the innocent Mikoa and other Catholic missionaries. The conspicuous parallelisms between these two scenes, which both dramatize their killings of innocent Black men through the motif of torches against a night sky, suggest that *Bienvenido, Padre Murray* deliberately begins its narrative at the same place where *Cristo negro* ends: with the martyrdom of the virtuous by uncivilized savages. By presenting its introductory lynching scene as a re-enactment of Mikoa's death at the end of *Cristo negro*, *Bienvenido* invites a comparison between anticolonial resistance in Africa and American lynchings. Yet the implication this comparison offers is rather disturbing: namely, that the global embrace of decolonization constituted a "lynching" of Spain's "innocent" empire. Such a logic reveals *Bienvenido*'s intention of capitalizing on the empathy generated by American Blacks' struggle for racial equality while stifling solidarity for African anticolonial resistance. By depicting imperial loss as a form of mob violence, *Cristo negro* and *Bienvenido* are both early examples of a "colonizer-as-victim" narrative that would emerge even more conspicuously at the end of the 1960s, especially through the motif of the Black rapist.

In sum, the Torrado-Muñoz trilogy of religious films, which included the saint film *Fray Escoba*, the missionary film *Cristo negro*, and the religious Western *Bienvenido, Padre Murray*, constructed Muñoz's star image as embodying a feminized, Black masculinity and exploited this image to romanticize Spanish imperialism as a civilizing source of whiteness and femininity for the world's supposedly savage races. Although neither of the sequels matched *Fray Escoba*'s success, they nonetheless imported the hagiographic genre's use of "miracle-time" not only to endow Muñoz's characters with saintly qualities, but also to highlight Spanish imperialism's miraculous ability to turn savages into saints. The multiple intertextual linkages between the three films, which were respectively set in seventeenth-century Lima, contemporary Guinea, and the old American West, emphasize that Muñoz's feminine aura was intended to glorify Spain's long-established and geographically expansive imperial legacy. Yet given *Cristo negro*'s Guinean setting, it also seems clear that the trilogy aimed to defend specifically the preservation of Spain's African colonies, where the feminization of Black masculinity was portrayed as still in progress, and where the "miracle" of civilization had not yet been fully achieved. In this way, Muñoz's screen persona exemplified not only the feminization of Black men, but also the imagined femininity of late imperial Spain, whose civilizing light was seen as a source of redemption for the innately barbaric masculinities of its colonial subjects.

Infantilizing Imperialism: Marisol as Missionary

Popular cinema's missionary imaginary was not only limited to religious films. Rather, it also surfaced in secular genres, including the sentimental musical comedies of the child actress Marisol, whose real name was Pepa Flores, and who was one of the greatest film stars of any genre during this period. Known for playing imaginative, yet mischievous child characters, Marisol belonged to Spanish cinema's *cine con niño* tradition of the 1950s and 1960s, which included other musical child stars like Joselito, Pablito Calvo, Pili and Mili, and Rocío Dúrcal. Although most famous for her roles as a child, she played adult roles from the late 1960s onward. She was especially renowned for her ability to perform both traditional *españolada* genres, such as flamenco, as well as the contemporary global pop (often referred to as *ye-yé* style) that took Spain by storm in the 1960s.

Although the narratives of Marisol's musicals ostensibly reinforced Francoist values, especially those that concerned gender, these films are often remembered for their ability to inspire and delight their large, diverse audiences, which included both children and adults, as well as for their ability to be interpreted against the grain. Tatjana Pavlovic, for example, writes that, in contrast to her peer Joselito, who was "stranded in the melancholic mode," Marisol demonstrated a "contagious optimism" and "occupied a space of future possibilities" (126). Alejandro Melero similarly notes that Marisol's ebullient music and dance numbers often made her films feel "liberating," but were also often laced with covert sexual subtexts that were meant to appeal to adult audiences ("Representation and Excess"). Rob Stone has further highlighted the counter-hegemonic possibilities of interpreting Marisol's cinema, noting that her films "let slip an occasional subversive attitude in the way her characters often triumphed over adults" (86).

A less examined aspect of Marisol's cinema, however, is its frequent engagement with colonial and racial themes. Like the *macho ibérico* comedy examined in chapter 1, Marisol's musicals, which almost always featured rags-to-riches narratives about a working-class girl who overcomes her humble origins, hinged on the theme of upward mobility. Furthermore, like *macho ibérico* comedies, Marisol's films dramatized the nation's economic mobility by emphasizing the mobility of Marisol's whiteness. As Peter Evans has argued, Marisol's ability to oscillate between recognizably Spanish musical genres and Anglo rock / pop was accentuated by the racialized contrast between the "dark Andalusian ethnicity" of her voice and the "slim, Aryan blondeness" of her looks (140). Her "Aryan" look, of course, was largely manufactured: early in her career, the producer who discovered her, Manuel Goyanes, insisted that she dye her naturally brown hair blonde, receive coaching on her Andalusian accent, and undergo plastic surgery on her nose (131). In this way, Marisol embodied an ambivalent, chameleonic whiteness that could be read as off-white or fully white, depending on the song. Hence, she simultaneously epitomized an "officially sanctioned, tourist-friendly and Costa del Sol-dominated 1960s Spain" (Evans 129), as well as the later regime's desire to "[evoke] closeness to Northern and Western Europe" (Triana Toribio 88). Finally, as in *macho ibérico* comedies, Marisol's fluctuating whiteness was frequently offset by Black characters, especially ones with connections to Equatorial Guinea.

Unlike *macho ibérico* comedies, however, Marisol's relationship to Black characters was not framed in terms of competition or sexual conquest; instead, it was depicted as innocent, feminine caretaking. We might consider, for example, Marisol's back-to-back smash hits *Tómbola* (dir. Luis Lucia, 1962) and *Marisol rumbo a Río* (dir. Fernando Palacios, 1963), which were both among the most successful domestic films of their respective years (Camporesi 124–6). In these films, Marisol is accompanied on-screen by a Black sidekick who was played by Equatorial Guinean child actress Joëlle Rivero. Like René Muñoz, Rivero constituted a rare instance of a Black actor who was credited for her work in Francoist film, but her film career did not continue past these two films, which is consonant with the broader erasure of actors of colour from Francoist cinema. In addition, in the two films Rivero did appear in, her characters' relationships with those played by Marisol is extremely stratified: unlike Marisol, Rivero lacks Marisol's music and dance abilities, and often engages in self-deprecating humour about her Blackness. Notably, the hierarchical screen relationship between Marisol and Rivero is softened by a certain maternal quality in which Marisol constantly showers Rivero with affection and bosses her around. In her brilliant analysis of *Tómbola*, Erin Hogan has argued that Rivero's character functions as a means of drawing a comparison between "Francoism's political use of children and the infantilization of its African ... territories" (18). Following this analysis, I read *Tómbola* and *Marisol rumbo a Río* as part of Spanish cinema's larger missionary imaginary, which personified Spanish colonialism as selfless, white, feminized caretaking of intellectually inferior races. The missionary imaginary of imperialism resurfaces again in a later film, *Las cuatro bodas de Marisol* (dir. Luis Lucia, 1967), which was also a major success, as it reached more than 2.5 million viewers in cinemas. In this film, which was partially filmed in Equatorial Guinea, Marisol plays one of her earliest adult roles: namely, an actress who earned fame by playing a Spanish missionary nun in Africa, but who plans to marry an American film director and continue her career in Hollywood.

Although these three Marisol films reproduce the missionary genre's cinematic imaginary of white beneficence towards Blacks, an important evolution can be traced between *Tómbola* and *Marisol rumbo a Río*, which were made in the early 1960s, and *Las cuatro bodas de Marisol*, which was released only one year before the declaration of Equatorial Guinea's independence in 1968. Like René Muñoz's performances of feminized Black masculinity, Rivero's Black sidekick characters in *Tómbola* and *Marisol rumbo a Río* are depicted as domesticated, subjugated, and in need of Spain's maternal protection. In addition, Rivero's roles linked Spanish imperialism in Africa to *desarrollismo*'s promises of upward geopolitical mobility. In both films, her characters suggest that just as Marisol could enjoy upward mobility while keeping a subservient Black friend, so, too, could African imperialism bolster Spain's imagined ascent into global whiteness. However, unlike these earlier films, *Las cuatro bodas de Marisol* demonstrates a seeming awareness that the last major colony would soon be lost. This highly self-referential film oscillates between glorifying Spain's missionary activities and accentuating the artificiality of the missionary imaginary as a construct of popular cinema. By portraying popular cinema's missionary imaginary as both nostalgic and campy, this latter film framed imperial loss as a step forward in Spain's upward geopolitical trajectory, implying that letting go of the empire, rather than holding on to it, would make the nation resemble the Anglo-European world.

In *Tómbola*, the colonial dynamic that shapes the relationship between Marisol and Rivero is reinforced through narrative, musical, and visual elements. One such element is *Tómbola*'s opening musical number, "Chiquitina," whose lyrics describe a young girl's desire to grow up. Marisol sings the song directly to Rivero's character, María Belén, as if Marisol were the adult and María Belén the child (Hogan 80). The association between María Belén's Blackness and her need for white protection is further emphasized by the film's plot, which presents two mirroring narratives. The film's main narrative recounts how Marisol orchestrates the return of a priceless artwork to a museum after initially witnessing its theft. It is preceded by a parallel plot in which Marisol mistakenly believes that her friend María Belén, the daughter of an African ambassador, has been kidnapped by an African rebel while the two girls are practising horseback riding near their school. Although María Belén's disappearance turns out to be a false alarm, the prospect of her kidnapping produces utter pandemonium: Marisol's search for her friend quickly metastasizes into a full-blown search-and-rescue operation in which even the Francoist military, who just happens to be training nearby, offers men, tanks, and a helicopter to help find the girl, who ultimately was safe all along.

By equating the loss and recovery of an African girl to the theft of a priceless artwork, the film implies that María Belén and the artwork are both valuable objects that belong to the patrimony of *Hispanidad*, and that their loss would rightfully generate panic and pandemonium. In this way, the plot about María Belén's kidnapping may be read as an allegory about Francoism's paternalistic vision of its African colonies in the context of global decolonization. In addition, the film's commentary on decolonization is interwoven with racialized anxieties about Spain's whiteness. This becomes abundantly clear in an encounter between the lost María Belén, who is wandering around the forest without knowing that everyone is looking for her, and an elderly Spanish man with a partially blackened face. Prior to María Belén's disappearance, Marisol had already spotted this man and wondered aloud if he might be an African rebel trying to disguise himself as white. However, when he befriends

María Belén in the forest, we learn that he is really an amicable Spanish railroad employee whose face is covered in soot. As the two converse, the man washes his face, explaining that his work often causes him to get his face dirty. María Belén's reply – "Usted sí, pero yo no" ("You can, but I can't") – contrasts the permanence of her own Black skin with the man's ability to "whiten" himself. By recalling the idea that Spain could wash away its Blackness, a notion that surfaced repeatedly in sex comedy films of the same period, María Belén's character symbolizes not only the regime's desire to hold on to its African colonies, but also suggests that maintaining the empire would allow Spain to remove the "Africanness" from its image as it asserted its European belonging.

Like *Tómbola*, the narrative of *Marisol rumbo a Río* also contains numerous thematic links to the unfolding drama of African decolonization, despite its Brazilian setting. In this film, which borrows extensively from Hollywood's *The Parent Trap* (dir. David Swift, 1961), Marisol and her mother Isabel (Isabel Garcés) endure great economic and personal sacrifice to pay for a boat voyage to Rio de Janeiro to be reunited with Mariluz, Marisol's twin sister, who was sent to live with her wealthy uncle after their father's death. This film portrays Marisol as experiencing a dramatic social ascent, in which she rises from literally sleeping among dogs on the boat to being surrounded by Black servants eager to wait on her in Brazil. Marisol quickly befriends one of the Black maidservants, Jöelle Rivero's character, who is ironically named Copito ("Little Snowflake"). In this way, the film unites its fantasy of economic development with a nostalgic portrayal of the racial supremacy that Spain once enjoyed as the seat of a global, multiracial empire.

The film's intertwined narratives of economic uplift and imperial nostalgia first become apparent in this film before Marisol has left Spain, and before Copito enters the plot. In a dream sequence that takes place just before Marisol boards the boat to Brazil, a sleeping Marisol dreams of having the ability to become a tourist anywhere in Latin America. At the beginning of the sequence, which consists entirely of music and dance with no dialogue, Marisol's pajamas are magically replaced by a stereotypically Spanish, bullfighting-themed costume, and she is transported to a fantasy realm marked by a bright red background, numerous male dancers, and an exuberant orchestral score. After dancing her way through a golden revolving door, a carriage full of money spontaneously appears in front of her. Next, a flight attendant offers her options of several possible travel destinations, including the Andes, Mexico, the Caribbean, and Brazil, each of which is signified by highly stereotypical costumes, music and sets. In each musical segment, Marisol, whose character is suddenly doubled, watches herself dance to a different Latin American rhythm in a point-of-view shot, but shakes her head with dissatisfaction at the idea of travelling to the Andes, the Caribbean, or Mexico. However, when she finally sees herself dancing the bossa nova in front of painting of Rio de Janeiro, she assents gleefully. The sequence is abruptly interrupted when Marisol wakes up, once again dressed in pajamas, with the sweeping orchestral score substituted by the buzzing of an alarm clock.

In this sequence, tourism, which the late-Franco regime had promoted to Spaniards as a panacea that would drive the nation's ascent into modernity, is also portrayed as a way for the country to regain its lost imperial splendor. Although a great deal of popular culture of late-Francoist popular cinema, especially comedy, emphasized Spain's ability to attract European tourists to its beaches as a path to prosperity, it was far less common for a film to depict Spaniards as having the economic power to be tourists themselves, especially in a locale as far away as Latin America. The film itself acknowledges the extreme difficulty with which most Spaniards of the time might have made such exotic travel dreams come true; after all, the dream sequence is preceded by scenes that represent Marisol and her mother's desperate struggle to pay for the trip to Rio and followed by Marisol's humbling sojourn sleeping among dogs on the ship. Yet, through tourism, the film implies, Spaniards can once again hope to obtain a prominent place in the world, especially by enabling them to enact a symbolic reconquest of Latin America.

The idea that Spain could achieve modernization and restore its colonial glory simultaneously is echoed by Marisol and Copito's friendship, which blossoms rapidly after Marisol's arrival in Brazil. Although Copito is represented as a loveable accomplice in Marisol's comical escapades, a striking aspect of her contribution to the film is her insistent, racist self-mockery, which as in *Tómbola*, implied that Spain was moving upward on a racialized spectrum of modernity from Blackness to whiteness. One of the most memorable examples of Copito's self-denigrating humour occurs in a scene in which Marisol, trying to save her family from an embezzlement scheme, is climbing on a ledge high above the ground, while Copito watches from a nearby window. When Marisol asks Copito to tell her a story to distract her from her fear of heights, the following dialogue ensues:

> COPITO: Érase una vez un negro que se encontró con un montón de nieve. El negro cogió un pedazo y le preguntó, "Oye nieve, ¿qué puedes hacer por mí?"
>
> MARISOL: ¿Y qué le dijo la nieve?

COPITO: "Quítate la ropa, negro, y báñate en mí." El negro se quitó la ropa, y se remojó en la nieve. Salió blanco, y le hicieron presidente de los Estados Unidos.

(COPITO: Once upon a time there was a Black man who found a pile of snow. The Black man took a piece and asked it, "Hey, snow, what can you do for me?"
MARISOL: And what did the snow tell him?
COPITO: "Take off your clothes, Black man, and bathe in me." The Black man took off his clothes and dipped himself in the snow. He came out white, and they made him President of the United States.)

Copito's story about a Black man bathing in snow and becoming not only white, but ascending to the presidency of the United States, strongly echoes the interaction between María Belén and the railroad worker in *Tómbola*. In both cases, racial transformation from Black to white illustrates that Spain's desire to offer racial uplift to its colonized subjects was interwoven with a desire to overcome its own status as an "Africa of Europe" so that it might participate fully in global whiteness, of which the United States is imagined as the apex. These overlapping meanings are further bolstered by the links between Copito's story and her name, which reiterates the idea of Black person being "whitened" by snow.

Copito's symbolic role as a cheerleader of imperialism and as an indicator of Spain's capacity for whitening is especially prominent in the climactic scene of *Marisol rumbo a Río*. In this scene, Marisol, her twin and Copito confront the perpetrators of an embezzlement scheme at the foot of Rio's enormous Christ the Redeemer statue, which is located atop Sugarloaf Mountain and is visible from many parts of the city. The camerawork in this scene is punctuated by numerous shifts between high and low angles as well as myriad contrasts in scale; hence, the characters are often physically dwarfed in relation to the physical enormity of the statue and the expansiveness of the cityscape that can be seen from the mountaintop. In multiple shots, the statue's face and outstretched arms tower over the action, especially on two occasions when the face is shown in close-up. As Marisol tries to rescue her sister, who has fallen over the ledge of the mountain and is holding on for dear life, a low angle medium shot shows Copito, who is again narrating stories to distract Marisol from her fear of heights, in the foreground of the frame with the statue looming over her. As the sisters struggle to climb to safety, Copito turns towards the statue, with her hands clasped in prayer, and prays fervently for their rescue, her voice hoarse with

Figure 2.3. Copito (Joëlle Rivero) prays before the Christ the Redeemer statue in *Marisol rumbo a Río* (dir. Fernando Palacios, 1963).

desperation (see figure 2.3). The image of a little Black girl showing such reverence before a statue of Christ, whose monumental quality is underscored by the low angle, is strongly reminiscent of René Muñoz films, especially *Fray Escoba* and *Cristo negro*, which often showed Muñoz in comparable moments of intense devotion before a religious image. Like those films, this scene, too, heralds Spanish imperialism's ability to transform the savagery of Blackness into obedience, docility, and loyalty. In particular, the contrast between the small, vulnerable Copito and the colossal statue is accentuated by a Black / white visual dichotomy, given the distinctness of Copito's dark skin tone against the whiteness of the statue. By showcasing the power of white Christianity and the humility of Black devotion, the scene dramatizes not only Copito's loyalty to Marisol, but also to the project of rebuilding Spain's whiteness, an ambition closely linked to imperial preservation.

The film's objective of imagining a racially whitened, economically prosperous Spain with its African empire intact and populated with "whitened" Blacks like Copito is further reinforced by the film's ending, in which Marisol, her mother Isabel, her sister Mariluz, and her uncle Don Fernando are all shown aboard a ship, about to return to Spain, within a single frame. The frame includes Copito, whom the newly reunited family is taking back to Spain with them (figure 2.4). According to this happy ending, Marisol and her mother, who previously suffered from tremendous economic hardship and precarity, can

Figure 2.4. Marisol and family at the end of *Marisol rumbo a Río* (dir. Fernando Palacios, 1963).

now return to Spain while partaking in the luxurious lifestyle of their wealthy Latin American relatives. In addition, the transatlantic family is also expanded through the adoption of a new child, specifically, one who is younger, darker-skinned, and not related to the others by blood. This ending mobilizes a rhetoric of Hispanic family ties to imply allegorically that *Hispanidad* – which includes not only Spain and its estranged American colonies, but also its "darker," "younger" colonies in Africa – must remain close-knit as Spain proceeds on its path towards prosperity.

The attempt of films like *Tómbola* and *Marisol rumbo a Río* to associate economic development with imperial preservation illustrate that in the early 1960s, the Franco regime still intended to project optimism about its efforts to maintain its empire. However, by 1967, the year in which *Las cuatro bodas de Marisol* was released, this guarded optimism had given way to pessimism, especially in regard to the Guinean colony. Between 1964 and 1967, various factors within Equatorial Guinea, such as the increased activism of nationalist movements and the failure of an economic development plan, caused many Guineans to feel increasingly frustrated with the colonial government and, consequently, to intensify their demands for independence (Álvarez Chillida, "El proceso" 79–80). By 1967, virtually all Francoist ministers other than Carrero Blanco had acknowledged that Spain's remaining colonies, including Equatorial Guinea, were more of an economic burden to Spain than a source of profit (81–2). Similarly, from 1966 onward, the increasing instability of Spanish dominion in Equatorial Guinea caused the number of Spaniards living in Equatorial Guinea to drop precipitously (80).

As the impending reality of Equatorial Guinea's independence became undeniable, popular cinema's depictions of African colonialism moved away from their reliance on Hispanotropicalist assertions that the Spanish empire was "different," more benign, or less racist than other European empires. Instead, many films began to suggest that the nation's upward geopolitical trajectory would require it to abandon its treasured imperial mission. This is precisely the case of *Las cuatro bodas de Marisol*, in which Marisol, who was twenty-one years old at the time of the film's release, plays an adult role. The film narrates several extended flashbacks in which Marisol recounts her previous relationships with an Englishman, a Spaniard, and a Frenchman to her fiancée, an American film director named Frank Moore, to make him jealous. In the end, however, she marries Moore and moves to Hollywood with him after all.

A distinguishing feature of *Las cuatro bodas* with respect to earlier Marisol movies is its overtly meta-cinematic quality: this film narrates the love adventures of a movie star, features several scenes of movies being filmed within it, and oscillates between the numerous temporal registers of the film's present and its various flashbacks. As such, we may read this 1967 film as an early example of a broader tendency in Spanish musical cinema in which, as Santiago Lomas Martínez has argued, the genre became increasingly self-reflexive and self-parodying during the last years of Francoism. A symptom of the genre's declining popularity, the pronounced self-reflexivity of musical cinema during this period conveyed a "distancing" and "demystifying" attitude towards outdated mythologies the genre had once enshrined, especially those pertaining to national identity and gender relations (Lomas Martínez 5–6). As we will see, the self-reflexivity of *Las cuatro bodas* portrays imperialism as one of Francoism's antiquated fictions that must be relinquished for Spain's upward global ascent to continue. In this way, the film attempted to sweeten the pill of Equatorial Guinea's looming independence, which occurred one year after its release.

The film's engagement with the theme of decolonization emerges primarily in two of the four extended flashbacks: first, one set in England, where Marisol meets her first love at a boarding school; and second, one set in Equatorial Guinea, which describes Marisol's romance with a French doctor. The British flashback addresses decolonization through dialogue, as it is replete with jokes that compare the mischievous, headstrong behaviour of teenagers with the ongoing disintegration of

European empires. For instance, in a voiceover that narrates Marisol's plan to escape from the extremely repressive school, Marisol declares: "A ver si me echaban del colegio, de Inglaterra, y del poco imperio que les iba quedando" ("I wanted to see if they would throw me out of the school, out of England, and out of the little bit of empire they still had left"). In a later scene, the stodgy headmistress, frustrated at her inability to control the delirious youths, tries to subdue them by appealing to their imperial sensibilities, crying out: "Ingleses, ¡escuchadme! ¡Salvemos a la Commonwealth!" ("English people, listen to me! Let's save the Commonwealth!") Yet another joke emerges in a scene that depicts Marisol and her love interest in an impromptu audience with Queen Elizabeth II. Speaking through a reverberating voiceover as if she were a deity, the Queen grants Marisol and her boyfriend a single wish each. Marisol's request, which she articulates by uttering only the word "Gibraltar," audaciously accentuates the later Franco regime's desire to recover Gibraltar from British rule. Predictably, this brazen quip sends all the English aristocrats present into a frenzy, thus ending the flashback and returning the narrative to the film's present.

The flashback's multiple jokes about decolonization serve a range of purposes. On one level, they extracted laughs by drawing a connection between rebellious adolescent behaviour and the ongoing rebellion of colonized peoples against European powers. On another level, however, these various jokes also sought to puncture the long-entrenched myth of imperialism during the sunset of Spain's identity as an imperial nation. This is evident not only in the headmistress's remark about the saving the Commonwealth, a community of Britain's former colonies that is analogous to Spain's *Hispanidad*, but also in Marisol's wish that Britain return Gibraltar to Spain. This latter remark reflected the hope of some late-Francoist ministers – most notably, as we will recall, Fernando María Castiella, the minister of Foreign Affairs – that if Spain were to voluntarily relinquish its African colonies, it might have greater leverage to regain control of Gibraltar, which the scene frames as a sort of postcolonial consolation prize. Yet perhaps the greatest consolation that these jokes offered was to emphasize that Spain, which was on the brink of losing dominion of its Guinean colony, was not alone in its experience of imperial loss. Rather, imperial loss made Spain resemble none other than Great Britain, a country whose role in producing youth-oriented pop culture, which is abundantly portrayed throughout this flashback, located it at the pinnacle of global modernity during the 1960s. Losing the empire, in other words, meant that Spain no longer had to see itself as "behind" Northern Europe; rather, imperial collapse was part of a process that signalled Spain's eventual absorption into global, white modernity.

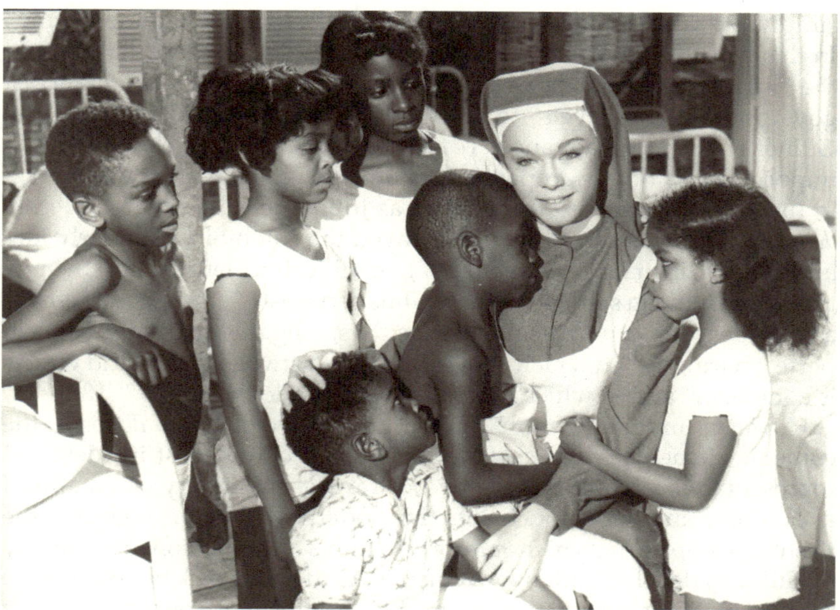

Figure 2.5. Marisol cares for needy African children in *Las cuatro bodas de Marisol* (dir. Luis Lucia 1967).

The effort of *Las cuatro bodas de Marisol* to assuage the humiliation of colonial loss by heralding Spain's upward global ascent is further emphasized in the flashback that is set in Equatorial Guinea. In this sequence, Marisol, encounters her love interest, a Frenchman, by happenstance while making a missionary film in the Guinean colony. This segment of the film was actually filmed in Equatorial Guinea and is peppered with images that showcase the supposedly idyllic quality of daily life in the colony: panoramic views of majestic landscapes; close-ups of exotic wildlife; happy townspeople waving at passing cars and vehicles; and lively celebrations involving traditional music and dance. This segment of the film particularly exploits the iconography of missionary films by featuring numerous images of Marisol taking care of or playing with African children while dressed in a nun's costume (figure 2.5). Curiously, despite the film's release in 1967, these scenes make no allusion to the brewing movement for independence, nor to the rapid exodus of Spanish settlers from the increasingly unstable colony. Instead, they portray Guinean life in a highly saccharine and romanticized light, as if the colony were a desirable tourist attraction simply waiting to receive Spanish visitors like Marisol with open arms. In this way, the film is congruent with what Alberto Elena has termed the "intense propaganda campaign" that was waged by the Francoist government "at all levels" to defend its waning presence in Equatorial Guinea as the 1960s advanced (*La llamada* 185). Cinema, clearly, was an important part of this propaganda campaign, given that other films set in the colony from the period, such as Julio Buchs' melodrama *Piedra de toque* ("Touch stone," 1963), portrayed the colony in a similarly idealized light (Elena, *La llamada* 185–7). Specifically, Elena writes, the picturesque Guinean settings of these films serve as a "privileged stage for a calm, peaceful existence in which settlers, religious and natives live in perfect harmony," in which "the integration between Blacks and whites is complete," and in which, overall, "everyone looks happy" (187).

However, unlike the more dramatic narrative of *Piedra de toque*, the comedic elements of *Las cuatro bodas de Marisol* undercut its idealized representation of Guinean life by portraying missionary cinema itself as outdated and out of touch with the modern world. This is clear in the flashback's opening, which features the film's only allusion to the reality of Guinean decolonization movements. As the flashback begins, we see Marisol walking through dense, bright green foliage, dressed in a nun's habit and carrying a case of first aid supplies, against a soundtrack of rapidly beating drums. Suddenly, a sparsely clad African man with a painted face emerges from behind the foliage and shoots an arrow into Marisol's back. Gasping in pain, she utters a prayer before collapsing. When she falls to the ground, a male director abruptly shouts, "¡Corte!" ("Cut!") He then tells Marisol: "[Usted] Es una gran estrella. Si hubiera existido el personaje que interpreta, no lo hubiera hecho de otra manera" ("You're a big star. If the character you're playing had ever existed, she wouldn't have done it any differently"). As Marisol approaches her trailer, with the arrow still protruding from her back, her mother (Isabel Garcés) chides her: "¡Quítate esa flecha, que no te favorece nada! ...Vamos a vestirte de ye-yé" ("Take off that arrow, it doesn't look good on you at all! ... Let's dress you up like a *ye-yé* girl").

Through its abrupt switching between diegetic levels and tongue-in-cheek dialogues, the flashback's opening scene accentuates the artificiality of the missionary imaginary. In particular, the scene pokes fun at the very themes that missionary films like *Misión blanca* or *Cristo negro* take seriously, such as the selfless generosity of priests and nuns in Africa, or the dangers they faced as decolonization movements progressed. The director's comment that Marisol's nun character never really existed, the fake arrow in her back, and her mother's suggestion that she quickly change costume all stand in stark contrast with the rest of the flashback's representation of Guinean life as idyllic and peaceful. By comically reworking serious narratives of missionary martyrdom, the segment accentuates the manufactured nature of not only of its own representation of colonial realities, but also the broader conventions of missionary film itself. And by portraying Marisol weaving in and out of her dual roles as film actress and missionary nun – a pattern that persists throughout the entirety of the Guinean flashback's meandering narrative – the sequence underscores the missionary imaginary itself as being just as artificial as any other genre of cinema, including any of Marisol's musicals.

In accentuating the campiness of the missionary imaginary, the Guinean flashback reiterates the British flashback's efforts to prepare viewers for the impending reality of imperial loss. In so doing, it prodded viewers to relinquish ideas that Francoist cinema had long championed – especially Hispanotropicalism, or the idea of Spain's unique imperial essence. Importantly, however, *Las cuatro bodas de Marisol* ends on an optimistic note: after the conclusion of the Guinean flashback, Marisol rejects her British, Spanish, and French suitors, and marries the American director, Frank Moore, as originally planned. Given the popular glorification of the United States as the pillar of global modernity, this ending strongly implies that letting go of the African empire will enable Spain to move closer towards a newer, more modern form of imperialism, namely, the cultural and economic supremacy that Hollywood so potently symbolized.

Like the Muñoz-Torrado trilogy, *Tómbola, Marisol rumbo a Río*, and *Las cuatro bodas de Marisol* personified Spain's long-held imperial identity in terms of white femininity. Furthermore, as Joëlle Rivero's characters illustrate, these films also celebrated the empire's ability to domesticate and subjugate colonized Africans. However, unlike the films that preceded it, *Las cuatro bodas de Marisol* reluctantly acknowledged that Spain's imperial identity was on its deathbed, and attempted to imagine a bright, post-imperial future in which colonial loss would align Spain with the harbingers of global modernity, such as Britain and the United States. Although subsequent articulations of the missionary imaginary would also acknowledge the reality of imperial death, they did not regard it with the same degree of lightheartedness.

The Erotics of Decolonization: The Myth of the Black Rapist

As the loss of the remaining colonies of Equatorial Guinea, Ifni, and Western Sahara became a reality, Spanish popular cinema began to reflect European paranoia about Africans inflicting gruesome vengeance upon their European colonizers. This paranoia spread throughout 1960s Europe because incoming news reports from various African countries detailed terrible acts of violence committed by Africans against white settlers in post-independence societies. Stories of Black men raping white women were particularly frequent. In Congo, as David Van Reybrouck states, political unrest following independence in 1960 generated numerous "worst nightmare" stories about African violence committed against Europeans (288). Noting that "there was no greater gap than that between the African man and the European woman" due to long-established colonial racial and gendered hierarchies, he explains that "It was the rumor of sexual violence that caused the most panic" (288). Similar patterns unfolded in the newly independent Equatorial Guinea, where rape-related rumours spread like wildfire after the country's independence in 1968 plummeted it into a dictatorship (Nerín 91–3). Although both authors contend that such rumours contained elements of truth but were most likely exaggerated, the anxieties that they generated surfaced in several Spanish films, such as the missionary film *Encrucijada para una monja* (dir. Julio Buchs, 1967), the musical melodrama *Esa mujer* (dir. Mario Camus, 1969), and the erotic horror film *La noche de los brujos* (dir. Armando de Ossorio, 1974). These films all feature extended, graphic scenes of white women being raped by Black or dark-skinned men in colonial settings.

Despite all three containing brutal rape scenes in colonial contexts, these films were very different from one other: they represented different genres, achieved different levels of box office success, and engaged imperial themes with varying degrees of realism. The only one of the three to address real-life decolonization with any level of seriousness is *Encrucijada*, which details how a Belgian missionary nun named Sister Maria is raped and impregnated by African rebels, causing her to abandon her religious order to raise the baby as a single mother. *Esa mujer* follows a comparable storyline, albeit one that is not grounded in any attempt of historical realism. A vehicle for Sara Montiel, one of the greatest musical stars of the era who was known for her "tragic diva" screen persona as well as for her substantial queer fan base, this film portrays Montiel's character as a happy missionary nun on a remote island until her rape by anticolonial rebels forces her to flee the convent, thus triggering her descent into a dissolute lifestyle. By contrast, *La noche de los brujos* is a lesser-known B-movie directed by Armando de Ossorio, one of Transition-era Spain's most prolific horror filmmakers better remembered for other works, such as his *Blind Dead* tetralogy of 1971–5. Derided by critics as "too hokey to be effective" (Stine 638) or "embody[ing] all that's worst in Euro-vamp films of the period" (Dendle 305), *La noche de los brujos* recounts how unsuspecting European researchers stumble into African lands haunted by the traumas of a colonial massacre and fall prey to gruesome postcolonial revenge. In addition to their genre-related differences, *Encrucijada*, *Esa mujer*, and *La noche de los brujos* achieved uneven box office results: *Encrucijada* was the most successful in its day, having sold about 2.8 million tickets, compared with *Esa mujer*'s more modest result of about 1.4 million or *La noche*'s paltry 348,000. *La noche*, however, has had the longest afterlife of the three, having been re-released on various VHS versions in the 1980s and on DVD in 2007 and 2017. Yet, despite their numerous differences, I argue that these films' collective reinforcement of the Black rapist trope during the era of decolonization is significant because it sustained myths about imperialism that obfuscated the realities of European violence in Africa at the time and that remain prevalent today.

The demonization of Black men as rapists, of course, was hardly a new phenomenon and not specific to Spain. On the contrary, such a myth had been propagated throughout Europe and the Americas since the dawn of European imperialism itself to the point of becoming "a necessary/permanent feature of the colonial landscape" (Loombia 79). In a foundational text on the subject, Angela Davis writes that "The myth of the Black rapist has been methodically conjured up whenever recurrent waves of violence and terror against the Black community have required convincing justifications" (173). To make sense of this myth's proliferation in Spanish films during the era of decolonization, we must consider what Tamari Kitossa has termed the "pornographic" and "propagandic" aspects of erotic racism in cinema. In his analysis of the highly influential, yet controversial American silent epic *Birth of a Nation* (dir. D.W. Griffith, 1915), Kitossa writes that the pornographic element of the Black rapist myth derives from its ability "to accomplish the desires of White scopophilia," that is, to stimulate white viewers' pleasure at the dehumanization of Black men, as well as to articulate repressed white fantasies of taboo activities such as interracial sex (32). The propagandic function of the myth, he writes, exploits already widely circulated beliefs and attitudes about Black men to fortify the boundaries of a given community, such as the racial boundaries that inform a white supremacist US nationalism (33–5).

The violent rape scenes in these three Spanish films served "pornographic" and "propagandic" functions in line with Kitossa's analysis. On the one hand, these scenes likely invited audiences to entertain a variety of socially proscribed pornographic fantasies, which could have ranged from women's or queer men's desires to escape sexual repression, straight men's fantasies of sexually possessing inaccessible figures like nuns, or anyone's desire for penetration by Black men's supposedly oversized genitalia, a key component of the rapist trope. On the other hand, the pornographic dimension of these rape scenes also served a propagandic purpose, but one that was not strictly nationalist. Rather, these brutal rape scenes aimed to construe not only late imperial Spain, but late imperial Europe more broadly as an innocent victim of dehumanized African savages. By portraying Black masculinity and white femininity as locked in a polarized battle of aggression and victimhood, these films erased the distinctions promoted by earlier Spanish films about imperialism, in which the Spanish empire was imagined as more benign, less racist, or otherwise "different" from other European empires. Instead, these films' portrayal of extreme African monstrosity made European whiteness seem internally undifferentiated, which accentuated the idea that Spain was a fully white, postimperial nation, rather than a so-called Africa of Europe.

As a Spanish-Italian co-production set between Congo and Belgium, *Encrucijada para una monja* is especially demonstrative of an emerging European imaginary of decolonization, rather than a distinctively Spanish or Hispanotropicalist one. The film's plot draws on widely reported stories of violence committed during Congo's Simba Rebellion of 1963–5, which emerged as a reaction to the assassination of Patrice Lumumba, the country's first prime minister.[6] As Van Reybrouck notes, the Simbas' disenchantment with Congolese independence – and, especially, their anger at Western powers for having orchestrated Lumumba's ouster – led them to enact a massive rebellion in which they managed to take control of a large swathe of eastern Congo (322–4). Given their "pronouncedly anti-American, anti-Belgian, and anti-Catholic" outlook, they were known for committing numerous acts of violence against whites, especially Belgian missionaries, including rape and murder (324). However, *Encrucijada*'s version of the events is decidedly Manichaean, as it utterly ignores the political context that gave rise to the Simba rebellion, as well as the responsibility of Western powers in producing the circumstances that led to it. The reductive quality of its narrative is clear from the opening scene, in which African rebels, armed with machine guns, creep through thick foliage until they reach a large, idyllic house inhabited by a white family and Black servants. The rebels suddenly begin shooting indiscriminately, and then set the house on fire – an unambiguous foreshadowing of the fate that will soon befall the nuns' mission. Although the scene is primarily filmed with long shots, several medium shots focus on the group's leader, Nangu, who bellows orders such as "¡Quemadlo todo!" ("Burn it all down!") with a demonic smile throughout the whole episode. Nangu's laughter endows the scene with a perversely pornographic quality, as it invites viewers simultaneously to feel horrified by the Africans' brutality as well as to relish the spectacle of destruction and carnage.

The association between Blackness and pleasurable monstrosity is reinforced by the opening credits that immediately follow this scene accompanied by a montage of photographs and newspaper text written in various languages that detail extreme bloodshed in Africa. Throughout the montage, occasional splotches of red emerge against the black and white newspaper background, a visual motif that accentuates the film's portrayal of a polarized, bloody struggle between Africans and Europeans. In particular, the word "Simba," which is recognizable in several languages, is repeatedly highlighted in red. Yet, despite the historical specificity of the Simba rebellion, the word "Simba" comes to be used throughout the film as essentially synonymous with "Black monster." For instance, much later in the film, in a scene that takes place after Sister María has resettled in Belgium, Sister María's mother bursts into tears when she is reminded that her grandchild will be a "pequeño simba saltando por los muebles" ("a little Simba jumping on the furniture"). In this way, the film strips the word of its historical meaning and instead redefines it as a universal signifier of Black savagery, enhancing the film's pornographic vilification of Blackness.

Undoubtedly, the sequence that most strongly advances the film's lurid portrayal of Black violence is the one that depicts Sister María's rape, which occurs just before the rebels attack the nuns' mission. One day, Sister María, cloaked in a starkly white habit, is approached by a young African boy, who requests that she travel to his mother's house because she has been bitten by a snake and requires treatment. Sister María at first hesitates because of the Mother Superior's orders not to leave the mission; however, when the child cries, "¡No te importa la vida de negros!" ("You don't care about Black people's lives!"), she relents, and sets out on the mission's utility vehicle to the boy's house. After treating the boy's mother, the woman's adult son escorts Sister María back to the mission. However, along the way, they must pass through a dark, thickly wooded forest from which eerie, high-pitched noises can be heard.

At the entrance to the forest, their vehicle is suddenly surrounded by rebels. Despite the pleas of Sister María's escort for mercy towards the "blanca buena" ("good white woman"), the rebels shoot him dead, causing Sister María to let out a piercing scream. The lead rebel, whose face is painted with white stripes and who is bare-chested except for a bullet belt, bursts into bellowing, nefarious laughter, causing several others to follow his example. Their laughter accompanies the next shot, in which Sister María, whose torn white habit contrasts sharply with her shadowy surroundings, struggles to escape on foot through the forest's thick foliage. In every direction she runs, a Black rebel materializes from behind a tree; meanwhile, the camera rapidly zooms in and out of extreme close-ups of several of the rebels' faces to punctuate their sadistic expressions and demonic laughter. With her face bloodied and her habit in shreds, Sister María eventually falls to the ground out of exhaustion. A particularly chilling shot shows her lying on the ground, with the lower body of one gun-toting rebel behind her, and the large, bare foot of another rebel in front of her in the foreground. As the ominous music intensifies, the lead rebel slowly approaches her, and the scene ends with another piercing shriek.

Although the scene does not show explicit sexual contact, it is replete with what Kitossa calls "metaphoric representations of genital significations" (35). These include the visual imagery of Sister María's white habit being ripped and stained, as well as the large foot in front of her face – images that are both echoed in the film's poster (figure 2.6). At the same time, this scene relies on several well-worn commonplaces of horror cinema, such as the spooky forest setting, the surprise emergence of hidden monster-villains, the rebels' maniacal laughter, the contrast between light and darkness, and, of course, the recurring sound of a woman's screams. Despite their lack of originality, these conventions effectively portray Black masculinity and white femininity not only as ingredients of a pornographic encounter, but also as moral opposites, in which the former personifies African decolonization movements as evil, brutal, and sexually aggressive, while the latter personifies imperialism as vulnerable, virtuous, and innocent. These interlocking binaries serve to utterly dehumanize the African rebels while construing Sister María and, by extension, the imperial project she represents, as a hapless and undeserving victim of Black monstrosity. According to this film, postcolonial Africa is, quite simply, a living horror movie, and Europeans, whose only role in the narrative is that of innocent martyr, have no choice but to retreat from it. By imagining Africans and Europeans as occupying opposite sides of polarized moral, sexual, and racial binaries, the film disregards Hispanotropicalist distinctions between Spain and other white countries, such as those that surface in René Muñoz's religious movies or in early Marisol films. Instead, given the film's ahistorical approach to postcolonial conflict, the scenario of Sister María's victimization can easily allegorize any European empire, or all of them at once, implying that all European empires shared comparable degrees of moral innocence and racial whiteness.

After *Encrucijada*, subsequent iterations of the Black rapist myth in popular cinema would seemingly try to outdo each other. This is

Figure 2.6. A poster for the film *Encrucijada para una monja* (dir. Julio Buchs, 1967).

notable in *Esa mujer*, a Sara Montiel film from 1969 that recounts the melodramatic fall from grace of Montiel's character, Soledad Romero. Although the film begins by showing Soledad on trial for the murder of a lover, a flashback transports us to a much earlier time in her life, when she was a nun stationed on a mission on a faraway, fictional island. The representation of Soledad's character draws on similar tropes to those in *Encrucijada*, such as her starkly white habit, as well as her initially being shown ministering to children. As Soledad teaches vowels to schoolchildren in a lighthearted musical number called "A, E, I, O, U," she is interrupted by a classic horror device, namely, a biting shriek that emanates from elsewhere in the convent. A two-minute sequence follows in which the entire community of nuns is ruthlessly raped by a gang of dark-skinned men, all of whom are wearing makeshift uniforms with bullet belts. Throughout the scene, the use of low-key lighting, another horror staple, creates dramatic shadow effects on the bare convent walls, which are as white as the nuns' habits. As in *Encrucijada*, the scene's soundtrack combines ominous music with the women's

Figure 2.7. Sister Soledad (Sara Montiel) is attacked in *Esa mujer* (dir. Mario Camus, 1969).

continued screams and grunts. The men, by contrast, are portrayed as little more than animals: in addition to not speaking or uttering a sound of any kind, they also rape several of the nuns in the stalls amongst the horses.

In many ways, this scene attempts to surpass the violence of the rape scene in *Encrucijada*. Whereas the former film only portrays the rape of Sister María, in *Esa mujer*, all the nuns are raped, and several, including Soledad, are impregnated as a result. Similarly, unlike *Encrucijada*, which refrains from showing the African rebels laying hands on Sister María (apart from the moment where one rips off her cross and tears her habit), in *Esa mujer*, we see the rebels violently manhandling and beating Sister Soledad and several of her companions. In several instances, two men are shown battering and overpowering a single woman. Furthermore, in *Esa mujer*, the aggressors rip the veils off the nuns' heads as they rape them, exposing their hair – a shocking image for audiences accustomed to seeing screen nuns in full habit (figure 2.7). Echoing the pornographic qualities of *Encrucijada*, such a scene, despite its brutality, could have easily stimulated sexual fantasies for a range of viewers, including those of married women trapped by sexual monotony, straight men excited to look under nuns' habits, or anyone enticed by the idea of a gang of dark-skinned men. At the same time, like *Encrucijada, Esa mujer* also releases European viewers from guilt about colonialism and its aftermath by portraying the colonizers as well-meaning victims who are helpless to defend themselves against the racialized brutality of anticolonial rebels. Notably, like *Encrucijada, Esa mujer* makes no effort to distinguish the Spanish empire from other European empires, as earlier films had insistently done. Instead, it follows *Encrucijada*'s lead of recycling an increasingly generic, universal European imaginary of decolonization as racialized evil pitted against white innocence.

The postcolonial anxieties articulated by the dramatic rape scenes in *Encrucijada* and *Esa mujer* were further bolstered by another element: namely, the films' refusal to represent the interracial children born of rape. Although the unborn child in *Encrucijada* is discussed in numerous dialogues throughout the film, the narrative ends before the baby is born, thus sparing audiences the discomfort of visualizing a future generation of interracial Europeans. Similarly, in *Esa mujer*, Sister Soledad's flight from the convent means that the daughter engendered by her rape, Eugenia, must be raised by the other nuns. Even though Soledad is eventually reunited with Eugenia as an adult, the film depicts Eugenia's character as blonde with pale skin, thus mysteriously erasing all traces of her interracial origin. The erasure of the trauma of interracial rape, which is evidenced by the absence of visibly interracial children, is also emphasized at the end of both films, when the female protagonists ultimately achieve independence from men altogether. In *Encrucijada*, Sister María not only leaves the convent, but also turns down an offer of marriage, choosing instead to raise her unborn child as a single mother, a daring proposition for the era. At the end of *Esa mujer*, Soledad is exonerated of killing her lover, who also happens to be her daughter's husband. In the final scene, Soledad and her daughter Eugenia, who are both dressed in black and united by grief, walk away from the courtroom together, free of the intrigues with men that have marred Soledad's life and strained the mother-daughter relationship almost to the point of breaking.

The parallelism in both films between the suppression or whitewashing of interracial children, on the one hand, and the idea of white women achieving freedom from patriarchy, on the other, mirrors the Franco regime's attempts to liberate itself of the postcolonial disasters associated with its youngest "child," the newly independent Equatorial Guinea. Although the regime's initial rhetoric about the independence was unsurprisingly self-congratulating, its self-flattery quickly gave way to coerced silence. On the day of Equatorial Guinea's independence, which took place on the unsubtly symbolic date of 12 October 1968, *ABC* featured an article entitled "Guinea en el día de la Hispanidad" ("Guinea on the day of *Hispanidad*"). Notably, it described Spain as a mother and Equatorial Guinea as a new child in the Hispanic family of nations:

> "España, que concibió a una comunidad de pueblos el 12 de octubre de 1492, en este 12 de octubre de 1968 alumbra con el gozo profundo de las madres una nueva nación, un nuevo miembro para la gran familia, a veces mestiza y siempre católica, de la Hispanidad."
>
> ("Spain, which conceived a community of people on 12 October 1492, on this day of 12 October 1968 gives birth with a mother's profound joy to a new nation, a new member for the great family of *Hispanidad*, which is sometimes mixed race and always Catholic.")

Despite this triumphant rhetoric, the newest member of the Hispanic family of nations would soon become an embarrassment. Within a year of assuming power, the newly elected president, Francisco Macías Nguema, seized control of the government as a dictator, and, in a paranoid effort to quash all opposition, submerged the fledgling nation into a bloodbath of terror and violence. The *materia reservada* law, which outlawed the publication of any information related to Equatorial Guinea throughout all of Spain, took effect in 1971 and would not be lifted until after Franco's death. Like popular cinema's depictions of Black savagery against innocent white women, the *materia reservada* law was clearly intended to exculpate the Franco regime from being associated with the unspeakable tragedies of the Macías regime.[7] Furthermore, like Sister Maria and Soledad, the Franco regime preferred simply to walk away from the disastrous entanglements of its imperial past.

Although the *materia reservada* law stifled discussion of Equatorial Guinea's plight for several years, popular cinema continued to circulate images of generalized African violence against Europeans. A particular example is the low-budget, zombie-vampire-sexploitation hybrid, *La noche de los brujos*. The film depicts a group of white researchers travelling through the fictional African country of Zambonia. They stumble into an area that was once traumatized by a colonial massacre and that is still haunted by the zombie spirits of African voodoo practitioners whose religion was never stamped out by European missionaries. Over the course of the film, the Black, voodoo zombies pursue the white women characters and subject them to highly eroticized and lethal tortures; the women then become zombie-vampires, who in turn develop their own bloodthirst for future victims.

The film's highly formulaic plot remixes well-worn tropes from European and global horror with soft-core porn, which flourished in Spain during the Transition and the very last years of Francoism. As Ian Olney notes, the narrative formula of well-meaning, white researchers travelling through formerly colonized lands and receiving a form of "poetic justice" (203) at the hands of racialized monsters for the misdeeds of colonialism was thoroughly rehearsed in numerous European horror films of the 1970s and 1980s, especially in the cannibal and zombie subgenres (199–216). In such films, these monsters were depicted as enacting violence against whites *not only* because of the former's innate savagery, *but also* because the whites deserved it, a pattern that creates ambivalence about who, exactly, is the real monster in such films (201).

Made in 1974, *La noche de los brujos* was an early example of this pattern for Spanish horror. The first decade of democracy witnessed the emergence of a plethora of comparable Spanish horror films that also combined colonial or postcolonial settings, racialized villains, and strongly pornographic elements. Several of these were directed by Jess Franco, one of Spain's best-known horror directors who worked in film in several European countries.[8] The horror genre served as an arena in which European erotic fantasies and nightmares about colonialism and its aftermath travelled between various national film industries and audiences, including those from Spain. The transnational quality of this imaginary was reinforced because, unlike other domestic film genres such as comedy, horror cinema in Spain was usually made to be marketed and distributed internationally and was often financed by several countries at once; as such, it tended to feature widely recognizable formulas and settings that were easily legible to foreign audiences (Lázaro Reboll 20–2). Indeed, although *La noche de los brujos* was financed only by Spain, the viability of its imaginary becomes clear when we consider that it was re-released on DVD in the United States and Canada twice in the twenty-first century despite its poor original run in theatres.

With this context in mind, we must evaluate the degree to which *La noche de los brujos* can be said to reflect Olney's argument that some European horror films evoke "the postcolonial notion of past imperialist injustices, buried but not forgotten, returning to haunt the present" (211). The theme of colonial trauma surfaces in the opening scene, which is set in "Bumbasa, 1910." As the film opens, we are introduced to a diabolical ceremony in which Black male voodoo practitioners tie a white woman named Agnes (Barbara Rey) between two trees, flog her until her clothes fall off, rape her, and behead her; subsequently, the African women bathe in her blood. Through cross-cutting, we learn that as the ceremony is proceeding, European soldiers are creeping through the thickly wooded forest towards the clearing where the Africans are practising their ritual. Peering through the trees, they arrive at the scene just after the woman is beheaded and watch the ceremony for a few moments before shooting all the Africans dead. At the end of the scene, Agnes's decapitated head grows fangs and starts to scream.

Despite the kitsch quality of the film's characters, costumes, setting, and special effects, this opening scene self-reflexively rehearses several of the patterns that we have traced in films of other genres like *Encrucijada* or *Esa mujer*. The depiction of white men ambushing an African ritual is an almost exact inversion of the opening scene of *Encrucijada*, in which African rebels launch a surprise attack on a colonial mansion. Likewise, the European soldiers' stopping to watch the ceremony for a few moments self-consciously emphasizes the scene's pornographic quality, as this detail mirrors that viewers, too, have taken time out of their lives to savour the pornographic pleasures of this lurid film. Yet the end of the scene, in which a close-up shows Agnes' head coming back to life and screaming, foreshadows the rest of the film's plot, in which the trauma of the colonial massacre becomes increasingly peripheral to the narrative. For, over the course of the film's narrative, the African vampire-zombies fade into the background, and are replaced by the film's true protagonists, the white women who become vampire-zombies themselves. By substituting the initial pornographic fantasy of Black rapists for a different fantasy of white women vampirizing each other, the film invites its audiences to forget the traumas of colonialism, and to celebrate instead the sexual availability and independence of white women, which are symbolized by their vampiric capabilities. Although the white women characters in this film are extremely objectified and hypersexualized, the film's emphasis on their vampiric power calls attention to their growing sexual and economic independence in real life. After all, in the film, their vampirism accomplishes more work than to merely make them spectacular sex objects; rather, as the film progresses, it enables them to attack their white male companions, thus destabilizing the latter's authority.

The film's effort to efface the trauma of colonial massacre by focusing on white women's sexual agency becomes especially clear in two subsequent ritual scenes, which are set in "Bumbasa, the present." The second ritual scene of rape and beheading occurs when Carol, one of the oblivious, European wildlife researchers, is wandering around the African ritual grounds at night to take pictures of it despite having been warned not to. In this scene, it is Agnes, the previously beheaded white woman, who captures Carol, ties her up, flogs her and beheads her, while African natives dance and play drums in the background. The African zombies' loss of agency in their own demonic ritual is further echoed in the third ritual scene, in which Agnes and Carol, who now are both vampire-zombies, lure a third white woman, Liz, out of her bed and into the ritual clearing, where she, too, is flogged, beheaded and transformed into a vampire-zombie. In this scene, once again, African natives dance, play music and shout in the background, but are denied a central role in the action. In both scenes, vampirism emphasizes white women's agency and the powerlessness of Africans, as white women characters use their evil powers to form an odd "sisterhood" that resists white patriarchal authority while marginalizing the Africans who gave them their power in the first place.

The relationship between vampirism and white women's agency is especially evident towards the end of the film, as white women vampires use their powers not only to recruit other female vampires, but also to attack their male companions. In one episode, the vampires Agnes and Carol sneak up on one of the expedition's leaders, Professor Jonathan Grant, while he is developing photographs in a darkroom. The female vampires shove his head in a tub of water, drowning him, and then tear up his photographs after he is dead. Similarly, in the film's final sequence, the expedition's other leader, Professor Rod Carter, uses the group's jeep to flee the haunted site with Tunika, a fourth white woman, who is bleeding because she, too, was recently bitten by Agnes and Carol. Not realizing that Tunika is a now a vampire, the professor says he wants to take her to a hospital immediately. Tunika, however, responds, "No hace falta" ("That that won't be necessary"), and reveals her newly sprouted fangs.

Although on one level, *La noche de los brujos* follows the narrative pattern of postcolonial "poetic justice" that Olney identifies, that narrative formula plays a very superficial role in this film, which marginalizes its initial story about African revenge for colonial violence by prioritizing another narrative about white women's sexuality. The film suggests, essentially, that Africans can transmit their savagery – a metonym, perhaps, for sexual power – to white women, who, in turn, can use it to undermine patriarchal authority. Consequently, this film recycles a pattern we see in other films, such as *Encrucijada* and *Esa mujer*. In all three films, the trope of the Black rapist enables each film to simplify and spectacularize the complex realities of postcolonial violence in Africa. At the same time, all three films imagine their rape scenarios as a trauma that, however paradoxically, places its white women protagonists on a journey that will ultimately free them from patriarchal control. By portraying decolonization and its aftermath through the lens of a polarized binary between an idealized white femininity and Black sexual aggression, these films departed from Spanish popular cinema's earlier depictions of colonialism in Africa, which insisted that Spanish imperialism was "different" from other empires. Rather, these films implied that the shared trauma of imperial loss had not only erased Spain's difference from other European countries, but also, that it "liberated" the nation from its colonial burden in a manner that was imagined as analogous to women's increasing independence from men.

Conclusion

In this chapter, we have seen how the missionary genre, a corpus of Spanish cinema whose consumption peaked during the early decades of Francoism, created an idealized imaginary of white, feminine beneficence towards nonwhite peoples, especially Blacks, that persisted beyond its initial popularity. This imaginary surfaced in numerous film genres of late Francoism, including hagiographic, Western, horror, and musical films. Due to their ability to reach large audiences, this multigeneric constellation of popular films played a critical role in shaping Spanish viewers' perception of the loss of Spain's African colonies, which occurred between 1956 and 1975. The importance of these films is further underscored because their depictions of decolonization were largely uncontested by opposition cinema, given the Franco regime's use of censorship and *materia reservada* laws to suppress critical perspectives about African struggles for independence.

In the early 1960s, both religious and secular films, such as René Muñoz's trilogy and some Marisol films, exploited Hispanotropicalist assertions of Spain's imperial uniqueness to justify preserving the empire. These assertions often overlapped with the rhetoric of *desarrollismo*, which aimed to portray Spain as catching up to Anglo-European modernity, while also characterizing the Spanish empire as "feminized" in a variety of ways. However, as decolonization advanced, popular cinema began to acknowledge the inevitability of imperial loss. Consequently, its efforts to portray Spain as being fully absorbed into European whiteness gradually overshadowed its earlier defence of Spain's unique imperial identity. Specifically, in films such as *Las cuatro bodas de Marisol, Encrucijada para una monja, Esa mujer,* or *La noche de los brujos,* imperial loss came to be imagined as a common thread that linked Spain to other European powers, diminishing the importance of earlier claims of Spanish imperial difference. In several of these films, Spain's racial whiteness was further accentuated by the Black rapist motif, which suggested that postimperial Spain was an innocent victim of African racial savagery, bore no responsibility for the disasters of decolonization, and ultimately, might even be "freer" without the burden of the empire.

Like the sex comedy analysed in chapter 1, the films that constituted late-Francoism's missionary imaginary bolstered the notion that Spain could free itself from its reputation as a colonial failure and from the burden of its postcolonial responsibilities. By portraying both preserving and relinquishing the empire as viable paths to the project of national whitening, these films call attention not only to the malleability of Spain's whiteness, but to the volatility of the logic used to exemplify its attainment. The turbulence and instability of Spain's claims to whiteness will become even more pronounced in the next two chapters, which highlight how the triumphant rhetoric of national whitening was punctured by intractable fears of racial degeneration and contamination.

Chapter 3

From Andalusian Gypsies to Urban *Quinquis*: Roma Identities in Popular Cinema

The film *Los últimos golpes de El Torete* ("The last blows of El Torete," dir. José Antonio de la Loma, 1980) narrates the misadventures of two notorious teenage delinquents whose characters were based on real criminals: El Vaquilla, who is of Roma descent, and El Torete, who is *payo*.[1] In a crucial scene, Begoña, a well-meaning *paya* radio host, discusses how the infamous duo became master criminals at a young age. Speaking on the air, she declares: "Dejemos de lado al Vaquilla, hijo y nieto de quinquis, porque de casta le viene al galgo. Centrémonos en el Torete, hijo de una familia andaluza pobre pero honesta" ("Let's forget about El Vaquilla, son and grandson of *quinquis*, because it runs in the family. Let's focus on El Torete, son of a poor but honest Andalusian family.")

Begoña's use of the term *quinqui* in this moment is noteworthy. This word is best understood today as a designation of young urban criminals, especially those who were glorified in the press and in popular cinema between the 1960s and 1980s. Yet historically, the term's meaning was racialized. An abbreviation of *quincallero*, a name for someone who practises scrap metal collection, the word evolved over time to imply a link between nomadism and criminality; consequently, it was used throughout much of the twentieth century to refer to traditionally itinerant, marginalized peoples such as the *mercheros* and the Roma[2] (García-Egocheaga location 3087; Pérez-Rodríguez 66–9). Far from disappearing during the Transition, the racial meanings of the word *quinqui* lingered during this period in a number of ways. For example, in the scene described above, Begoña's remark implies that El Vaquilla cannot avoid criminality because such behaviour "runs in the family," thus reinforcing the perception of the Roma as innately inclined to delinquency (Martín Cabrera 122, Florido Berrocal 146–7). By contrast, she implies, the criminality of a non-Roma youth like El Torete is a consequence of sociological factors, and can be ameliorated with the appropriate intervention.

Although the stereotype of innate Roma criminality dates back to early modern times, *quinqui* cinema's fusion of action and social realism during the 1970s and 1980s marked a notable shift away from long-established patterns that had characterized representations of the Roma in earlier periods of Spanish cinema. *Los últimos golpes de El Torete*, for instance, had little in common with the upbeat folkloric musicals appearing from the 1920s to the 1950s, which were usually set in Andalusia and narrated the assimilation of comical, musical Roma women into mainstream society by way of marriage to *payo* men. Instead, *quinqui* films portrayed a racially mixed underworld in which Roma people, southern migrants, *mercheros*, and interracial descendants of these groups lived on the outer edges of Spain's major cities like Madrid, Barcelona, and Bilbao. These underserved urban ghettoes were construed as hotbeds of violence, poverty, and drug abuse, and were breeding grounds of famous male delinquents like El Vaquilla, El Torete, and others. Many *quinqui* films portrayed their seedy urban settings as distinctively marked by Roma contamination, given the films' frequent narrative focus on *payo*-Roma love stories, *payo*-Roma criminal friendships, or Roma protagonists, as well as their abundant reliance on Roma music and slang.[3] Hence, *quinqui* cinema reversed the racial assimilation narratives of folkloric films: while folkloric musicals imagined how *payos* could domesticate the Roma, *quinqui* films portrayed the Roma as contributing to the decay of *payo* society.

Popular cinema's shift from narratives about Andalusian Gypsy women to narratives about urban *quinqui* men was a gradual process that began in the 1960s. During this decade, the Franco regime's promotion of tourist-friendly myths about colourful, folkloric Gypsies existed in tension with ever-intensifying fears about Roma encroachment on society. These fears were a consequence of large scale rural-to urban migrations during the mid-twentieth century, which drove the proliferation of deprived slums on the peripheries of Spain's major cities. Although both *payo* and Roma Spaniards were swept up in these rural-to-urban migrations, the peripheral urban ghettoes that emerged to house them featured markedly disproportionate concentrations of Roma inhabitants (Río Ruiz 40). This pattern intensified as *payo* residents were generally able to move into better-served neighbourhoods much faster than their Roma counterparts (Río Ruiz 41–2; Saavedra 253–5). Consequently, popular culture such as *quinqui* cinema established a link between these underserved ghettoes and Roma racial degeneracy. During the late 1970s and the 1980s, as audiences flocked to watch *quinqui* films in theatres, state-sponsored efforts to resettle Roma communities provoked vigorous resistance from *payo* neighbourhood associations throughout the country who did not want to accept Roma neighbours (Calvo Buezas 15–19).

This chapter discusses the shapeshifting cultural myths about the Roma during late Francoism and the Transition that harnessed anxieties about Spain's imagined ascent into global modernity and Euro-American racial whiteness. Although the late-Franco regime aimed to capitalize on the myth of the folkloric Gypsy to promote tourism, the growth and proliferation of impoverished urban peripheries with large Roma populations generated fears that the nation's imagined ascent into modernity might be derailed by its internal racial contamination. Hence, while the first two chapters of this book illustrate an imagined journey towards whiteness, this chapter and the next illustrate how fears of whiteness's volatility – that is, its ability to be lost after having been gained – were a marked preoccupation of Spanish popular cinema between the 1960s and 1980s.

Our examination of the Roma in popular film begins with a review of how duelling myths about the Spanish Roma, the folkloric Gypsy, and the urban *quinqui* came into being. With this context in mind, we examine how entangled depictions of folkloric Gypsies and urban *quinquis* during late Francoism and the Transition epitomized larger struggles over Spain's national and racial identity. To do so, the star images of three male actors of the era are analysed: first, Manolo Escobar, an Almerian *payo* known for starring in *macho ibérico* comedies and performing *copla* songs; second, Peret, a Catalan Roma singer, composer, and guitarist who also starred in *macho ibérico* comedies; and third, Ángel Fernández Franco, a real-life *quinqui* delinquent who starred in José Antonio de la Loma's *Perros callejeros* ("Street dogs") trilogy. Focusing on the "structured polysemy" of these actors' star images – that is, their ability to produce a "multiplicity of meanings and affects" in which some meanings "are foregrounded and others are masked or displaced" – demonstrates how their screen personas channeled and responded to deep-seated anxieties about the presumed degeneracy of the encroaching Roma (Dyer, *Stars* 3). In particular, the contradictions and ambiguities of these male stars call attention both to the nonlinear, volatile quality of Spain's whitening, which was imagined as moving in forward and backward directions at the same time, as well as to the instability of the boundaries of whiteness itself.

Performing Race: The Precarious *Payo* / Roma Boundary

Popular film from the 1960s to the 1980s was characterized by duelling myths about the Roma: on the one hand, the singing and dancing folkloric Gypsy; and on the other, the figure of the urban *quinqui*. While the former can be traced back to early modern times, the latter emerged as a consequence of mid-twentieth century mass migrations. Drawing on theories of racial performativity and whiteness as a wage, in this section, we examine how these competing stereotypes harnessed Spanish fears of racial precarity, the idea that the dominant narrative of national whitening during late Francoism and the Transition could be thwarted by Roma racial contamination.

The intermingling of myth and reality has characterized social perceptions of Roma peoples since their earliest days in Spain. For instance, although it has been known since the eighteenth century that Roma languages were descended from Sanskrit (Charnon-Deutsch 89), popular belief held that Spain's Roma population were of Egyptian origin until well into the twentieth century.[4] The myth of the Roma as Egyptian gave rise to the word "gitano" (a derivative of "egipciano"), the most commonly used Spanish term to refer to this heterogeneous community. The Roma's supposedly mythical origins contributed to their romanticization through tropes such as mystery, primitiveness, musicality, and passion, thus engendering the iconic character of the bohemian, musical Spanish Gypsy. Although this character was already evident in the seventeenth-century in texts like Cervantes' *La gitanilla*, it became especially solidified and popularized throughout Europe during the late eighteenth and nineteenth centuries. During this period, European travellers who visited Spain were especially drawn to Andalusia because of the perceived Orientalism and exoticism of its conspicuous Islamic heritage and its large Roma population (Charnon Deutsch 50–4). By the mid-nineteenth century, representations of Andalusia as an exotic, premodern realm where travellers could admire primitive, passionate Gypsies had proliferated in art, music, and literature, with Prosper Mérimée's novel *Carmen* (1845) and the eponymous opera by Georges Bizet (1875) serving as quintessential examples (Charnon Deutsch 54–9). The overwhelming prevalence of female Gypsy protagonists in these narratives served not only "to make racial difference more palatable" by feminizing it, but also to highlight women's inherent inclination to disorder by racializing them (240). Over time, the association of Andalusia with mythical Gypsies, especially Gypsy women, caused the two identities to become "collapsed" in the European imagination, and the trope of the Andalusian Gypsy "came to stand for Spanishness both outside, and, to an extent, inside Spain's cultural arena" (11).

The figure of the musical Gypsy woman travelled between European and Spanish cultural representations, and became especially hegemonic in folkloric musicals, a genre of Spanish popular film that reached its heyday between the 1920s and 1950s. During this period, stars like

Concha Piquer, Imperio Argentina, Raquel Meller, Lola Flores, and others became staples on Spanish screens for their roles playing Gypsy women despite almost all of them being *payas*.[5] The majority of these films were set in Andalusia and narrated the assimilation of rural, peasant, yet indomitable Gypsy women into mainstream society by way of marriage, usually to a *payo* landowner. For Jo Labanyi, these narratives of racialized and gendered subordination emblematized the dictatorship's intention to "secure, with the final marriage, the fascist dream of a society transcending capitalist class conflict" ("Musical Battles" 211). In her landmark study *White Gypsies*, Eva Woods Peiró further argues that the effort of such films to "situate Spain's racial identity as coherent and contained" also constituted an attempt to portray Spain as "'catch[ing] up' to European modernity" (2–3). In other words, narratives of the screen Gypsy's assimilation articulated a desire to contain Roma difference while imagining Spain as achieving parity with Europe. Significantly, both Labanyi and Woods-Peiró also call attention to the folkloric film's ability to invite subversive identifications and interpretations, especially from its female, working-class, and queer audiences.

Despite its legibility as a cultural icon for large and diverse audiences, the folkloric Gypsy trope has always stood in stark contrast with the brutal ostracism and oppression imposed on Spain's flesh-and-blood Roma communities. Since this community's arrival in the Iberian Peninsula in the early fifteenth century, literally dozens of laws were enacted that aimed to suppress Roma languages, dress, itinerant lifestyles, and traditional livelihoods. The first of these was the Catholic Monarchs' *Pragmática real de Medina del Campo* (Royal Decree of Medina del Campo) of 1499, which subjected the Roma to a range of penalties if they did not assume a sedentary lifestyle and practise a known profession (Martínez Martínez 368). A number of subsequent laws aimed to expel the Roma from various territories, such as those enacted in Valencia in 1547, in Navarre in 1549, and in Catalonia in 1623 (Martínez Martínez 369). Likewise, raids were frequently conducted to forcibly exploit Roma labour for mining, agriculture, public works, or rowing in galleys, such as those carried out in 1539, 1571, 1639, and 1749 (de León 1). The last of these raids, which is known as "La gran redada" ("The Great Gypsy-Round-up"), is especially infamous because it involved a carefully orchestrated, nationwide attempt to arrest Spain's entire Roma population and deport them permanently to labour camps. Although the captured Roma were subsequently released in phases and achieved full liberation in 1763, Carlos III's *Ley asimiladora* ("Assimilationist Law") of 1783 reinforced earlier prohibitions on the use of Roma customs, language, and dress while forbidding any acknowledgment of Roma cultural difference, including the word *gitano* itself (Martín Sánchez locations 338, 536).

Underlying these numerous instances of historical anti-Roma racism was a deeply ingrained perception of Roma peoples as inherently inclined to criminality, which has persisted from early modern times until the present day. For instance, a 1586 law required the Roma to possess notarized proof of residence to sell merchandise because it was assumed that their goods were likely to be stolen (Martínez Martínez 353). Likewise, nineteenth-century criminologists like Cesare Lombroso and Rafael Salillas famously claimed that the Roma belonged to a group of inferior races that had inherited a biologically immutable tendency towards criminal behaviour (García Sanz 150). A similar essentialism informed the Franco regime's view of the Roma, whom it targeted with specific laws like the *Ley de vagos y maleantes* ("Law of vagrants and criminals") of 1934[6] as well as its successor, the *Ley de peligrosidad y rehabilitación social* ("Law on dangerousness and social rehabilitation") of 1971 (Rothea 14–15). Both of these laws identified the Roma as belonging to the category of "vagos" ("vagrants"), despite their traditional nomadism having largely waned by the mid-twentieth century. As Carolina García Sanz has argued, the imprisonment of Roma citizens under these laws during the Franco regime often had less to do with specific crimes committed by individuals than with "an assigned group personality" associated with all Roma people (146).

During Francoism, the internal code of the *Guardia Civil* (Civil Guard), Spain's oldest police agency, was explicit in its effort to treat the Roma as perpetual criminals. The following articles, which were active from 1943 to 1978, read as follows:

> Artículo 4°. Se vigilará escrupulosamente a los gitanos, cuidando mucho de reconocer todos los documentos que tengan, observar sus trajes, averiguar su modo de vivir y cuanto conduzca a formar una idea exacta de sus movimientos y ocupaciones, indagando el punto al que se dirigen en sus viajes y el objeto de ellos.

> Artículo 5°. Como esta clase de gente no tiene por lo general residencia fija, se traslada con frecuencia de un punto a otro en que sean desconocidos, conviene tomar de ellos todas las noticias necesarias para impedir que cometan robos de caballerías o de otra especie.

> (Article 4. The Roma will be scrupulously watched, with care to recognize all the documents they carry, to observe their dress, to ascertain their way of life and whatever else is necessary to form an exact idea of their movements and occupations, including learning the destination and goals of their travels.

Article 5. Since this class of people generally does not have a fixed residence, frequently moves from one place to another in which they are un-
known, it is necessary to gather all the information about them necessary
to prevent them from committing robberies, such as those of horses or any
other type.) (qtd. in Cabanes Hernández et al. 91)

Although the *Guardia Civil's* code was updated during the Transition,
the fraught relationship between Roma communities, the police, and
the carceral system has persisted beyond the end of the dictatorship
and into the present era. In 1988, for instance, the Spanish Supreme
Court condemned the municipal government of Madrid for overpolic-
ing Roma communities in Vicálvaro (Calvo Buezas 27). Likewise, a 1999
study indicated that 25 per cent of Spain's incarcerated women were
Roma, although the Roma had never comprised more than 2 per cent
of the national population (Martín Palomo 149). Similarly, a 2013 study
on racial profiling by the Spanish police indicated that Roma Spaniards
were about 10 times more likely to be stopped by the police than white
Spaniards – a rate higher than North Africans, who were 7.5 times more
likely, and Afro-Latin Americans, who were 6.5 times more likely to be
stopped (García Añón et al. 29).

During late Francoism, the idea of the Roma as irredeemable delinquents who were all but predestined to become fodder for the criminal justice system intersected and overlapped with the emergence of
the *quinqui* figure, which arose first in the press and later in cinema.
As discussed earlier, the word *quinqui* was not a perfect synonym for
the Roma, but rather, an ambiguous term that implied a link between
nomadism and criminality; as such, it was also associated with other
marginal groups such as the traditionally itinerant *merchero* ethnicity,
and, after the Transition, with delinquents of any background. The
term achieved widespread use in the press during the 1960s and 1970s
due to the notoriety achieved by several young male delinquents,
whose myriad criminal exploits were sensationalized by abundant
press coverage and, from the late 1970s onward, *quinqui* cinema.
Some of the most memorable included El Lute (Eleuterio Sánchez),
a *merchero* who is often regarded as the most famous *quinqui*; El Vaquilla (Juan José Moreno Cuenca), a Roma criminal whose life story
became the basis of de la Loma's *Perros callejeros* ("Street dogs") trilogy; and Ángel Fernández Franco, a *payo* criminal who starred in
the trilogy. Although not all *quinquis* were Roma, the pronounced
overlap between the two cultural imaginaries was a significant part
of what made the *quinqui* a fascinating, yet terrifying cultural figure.
As Luis Martín Cabrera has argued, the *quinqui* was a byproduct of

an "impure and monstrous racial formation" that emerged from the intermixing of Roma, *merchero*, and southern migrants on the outer edges of Spain's major cities, and was imagined as possessing a contagious degeneracy that could infect the working classes more broadly (122). Paula Pérez Rodríguez corroborates this argument, observing that the *quinqui* figure was construed, in essence, as a *payo agitanado* ("Gypsified payo") whose "racial indistinction ... confuses the limits of conduct that should guide the citizenry" (69).

The *quinqui* figure's racial ambiguity, as well as his presumed cultural and behavioural proximity to the Roma, caused the terms *quinqui* and *gitano* to be used interchangeably or in conjunction with each other on many occasions in the Spanish press throughout the twentieth century, including well into the 1970s (Pérez Rodríguez 68–73). The blurring of the *quinqui* and Roma cultural imaginaries is also evident in a wide range of films from the 1960s and 1970s, in which the emergent stereotype of the urban *quinqui* criminal became enmeshed with the traditional folkloric Gypsy trope. One of the earliest films in which the folkloric Gypsy image acquires *quinqui* overtones is the arthouse film *Los Tarantos* ("The Taranto clan," dir. Francisco Rovira-Beleta, 1963), which recast the Shakespearean Romeo and Juliet narrative as a drama about rivalling Roma families on the outskirts of Barcelona. As Bohumira Smidakova has argued, this film, which combined flamenco-driven musical numbers with an ethnographic tone, offered a highly idealized and nostalgic portrayal of Roma life by projecting an image of Spain that was both "exotic" and "immune to the changes of the time" (68). Nonetheless, despite rehearsing the myth of singing and dancing Gypsies, this film also prefigured later aspects of *quinqui* cinema through its violence-driven narrative, its tragic ending, and, especially, its setting on Barcelona's urban periphery, all of which departed from the conventions of earlier folkloric cinema. Similar patterns would surface in subsequent Roma-themed films like *Con el viento solano* ("With the eastern wind," dir. Mario Camus, 1966), *Amor brujo* ("Bewitched love," dir. Francisco Rovira Beleta, 1967), and *La ley de una raza* ("The law of a race," dir. José Luis Gonçalvo, 1969). Like *Los Tarantos*, all of these films were set outside Andalusia and featured tragic plots that revolved around Roma violence and criminality; in addition, a majority of them focused on male protagonists and were also set in or around major cities. In this way, despite retaining the folkloric genre's significant emphasis on music and dance, these arthouse films, which were aimed primarily at film festival or foreign audiences, illustrate the extent to which the folkloric Gypsy imaginary was gradually being divested of its rural, Andalusian image and was instead moving towards the urban *quinqui* stereotype that would pervade popular cinema the 1970s and 1980s.

The entanglement of the folkloric Gypsy and *quinqui* stereotypes is also evident in popular cinema genres of the 1960s and 1970s, especially *macho ibérico* films, such as those that starred Manolo Escobar, a southern *payo*, or those that starred Peret, a Catalan Roma singer and actor. In contrast to the previously described arthouse films, the *macho-ibérico*-themed musical comedies of Escobar and Peret were directed at domestic, working-class viewers who themselves had recently emigrated from rural areas to cities. While the *macho ibérico*'s ambiguous whiteness was often articulated as moving between racial whiteness and Blackness (see chapter 1), it also was often depicted as alternately embracing and disavowing Roma identity and its multiple cultural significations. Escobar's musical persona, for instance, heavily exploited the folkloric Gypsy myth; his films, however, often attempted to distance him from Roma degeneracy by portraying the *quinqui* criminal as a distorted version of Escobar. By contrast, Peret's music and films celebrated the singer's intersecting Roma and Catalan identities, which revised the dominant imaginary of the Roma as Andalusian. At the same time, Peret's work also insistently critiqued the emerging *quinqui* trope by accentuating the marginalization and criminalization of Roma communities, especially by the police. As late Francoism gave way to the Transition, anxieties about interracial contact between *payos* and the Roma became especially palpable in *quinqui* films, many of whose protagonists could be described as *payos agitanados*, or "Gypsified payos."An especially compelling example is the star image of Ángel Fernández Franco, whose portrayals of the character El Torete in José Antonio de la Loma's *Perros callejeros* trilogy (1977–80) were based on a real-life Roma criminal, El Vaquilla (Juan José Moreno Cuenca). Like other *quinqui* stars, Fernández Franco was admired by a large fan base, especially by adolescent boys; yet, his performances nonetheless called attention to the ills of Roma cultural influence at a time when *payo* resentment against Roma resettlement was intensifying throughout the country.

A key element in the intertwining of the cultural imaginaries surrounding the Roma and *quinquis* during late Francoism and the Transition is that both groups were strongly associated with urban peripheries. The marginal neighbourhoods portrayed in *quinqui* films of the 1970s and 1980s, such as Barcelona's La Mina, Bilbao's Otxarkoaga, or Madrid's Vallecas, are often referred to in both popular and scholarly discourse as *chabolismo vertical* ("vertical slums") because they were, for the most part, hastily built housing developments that were constructed during late Francoism to replace makeshift shanty towns made up of *chabolas* (shacks). These housing developments were barely an improvement over what they replaced, as they often lacked basic amenities and offered substandard living conditions (López Simón 186–90). It is no coincidence that during this period, urban peripheries also housed large concentrations of Roma citizens. Río Ruiz estimates that in 1978, 75 per cent of Spain's total Roma population lived in shanty-town neighbourhoods, and thus the Roma made up about 52 per cent of Spain's overall shanty-town population (40). The ethnic segregation of peripheral slums would continue throughout the 1980s: although the overall shanty-town population declined significantly during this decade due to state-sponsored resettlement projects, by 1990, 90 per cent of Spain's remaining shanty-town population comprised Roma inhabitants (45). Large-scale surveys conducted on Spanish teachers and schoolchildren in the 1980s by the social anthropologist Tomás Calvo Buezas, whose results are gathered in his groundbreaking study *España racista: voces payas sobre los gitanos* ("Racist Spain: non-Roma voices about the Roma," 1990), indicate that the assumption that most or all Roma people lived in *chabolas* was widespread among school-aged youth in the 1980s (75–82). The ethnic concentration of Roma communities on urban peripheries was the result of overlapping processes of displacement and resettlement, as economic migratory waves of Roma from across Spain often intersected with the forcible resettlement of Roma communities from other areas of cities due to urban development projects. It also resulted because *payo* residents were able to move out of peripheral ghettoes and into more established working-class neighbourhoods much faster than their Roma counterparts. As such, the imaginary of the urban periphery was largely racialized during this period. Teeming with heavily stigmatized Roma inhabitants, these peripheries were imagined as the cradle of the racially ambiguous *quinqui* stars that populated Spain's movie screens during the 1970s and 1980s.

To fully make sense of the affinities and tensions between the folkloric Gypsy and the *quinqui* stereotypes in late-Francoist and Transition-era cinema, we must understand the ways in which the *payo* / Roma racial boundary offered, in Du Bois' terms, a "psychological wage" associated with being *payo* or white. We will recall, for a moment, W.E.B. Du Bois' argument, which was based on a US context, that whiteness offered those who were able to benefit from it "the security of knowing that there would always be a group below them, that there was a floor below which they could not fall" (Lipsitz 98). In Spain, the *payo* / Roma racial boundary arguably offered Spanish *payos* two distinct yet interrelated psychological wages. On the one hand, the myth of the folkloric Gypsy offered Spaniards an opportunity to invest in a unique, eternal, and desirable national identity in an increasingly globalized and homogeneous Western world. On the other, as I argue in chapter 1 with reference to discourses of Blackness, Roma racial difference offered many Spaniards, especially working-class *payos* who felt destabilized by migration and rapid social changes, a feeling of safety that there would always be another racialized group beneath them.

Although popular cinema exploited both the *payo*/Roma and Black/white racial boundaries, the *payo*/Roma boundary was unique because it was not predicated primarily on skin colour. Rather, in cinema, Roma identity was rendered legible more by a character's actions and behaviours than by immutable visual or corporeal markers. In other words, what made someone recognizable as a "Gypsy" in folkloric cinema was their musicality, dancing ability, and the use of recognizable customs like dress or speech; likewise, what made someone recognizable as a *quinqui* was the tendency to rob and commit crimes, to flout the justice system, to use Roma-inflected slang, etc., rather than any specific physical features. The idea that the *payo* / Roma racial boundary was based more on behaviour and costume than on body type is especially notable given the frequency with which, in both folkloric and *quinqui* films, Roma characters were played by *payo* actors who made no effort to darken their skin or hair.[7] This marks a stark contrast with the representation of Blacks, Arabs, and Indigenous peoples, for whom the use of dark make-up by white actors was commonplace in both Francoist and post-Franco cinema.[8] In this way, in addition to offering a psychological wage associated with being *payo* or white, the *payo* / Roma racial boundary in cinema of the 1940s to 1980s was distinguished by its phenotypical ambiguity. In cinema, it was one's behaviour, rather than one's body, that most tellingly made Roma identity legible.

The visual indeterminacy of the *payo*/Roma boundary made it especially precarious: even though it was an omnipresent marker of racial and class hierarchies, it was also easily transgressed, subverted, and blurred. Following Charlotte Chadderton, who has theorized racial performativity from a Butlerian viewpoint, we can observe that in popular film, the *payo* / Roma boundary "functions as a performative" because it is "made to be 'real,' in some sense, through the accumulation of both explicit and implicit speech acts, or citations of norms" (111). However, although repetition and citation serve as "the way in which racial norms and discourses are maintained" (110–11), Chadderton also argues that:

> the fact [that racial norms] have to be repeated to be effective means that there is the possibility for transformation in the repetitions. As norms are constantly being remade, there is space for opposition, or of failing

to constitute accurately … [A]t any moment, norms are only *precariously* inhabited, and they can be reconstituted. The subject may for example fail to successfully inhabit the norms by which she has been interpellated as a racial subject. (112–13, emphasis mine)

In this passage, Chadderton demonstrates that the performance of racial difference is marked by an underlying precarity. This precarity stems from the ability of racial categories to be transformed or reshaped by the repetition of norms, which includes the possibility of failure to correctly embody a racial identity. Although any racial boundary can be vulnerable to such a failure, I argue that the *payo* / Roma boundary was especially fragile due to its visual ambiguity: the manifold discrepancies and overlaps between Roma and *payo* identity, both on-screen and in real life, called attention to the unsettling possibility that *payos* and Roma might simply fail to be meaningfully different from each other, thus threatening the psychological wage of being *payo*. This notion became especially prevalent as mid-twentieth century migrations eroded traditional forms of segregation between *payos* and Roma, and consequently engendered ethnic conflicts in urban peripheries and in cities themselves. Recalling Martín Cabrera's argument that the *quinqui* was construed as a racially monstrous figure with the ability to infect Spain's working classes, we may understand the fear of contagion that this figure evoked as a consequence of the *quinqui* figure's performativity. The *quinqui*, in other words, signalled the ability of *payos*, who in many cases might already *look like* the Roma, to *become like* the Roma by *acting like* the Roma. According to this logic, the monstrous racial mixture that was brewing on Spain's urban peripheries might cause *payos* to reproduce Roma racial norms, rather than the other way around, thus jeopardizing the nation's upward ascent into modernity.

What follows examines how the star images of male actors like Manolo Escobar, Peret, and Ángel Fernandez Franco harnessed anxieties about the precarious *payo* / Roma boundary. To do so, we will examine how a range of case studies from each actor's oeuvre both mobilized and responded to emerging fears of the precarity of Spain's whiteness and Roma racial degeneracy.

Southern but Not Gypsy: The Racial Precarity of Manolo Escobar

Thanks to his fifty musical albums and starring roles in nineteen films, the face and voice of Manolo Escobar are indelibly associated the *macho ibérico* trope of late-Francoist culture. Although Escobar's performance of southern identity exploited a folkloric Gypsy imaginary, his supposed Romaphilia was often contradicted by his films' efforts to distance him from real-life Roma communities, who were seen as incompatible with the nation's ascent into modernity. As mass migration created intersecting imaginaries associated with being southern, Roma, and *quinqui*, Escobar's films sought to restore the differences between these identities by reaffirming Escobar's racial whiteness while casting the Roma as profoundly unassimilable into mainstream society.

Escobar's star persona intertwined the late-Franco regime's promises of upward mobility with its suspicion of foreign cultural influences. In his essay *Crónica sentimental de España* ("Sentimental chronicle of Spain"), Manuel Vázquez Montalbán writes that Escobar was "an idol of older and younger multitudes, especially of proletarian origin," noting that his music was consumed and sung in working-class spaces like construction sites and jails (121). Escobar's appeal to working-class audiences was undoubtedly related to his own life story as an emigrant who moved from the southern region of Almeria to Catalonia, where, in addition to achieving commercial success, he also married a German tourist whom he met on the beach – a biography that vivified the *sueca* narratives that many of his films deployed. At the same time, for the regime, Escobar's popularity was a cultural weapon with which to "confront the foreign influences" that were gaining traction in the 1960s and 1970s (Vázquez Montalbán, *Crónica sentimental* 87). Musically, Escobar was best known as a performer of the *canción española* or *copla*, a classic genre of Spanish popular song that combined sentimental narratives with Andalusian folkloric elements, and which had achieved maximum popularity from the 1920s to the 1950s. Yet, Escobar's *coplas* of the 1960s and 1970s represented a marked shift compared with earlier *coplas*, which were sung primarily by women and centred on marginal characters like "whores, sailors in dingy joints, escaped convicts, and so on" (Silvia Martínez 93). Instead, Escobar's music exemplified the *copla*'s turn towards a "defense against otherness," which it articulated through an array of ideologically conservative values like "nostalgic agrarianism, the religious, almost mythical exaltation of women, the exaltation of the homeland, and the macho demonstration of virility" (Arce 175).

In Escobar's films, the *copla* was construed as a bulwark against foreign cultural influences such as Anglo-American pop and rock. This tendency is especially notable in films like *Pero… ¿en qué país vivimos?* ("But… what country are we living in?" dir. José Luis Sáenz de Heredia, 1967), in which Escobar plays a singer of *canción española* who defeats a free-spirited, female pop singer played by Concha Velasco in a national music contest. Yet, Escobar's star persona also addressed internal forms of otherness – especially the question of the Roma. Although the *copla* had long exploited flamenco rhythms and cadences, narratives about stock Gypsy characters, and loan words from the Roma language *caló*, in Escobar's films, the folkloric Gypsy imaginary evoked by his music coexists in tension with a pronounced vein of anti-Roma racism. Hence, his cinematic embodiment of an eternal Spanish essence was interlaced with a disavowal of Roma racial otherness.

A striking example of the anti-Roma dimension of Escobar's star persona can be found in one of his best remembered and most analysed films, *Un beso en el puerto* ("A kiss at the port," dir. Ramón Torrado, 1965), which glorifies the newly built beach resort of Benidorm. Justin Crumbaugh has brilliantly analysed this film, which reached over four million viewers in cinemas, as an attempt to offer a "spectacle of consumer and sexual freedom [as a substitute for] socio-political freedom" ("Spain Is Different" 267). In the film, Escobar plays a small-town emigrant named Manolo Espinar who has come to the cosmopolitan touristic oasis in hopes of seducing foreign women. On two occasions, the misadventures stemming from his exploits land him briefly in jail. Although he is quickly released on both occasions, the two jail scenes put Escobar's character in contact with a gaggle of Roma men, who are all confined in the cell next to his. The characters are identifiable as Roma through their speech, which bears recognizable influences of the *caló* language, and through dialogues, given that several characters refer to them as "gitanos" and "quinquis." As in multiple other films studied in this chapter, the word *quinqui* in *Un beso en el puerto* is used interchangeably with the term *gitano*, which underscores its insinuation of an immutable link between racialized origin and criminal behaviour.

The jail scenes in *Un beso en el puerto* illustrate a delicate balancing act between lauding Manolo for possessing a Gypsy-like musical prowess, while also emphasizing Manolo's moral and racial superiority over the Roma characters. For instance, upon entering his cell, Manolo immediately declares that he has been jailed "por un error" ("by mistake"); one of the Roma characters, an elderly man, responds sarcastically while his companions chuckle in the background: "Lo mesmo que nosotros. También fue por un erró. Y si no, ¡mira la cara de inocente que tenemos todos!" ("Same as us. Also by mistake. And if you don't believe it, look at our innocent faces!") The tongue-in-cheek quality of this response is reinforced because it is never revealed why these characters are in jail; instead, it is assumed that the men's Roma identity and speech naturalize their presence there. Subsequently, another Roma character attempts to lift Manolo's spirit by inviting him to engage in "un poquito de jolgorio" ("a bit of fun"); this leads Manolo to launch into the performance of a song which, like the film's title, is called "Un beso en el puerto," while the Roma characters dance and provide musical accompaniment but do not sing along. The subordinate status of the Roma is further emphasized by the camera, given that most of this scene is filmed in medium shots from inside Manolo's cell with Manolo at the centre of the frame. As a result, the viewer is made to feel as if we are sharing Manolo's cell while looking at the Roma characters from his point of view, and therefore, through the filter of jail bars, which separate the camera from the Roma characters in almost every shot. In many ways, this scene epitomizes the late-Francoist view of the Roma: although still admired for their musical abilities, they are reduced to mere accompaniment for the performance of a *macho ibérico*, a *payo*, from whom they are spatially segregated by being kept in a different cell. The scene's visual and musical strategies jointly suggest that Escobar's star identity, a hegemonic symbol of Spain's s national identity, could draw on Gypsy tropes and myths as long as it was clearly delineated as separate from, and superior to, actual Roma communities, who were indelibly associated with criminality and degeneracy.

Unlike the first scene, however, the second jail scene reveals how the discourse of Roma inferiority masked deeply embedded fears of national and racial degeneration. In this scene, Manolo, in jail once again, is portrayed as exhausted and barely able to stay awake. The Roma characters, who remain in the next cell over, are delighted that he has returned. One of them happily declares that "En cuantito salgamos de esta grillera, tengo yo el gusto de invitarte a una copa en nuestro campamento ... ¡Un campamento gitano es una cosa muy seria, compare!" ("As soon as we get out of this cage, it would be my pleasure to invite you to a drink at our camp ... A Roma camp is a very serious thing, man!") Enlarged by a low angle, the Roma characters erupt into maniacal laughter, and Manolo drifts into sleep; a disorienting dissolve slowly leads us to Manolo's nightmare, in which he imagines himself as living in a Roma camp. In his nightmare, a number of stereotypical Roma women in brightly coloured flamenco garb dance in a sinister manner around a campfire as if practising a ritual; they are accompanied by an ominous soundtrack of string instruments and fast-paced drums. Subsequently, the film's various *payo* protagonists, including Manolo, his love interest Dorothy, and her father Luis, all appear on the scene, but are dressed in highly caricatured Roma clothing. After Manolo performs the musical number "Un bolero para ti" ("A love song for you"), a Roma man wielding a knife appears out of nowhere; he proceeds to grab Manolo's neck with one hand and try to stab him with the other (figure 3.1). The suspense of the nightmare is accentuated by a lingering medium shot that shows Manolo in a kneeling position with face

Figure 3.1. Manolo Escobar's nightmare in *Un beso en el puerto* (dir. Ramón Torrado, 1965).

contorted, head tilted backwards, and a dagger pointed at his throat as the Roma attacker overpowers him. As the orchestral score swells, special effect fog clouds the frame; when it clears, we see Manolo in close-up on his jail bed, clasping his neck as if to protect himself from being strangled. His Roma comrades, once again shown in a point-of-view shot on the other side of the jail bars, look on in surprise from their cell and tell him it was only a bad dream. Conveniently, Manolo is released from the jail shortly thereafter.

As I explain in the introduction of this book, this nightmare sequence belongs to a genealogy of similar dream scenes in Spanish cinema in which Spanish characters imagine themselves as being devoured, conquered, or overpowered by inferior races. We may recall, for instance, a nightmare scene from *Bienvenido Mr. Marshall* ("Welcome Mr Marshall," dir. Luis García Berlanga, 1951), in which the character Don Luis dreams that he is cannibalized by natives after discovering the Americas. Similarly, we may remember nightmare scenes from the 1926 and

1951 versions of *El negro que tenía el alma blanca* ("The Black man with a white soul," respectively dir. by Benito Perojo and Hugo del Carril), in which Emma, a white Spanish woman who is partnered to dance with a Black Cuban man, dreams that she is thrown into a gorilla's mouth or that she becomes Black herself, only to wake up screaming. Tellingly, various elements from these scenes also occur in Manolo's nightmare, such as the motif of dancing around a fire, the pronounced beat of drums, and the idea of being killed or cannibalized. Through these recurring tropes, all of these scenes deploy a generalized iconography of racialized savagery that was liberally applied to various groups such as Blacks, Indigenous people, and the Roma in popular cinema. What makes Manolo's nightmare especially interesting, however, is that its denigration of the Roma as ruthless savages coexists with the scene's simultaneous exploitation of a folkloric Gypsy imaginary. For, despite its nightmarish quality, the scene also features a love song in which Manolo and other characters, whom we know to be *payos* in the film's main diegesis, perform a patently theatrical version of Gypsy identity as entertainment for the film's viewers.

The scene's logic is both transparent and self-contradictory. On one level, the commercial allure of the folkloric Gypsy imaginary remains a useful strategy for Escobar to craft and sell his star image. In particular, his identity as a southern Spaniard who sings *canción española* makes his performance of Gypsiness through music and dress in the film both palatable and predictable, given the longstanding overlap between southernness and Gypsiness in Spanish culture. On another level, the scene also aims to disentangle Escobar's identity as a southern *payo* from the Roma characters who are jailed next to him. His nightmare emerges as an expression of his utter terror that his proximity to the Roma in the jail has caused him to descend to their level. By sharing space with the Roma, the scene implies, Escobar – and, by extension, the Spanish nation he represents – come dangerously close to *becoming like* them, and, consequently, to inhabiting a racialized alterity confined to the margins of modernity. To escape this horrifying prospect, the film unequivocally reasserts Escobar's *payo* or white identity by allowing him to wake up from his nightmare of racial debasement and walk free from the jail, even as the Roma characters are seemingly stuck there permanently.

Another one of Manolo Escobar's most famous films, *Me has hecho perder el juicio* ("You've made me lose my mind," dir. Juan de Orduña, 1973), rehearses similar ideas about the Roma through its use of a jail scene and through its comparisons of Escobar to Roma or *quinqui* characters. In this film, which reached almost two million viewers in cinemas, the protagonist Manolo (Manolo Escobar) schemes to become a popular singer after failing to achieve success in other jobs like bull-fighting or acting. Early on in the film, he and his friend Diego (Andrés Pajares) are jailed when Manolo angers spectators and local authorities by withdrawing from a bullfight at the last minute. As in *Un beso en el puerto*, Manolo is confined in a jail cell next to a Roma family, which, this time, includes a man, a woman and several children. And again, the dialogues between them emphasize the camera's physical closeness to Manolo and his perspective of the Roma characters, who are always framed by jail bars. Similarly to *Un beso en el puerto*, the Roma characters incite Manolo to sing to lift his spirits and play a subordinate role in the performance by accompanying him with flamenco-inspired dancing, clapping, and guitar playing. When the police chief's wife, who lives nearby, hears the music emanating from the jail, she intercedes on Manolo's behalf. As a result, the police chief releases Manolo and Diego, whose faces are repeatedly shown in close-up in the last part of the sequence. Meanwhile, the Roma characters, who are relegated to the margins of the frame or who are left off-screen altogether as the scene progresses, remain imprisoned.

A notable aspect of this scene is its depiction of the Roma not only as criminals, but as social parasites, a notion that surfaces repeatedly in subsequent films. The jailed Roma patriarch makes his laziness evident through the following dialogue, in which he introduces himself to Manolo:

PADRE: Yo soy quinqui. Y los quinquis somos muy españoles. Lo nuestro son las cárceles nacionales. Ya estoy entrenando a la familia.
MANOLO: ¿Y lo dice tan tranquilo?
PADRE: ¿Y qué quiere? A mí la cárcel me va.
NIÑO: ¡Y a mí, papá!
PADRE: ¿Lo ves? Se come caliente, se duerme bajo un techa'o, da una sensación dorá. Calor de ni'o.

(FATHER: I am *quinqui*. And we *quinquis* are very Spanish. We prefer national jails. I'm already training my family.
MANOLO: And you say it so calmly?
FATHER: What do you want me to say? Being in jail suits me just fine.
CHILD: Me too, Dad!
FATHER: See? You eat hot food, you sleep under a roof, it's a golden sensation. The warmth of a nest.)

In this scene, the father's reference to himself as a *quinqui* works in tandem with his exaggerated accent and his family's spontaneous, flamenco-inspired performance to align these characters with a Roma imaginary that straddled stereotypes of folkloric musicality and urban criminality. In this film, then, as in others discussed in this book, the term *quinqui* is used as a synonym for *gitano* and strongly connoted a link between racial origin and criminal behaviour. This link becomes especially evident when the little boy chimes in that he, like his *quinqui* father, feels at home being in jail. After all, the film assumes, what other future could a little *quinqui* boy possibly aspire to?

The dialogue invites the film's audiences, which consisted largely of newly urbanized immigrants, to simultaneously identify and disidentify with the Roma characters. In particular, the incongruent notion that living in jail could be an improvement in one's lifestyle would have likely provided comic relief to many *payo* viewers, who may have felt comforted by the opportunity to laugh at a racial group who occupied a lower social rung than they did. In this way, the scene offers a "psychological wage" associated with being white or *payo* to the film's working-class audiences. At the same time, it is not difficult to imagine that some viewers might have empathized with the jailed Roma family, as they may have personally known friends or family members who had been incarcerated for committing petty crimes or for their subversive political activities. What is certain, however, is that the scene portrays the Roma as occupying the lowest social level imaginable and Manolo as being *almost* just like them. After all, like the freeloading family, Manolo is musical, embodies numerous tropes of a southern and working-class background, and is confined to a jail for his misbehaviour. Through his dialogues with the Roma family, it is as if Manolo sees himself in a distorted mirror that portends his own fate if his transgressive behaviour keeps landing him in jail. Even so, while the scene imagines Manolo's supremacy over the Roma as being destabilized, it is never completely eroded, given Manolo's role as lead vocalist in the musical number, the extreme caricatures of Roma criminality and sloth, and the spatial segregation of *payo* and Roma inmates.

Later on, however, the film's underlying paranoia that Manolo, a southern *payo*, may be frighteningly close to embodying Roma or *quinqui* identity resurfaces. The anxiety about Manolo's racial proximity to the stigmatized figure of the *quinqui* becomes especially evident when Manolo, guided by the duplicitous lawyer Pepe (José Sazatornil), must defend a phony lawsuit in court, even though the lawsuit's real purpose is to achieve publicity for Manolo's singing career. The following dialogue, in which Manolo is cross-examined by the opposing lawyer, underscores Manolo's resemblance to racially inferior groups:

ABOGADO: No es cierto que gracias a la publicidad que le ha dado esta
   incalificable farsa, ¿es usted un cantante conocido y cotizado?

MANOLO: Eso es cierto, pero no creo que sea gracias a la publicidad, porque también es popular El Lute, y sin embargo, que yo sepa, nunca ha tenido éxito como cantante.
ABOGADO: Entonces, ¿cree que existe algo en común entre usted y El Lute?
PEPE: …. ¡Protesto! Porque cosa torcida es que mi ilustre colega compare a mi patrocinado con el Manolete de las fugas.

(LAWYER: Isn't it true that thanks to the publicity that you have gained from this indescribable farse, you are now a well-known and highly sought-after singer?
MANOLO: That's true, but I don't think it has to do with publicity, because El Lute is also popular, and yet, as far as I know, he's never had any success as a singer.
LAWYER: So, you think there is something in common between you and El Lute?
PEPE: … Objection! Because it is twisted for my illustrious colleague to compare my client to the Manolete of jailbreaks.)

This dialogue contains allusions to two figures who were well known to viewers of late-Francoist popular comedy. The first, El Lute, refers to Eleuterio Sánchez, a notorious criminal of *merchero* ethnicity whose life story, like that of El Vaquilla, became a sensation in the press and later in *quinqui* film.[9] The second allusion refers to Manolete Lejostierra, a well-known bullfighter of the 1940s, whose superior skill in the sport is invoked when Pepe refers to "El Lute" as the "Manolete of jailbreaks." By comparing Manolo Escobar with these two figures, a bullfighter and a racialized criminal, the dialogue accentuates Escobar's own racial ambivalence. For by capitalizing on his southernness to embody an essential Spanishness, Escobar cannot help but also approximate the racial alterity of groups like the Roma or the *mercheros*, who, in this period, were caught between overlapping imaginaries of colourful folklore and urban criminality. This is especially evident when Pepe, Manolo's lawyer, declares that it is "twisted" to compare Manolo with El Lute. According to the film's logic, it is appropriate and beneficial for Escobar to be associated with singers and bullfighters, professions that were closely associated with the mythical Gypsy; however, Escobar should *not* be compared with "El Lute," who represented the emerging myth of the urban *quinqui* criminal.

Although the racialized figure of the *quinqui* only makes relatively brief appearances in *Un beso en el puerto* and *Me has hecho perder el juicio*, it plays a central role in the crime musical *Cuando los niños vienen de Marsella* ("When the kids are from Marseilles," dir. José Luis Sáenz de Heredia, 1974), in which Escobar plays a Roma protagonist. Released in the final years of the dictatorship, this film, which reached just under one and a half million spectators in cinemas, sensationalizes the real-life unmasking of a Spanish Roma criminal network that operated between Marseilles and Barcelona and that manufactured false identities of children in order to defraud the French social security system.[10] Its plot follows several Roma characters including Manolo Moreno (Manolo Escobar), his love interest María (Sara Lezama), and their accomplices from the deprived urban peripheries of Marseilles through a life of criminality between France and Spain and, finally, to a Spanish prison. On one level, this film reproduces the "screen Gypsy" trope of folkloric musicals by showcasing not only Escobar's vocal performances, but also Lezama's dazzling skills as a flamenco dancer. On another level, the film anticipates *quinqui* cinema by spectacularizing the link between urban peripheries, marginal populations, and delinquency, and by ending its narrative with the imprisonment of its Roma protagonists. Echoing previous Escobar films, this film portrays jail as the only space where the Roma belong and reassures audiences that the dominant order of *payo* society will prevail over Roma depravity. Furthermore, despite its reliance on the "screen Gypsy" trope, this film weakens the traditional association between Roma identity and Spanish nationalism by portraying its criminal protagonists as itinerant opportunists who move between France and Spain without particular loyalty to either nation, draining the resources of each state as they can.

The battle between the duelling stereotypes of the folkloric Gypsy and the urban *quinqui* unfolds throughout *Marsella*. In the film's opening sequence, a montage of newspaper clippings in Spanish and French detail a sordid tale of Roma criminality, with the French words "gitans" or the Spanish word "gitanos" appearing prominently in numerous headlines. Subsequently, an establishing shot locates us in a seedy, suburban neighbourhood of Marseilles at nighttime, whose residents are all Roma and live in trailer homes. Inside one of the homes, Pilar and her partner José are caring for two small children when suddenly, an armed man named El Rufo breaks in and shoots the adults. José dies immediately but Pilar is taken to a hospital, where she dies only after begging her friend Manolo to entrust her children to the care of her sister María, who lives in Corsica. Upon arriving in Corsica, Manolo learns how to exploit the French welfare system by falsifying his own identity and by inventing nonexistent children. His criminal enterprise expands until it becomes so big that he is concerned it will become obvious to French authorities; he thus moves the business to Barcelona, but the plot is ultimately discovered by Spanish police.

The film's effort to dilute the nationalist connotations of the folkloric Gypsy imaginary become especially apparent not only through its transnational setting between France and Spain, but also through a pronounced subtext that concerns France's postcolonial relationship with Algeria. Upon Manolo's arrival in Corsica, María, his partner in crime who later becomes his love interest, explains that in order to care for Pilar's orphaned children, she needs to receive social security benefits from the French state, but cannot file for them herself because the state knows her real children already. Instead, she tells Manolo that he can do it for her by pretending to be a widowed father who recently immigrated to France from Algeria, a former French colony that achieved independence in 1962. Manolo is told to say that his documentation was destroyed in the Algerian War of Independence and is reassured that the veracity of his origins can be certified by local Roma witnesses who will be willing to lend a hand. Upon realizing how easy it is to falsify his identity and nationality, Manolo hatches the idea of inventing nonexistent children to milk the French welfare system.

The Algerian subtext in this film serves to feminize the French nation by suggesting that the former metropolis has made itself vulnerable to freeloading foreigners due to its excessive generosity. Through this logic, France becomes a model of what Spain should *not* become: namely, a formerly great nation rendered "soft" by imperial decline, by its postcolonial sense of duty to its former colonies, and by its easily exploited welfare state. By contrast, Spain, the country where the Roma criminal network is unmasked and uprooted, and where the protagonists are ultimately imprisoned, is shown to be the "strong" state whose authoritarian rule and massive police apparatus are the only solution through which order can be re-established. (Tellingly, the film contains no references to Spain's then-ongoing process of decolonization, the discussion of which was thoroughly suppressed by *materia reservada* [classified information] laws that forbade any public mention of Equatorial Guinea from 1971 to 1976 and Western Sahara from 1974 to 1976.) While a feminized France allows the Roma characters to spread their degeneracy unchecked, a virile, authoritarian Spain exerts the power to subdue and punish the deviant Roma. In this way, the film's idea of Spanish nationalism derives most strongly from its portrayal of the state's ability to contain the threat of racial degeneration posed by this unruly population, which was filling the peripheries of Spanish cities and which could just as easily enact similar chaos on society if not kept under tight surveillance.

The film's disavowal of Roma heritage as a national emblem is perhaps most tellingly illustrated in a scene in which Manolo and various other Roma men plan to enact revenge on El Rufo in the wake of Pilar's death. Gathered in a common space amongst the trailers in their impoverished Marseilles neighbourhood, the men find themselves seated around a table, contriving a violent plot. Manolo, expressing frustration at this reality, stands up and reprimands them as well as the entire Roma community:

> MANOLO: Toda la vida igual. Llevamos dos mil siglos empioja'os … Dos mil siglos, ¡sí! Ni uno menos. A estas dos criaturas ya se les están buscando para matarlas otras que aún no han nacido.… En vez de tantos tiros y puñaladas lo que podíamos empezar a dar son otras cosas.
>
> GITANO 1: ¿Como qué?
>
> MANOLO: Cosas más importantes. Médicos, ingenieros, y hombres de empresa … No hemos dado ni uno en dos mil siglos.
>
> GITANO 2: Ni falta que nos hace. Tampoco hemos da'o ciclistas ni obispos. Cada uno da lo suyo. La gallina da el huevo y la vaca, la leche.

> (MANOLO: It's been the same all our lives. We've been living in squalor for two thousand centuries ... Two thousand centuries, yes! Not a bit less. These two little kids are already being hunted down by other kids who haven't even been born yet ... Instead of all these shootings and stabbings, we should start doing other things.
>
> ROMA 1: Like what?
>
> MANOLO: More important things. Doctors, engineers, businessmen … We haven't produced a single one in two thousand centuries.
>
> ROMA 2: Nor do we need to. We also haven't produced any cyclists or bishops. Everyone does what they can. The chicken lays eggs and the cow gives milk.)

Despite Manolo's fictional identity as a Roma character, this scene capitalizes on Escobar's extradiegetic fame to distinguish him temporarily from the other Roma characters. Known as a southern *payo* and as a dominant cultural representative of Spanish nationalism, Escobar's character is the only one present in the scene who has the vision and intellect to lament the lowly social stature of his Roma comrades, who are generally portrayed to be too short-sighted and stuck in their ways to even begin to imagine how to improve their lot. The camera emphasizes this point through point-of-view shots that reflect Manolo's viewpoint as he looks down, both literally and metaphorically, from his standing position towards his seated comrades as he berates them. In this way, the camera construes Manolo as briefly stepping back into whiteness, which becomes a vantage point from which to denounce Roma degeneracy while shoring up Escobar's star image as the embodiment of a *payo* Spanish essence. His assertion that the Roma have produced no one and nothing worthy of admiration in "two thousand centuries," a grossly inaccurate time frame, is particularly striking, given that he and his *paya* co-star Lezama abundantly exploit and appropriate the trappings of Roma identity through their musical and dance performances. Manolo's temporary recovery of whiteness in this scene is especially notable because it inverts the racial dynamics of the jail segments we see in earlier films like *Un beso en el puerto* or *Me has hecho perder el juicio*. In those, Escobar's *payo* characters almost descend into the hell of Roma identity, but ultimately escape and preserve their whiteness. In this scene, Escobar's Roma character briefly steps outside his racialized condition and embodies the intelligence and ambition of a *payo*. Even so, over the course of the film, he proves unable to resist his racialized flaws, and succumbs to the same vices he denounces by hatching the fraud scheme.

As we have seen, *Cuando los niños vienen de Marsella* aims, paradoxically, to commercially exploit the "screen Gypsy" trope while simultaneously stigmatizing flesh-and-blood Roma communities as a threat to late-Francoist dreams of upward mobility. In this way, it follows a pattern established in *Un beso en el puerto* and *Me has hecho perder el juicio*, given that all three films harness the figure of the urban *quinqui* to construe Roma identity as having a corrosive effect on society, even as they attempt to preserve the commodifiable aspects of the folkloric Gypsy myth. At the same time, these films accentuate the volatility of the *payo* / Roma boundary by showing how easily whiteness can be gained or lost. By exploring the limits of Spain's racial identities, these films anticipate a paranoia that would become more explicit in later *quinqui* cinema; namely, the idea that *payos* becoming like the Roma might not only be a nightmare, but a reality.

Between *Macho ibérico* and Roma Icon: Peret as Racial Mediator

A counterpoint to Manolo Escobar in the pop cultural universe of late Francoism is the Catalan Roma singer, guitarist, composer, and film actor Peret. Like Escobar, Peret's musical breakthrough occurred in the early 1960s, and his film career developed as an extension of his musical success. After first appearing as a guitarist in the arthouse film *Los Tarantos*, Peret starred in a number of popular comedy films in the 1960s and 1970s that served as commercial vehicles for his most successful songs. Also like Escobar, Peret's filmic persona was closely linked to Francoist hegemonic fictions like the *macho ibérico* trope or the "Spain Is Different" campaign. Consequently, Peret, like Escobar, became a national symbol; for example, he was chosen to represent Spain in the 1974 Eurovision contest and later performed at the 1992

Barcelona Olympics. Yet, while Escobar gravitated towards the traditional *copla* and mostly performed songs written by other composers, Peret became known for popularizing a new musical style known as *rumba catalana*. A fusion of *rumba flamenca* with Caribbean rhythms and pop-rock, this newer genre was "based on a new strumming with percussion on the body of the guitar called *ventilador* (fan)," and often included "a second guitar and handclaps" as well as "sometimes bongos and piano" to highlight its Latin American influences (Folch 21). In addition to being a pioneer of this style, Peret also wrote the music and lyrics to many of his own greatest musical hits. Furthermore, unlike Escobar, Peret was Catalan and of Roma origin; as such, he wrote and performed not only in Castilian, but also occasionally in Catalan and *caló*. This next section will demonstrate how Peret's incarnations of the *macho ibérico* character aimed to soften his viewers' anti-Roma prejudices by promoting a cosmopolitan, yet palatable vision of Roma identity in which he strategically inhabited and disengaged from folkloric and *quinqui* stereotypes. In particular, a close analysis of Peret's lyrics reveals an insistent critique of Roma-police relations that often went unnoticed by his large audiences due to the upbeat, feel-good rhythms of his music. This invites us to read Peret's oeuvre as a response to the increasingly prevalent *quinqui* myth, which implied that the Roma were contaminating Spain's cities and needed to be contained or subdued by *payo* disciplinary institutions.

In his era, Peret was often dismissed as a lowbrow figure whose music amounted to little more than the fodder of youthful merriment. For example, a well-known journalist of the period, Lauren Postigo, told Peret to his face in a 1976 interview on Televisión Española that: "Tus letras son intrascendentes. Sirven para el cachondeo; sirven para la madrugada; sirven para la hora de la copa" ("Your lyrics are banal; they are appropriate for parties, for late nights, for drinking") (qtd. in *Peret: jo soc la rumba*, dir. Paloma Zapata, 2018). Likewise, researchers Carlos Aguilar and Anita Haas describe Peret's music as "purely commercial," arguing that it was "conceived of with no purpose beyond easy entertainment" (344). However, not all commentators shared this flattening vision of his work. In a 1969 article titled "The Catalan Roma," Manuel Vázquez Montalbán argued that many of Peret's songs were polysemic, noting that they appealed both "to the consumer of Manolo Escobar and to the consumer of Michel Foucault" (16). Vázquez Montalbán also argued that some of Peret's songs, such as his 1968 Catalan language hit "El mig amic" ("The half friend"), could be described as "profoundly serious, historically tragic" (17). For Vázquez Montalbán, Peret's significance derived from his ability to shed light on flesh-and-blood, contemporary Roma communities, such as those of Catalonia, who had long been overshadowed by dominant stereotypes of Andalusian Gypsies. These "other" Roma of Catalonia, as Vázquez Montalbán calls them, were of diverse social classes; they could be found in the city, suburbs, or countryside; and many of them were "clean, Catalan-speaking … with the security offered by a savings booklet" (15–16).

"El mig amic," one of Peret's most successful and best-remembered hits today, is especially illustrative of his effort to refashion the folkloric Gypsy myth and the monolithic vision of national identity that it signified. In this song, Peret separates Roma narratives from Andalusian tropes and reorients them within discourses of Catalan identity; in doing so, he undermines Francoist fictions of internal linguistic and racial homogeny while also accentuating the intersectionality of presumably unrelated identities like "Catalan" and "Roma." Although the refrain of the song was performed in the cheerful *rumba catalana* style with background singers, multiple guitars, and percussion, its verses were sung at a slower tempo with a more melancholic tone and only a single voice and guitar. The stylistic disjuncture between the refrain and the verses may have been an invitation to listeners to concentrate on the narrative outlined in the verses.

The song's title refers to Peret's father, an itinerant cloth seller, who was known as a "half friend" because of the contrast between his cunning, often deceptive sales skills and his willingness to lend a hand to anyone in need. The song's lyrics read as follows:

I enredant per allà	And deceiving over there,
i enredant per aquí,	and deceiving over here,
d'aquesta manera	this is how
em va pujar a mi.	he raised me.
Teixits venia el meu pare	My father sold fabric
per la comarca de Vic	in the area around Vic
i la gent que li comprava	and the people who bought from him
li deien el "mig amic."	called him a "half friend."
Qui és que es vol deixar enredar	Who wants to be deceived
per un gitano eixerit?	by a lively Roma man?
A qui em compri una camisa,	If someone buys a shirt,
li regalo un cobrellit!	I give him a bedspread!
Així es guanyava la vida	That's how my father, the "half friend,"
el meu pare, el mig amic,	earned a living.

i el pobre del que li comprava

se'n quedava ben lluït.

Però ho feia amb una gràcia
i hi posava tant d'estil
que inclús havia venut trajos
a algun guàrdia civil.

and the poor man who bought
from him
always looked splendid.

But he did it with such grace
and he had so much style
that he even sold suits
to a few policemen.

(Printed with permission from BMG and Warner Chappell)

Sung in Catalan and located in the "area around Vic," the song's narrative unequivocally disengages from long dominant Andalusian tropes of Roma identity. Similarly, although it plays with the stereotype of Roma deceitfulness, it adds complexity and depth to that image by also underscoring the generosity, intelligence, and economic power of Peret's father. The third stanza, for instance, in which the speaker declares, "If someone buys a shirt, / I give him a bedspread," can be interpreted either as a form of trickery or as an expression of kindness, since a bedspread, generally, is likely to be more economically valuable than a shirt. Likewise, the fourth stanza indicates that the speaker takes great pains to make sure that his less wealthy clients are always well served by the clothes they purchase.

The last stanza, however, raises an issue that surfaces repeatedly throughout Peret's music and films: namely, the tense relationship of the Roma to the *Guardia Civil*, Spain's oldest police force. For policemen, the speaker reserves a different approach: one in which his "grace" and "style" enable him to enact subtle revenge on them. According to the song, it is only through crafty or deceptive means that Peret's father, a travelling Roma salesman, is able to sell clothes to the enforcers of the state's institutional racism. Although the song doesn't give us any indication of what the deceptive strategy is, we may surmise that Peret's father might fool the police in a number of ways, such as by pretending to be *payo*, by selling them defective or counterfeit products, or by overcharging them, among others. Coupled with his "grace" and "style," such tactics enable Peret's father not only to overcome the police officers' anti-Roma prejudice, but also to exploit them economically.

The intertwined objectives of "El mig amic," which include Catalanizing Spain's imaginary of the Roma and critiquing police enforcement of anti-Roma prejudice, are both equally palpable in the first film in which Peret played a leading role, *Amor a todo gas* ("Love at full speed," dir. Ramón Torrado, 1969). This musical comedy film was made to showcase several of Peret's musical hits, including "El mig amic," and reached more than 1.8 million viewers in cinemas. Set in Madrid, it features three scenes in which Peret's character, a taxi driver also named Peret, has dust-ups with a curmudgeonly police officer (José Sazatornil), who repeatedly punishes Peret for trivial, trumped-up infractions. In the first instance, the policeman fines Peret fifty pesetas for honking the horn of his taxi, but subsequently raises the fine every time Peret speaks, accusing him of "engaño a la autoridad" ("deceiving authority"), "desacato a la autoridad" ("disrespecting authority") and "por llamarme 'hombre'" ("for calling me 'man'"). In the second scene, the policeman fines and arrests Peret for driving through a park while chasing after his love interest, Elena; thus, Peret is forced to spend a night in jail surrounded, in his own words, by "asesinos, quinquis y pirómanos" ("murderers, *quinquis* and arsonists"). As in all the films discussed so far, the term *quinqui* retains overtly racial connotations, but Peret harnesses those connotations in order to contrast the racialized stereotype of the *quinqui* delinquent and his own image as a lovable *macho ibérico*. In doing so, his use of the term undermines the oft-repeated association between Roma identity and urban criminality – a perception that clearly informs the policeman's incessant efforts to harass and punish him.

In the third scene, the police officer is enraged to find that an entire cluster of taxi drivers have abandoned their taxi stand to watch Peret perform nearby, thus upsetting multiple customers. He threatens to fine Peret once again, this time for "abandono de servicio público" ("abandoning public service") and a litany of other absurd charges. This time, however, Peret promises the police officer that he has not abandoned any responsibilities because is now a professional musical artist. He reassures the officer by telling him: "Palabra de catalán, y los catalanes nunca mienten" ("I give you the word of a Catalan, and the Catalans never lie"). The police officer, stunned to learn that Peret is Catalan, reveals that he is Catalan as well, and declares Peret his "paisano" ("countryman"). The two embrace and speak in Catalan while laughing and smiling to the astonishment of onlookers. As they reconcile, Peret coaxes the policeman into promising that he won't fine him anymore. The harmonious quality of this moment is further accentuated because it is filmed in medium close-up, a strategy that transmits a feeling of familiarity, intimacy, or closeness between the characters and the viewer. This also marks a contrast with the previous two encounters between Peret and the police officer in which the camera's greater distance from the characters emphasizes the tension between them.

The ease with which knowledge of Peret's Catalan identity completely transforms the policeman's perception of him calls attention to the ways in which identities like "Roma" and "Catalan" had been constructed in the popular imaginary as incompatible with each other. It is logical to assume that the policeman is aware of Peret's Roma origin, just like the audience, who had already been familiar with Peret's music for several years, would certainly have been. Yet, given the overwhelmingly dominant imagery of the Roma as Andalusian, Peret's Catalan identity is portrayed as an unexpected surprise, and becomes the key to breaking what would otherwise have remained a vicious circle of accusation and punishment. In this way, Peret's interactions with the police officer in *Amor a todo gas* mirror his father's relationship with them in "El mig amic": in both texts, a Roma character uses "grace" or "style" to soften the biases of the police and to extract economic gain from them, whether by selling them suits, as in the song, or by avoiding their fines, as in the film. Furthermore, by using the Catalan language to accentuate the intersectionality of Roma and Catalan identities, both the song and the film challenge the Francoist vision of a homogenous national identity and defend the value of Spain's linguistic and racial diversity.

Although the critique of police abuse in "El mig amic" and *Amor a todo gas* is subtle, it is more overt in songs like "Cumaco San Juan" ("The *cumaco* drum of St. John", 1967) and "El gitano Antón" ("Antón the Gypsy," 1968). Both of these are *rumba catalana* adaptations of Latin American songs from the 1950s whose original lyrics address anti-Black racism. The former is based on "El cumaco de San Juan," a Venezuelan merengue, while the latter is based on "El negrito bembón" ("The big-lipped Black man"), a Puerto Rican salsa song.[11] In both cases, Peret not only updates the songs' rhythms in the style of *rumba catalana*, but also readapts their lyrics to meditate on the police's role in enforcing anti-Roma racism in Spain. In "Cumaco San Juan," Peret's lyrical adaptation is minor but consequential. The first two stanzas of the Venezuelan original read as follows:

Yo soy el negrito fino,	I am a fine Black man,
fino, fino, fino, fino	fine, fine, fine, fine,
con mucha *ciricunstancia*	with a lot of circumstance,
como no tengo arrogancia	since I'm not arrogant,
a mí me tratan como un cochino.	I'm treated like a pig.
Guardia, no lo deje entrar,	Guard, don't let him in,
guardia,	guard,
porque es un ladrón	because he's a thief!

<table>
<tr><td>

Guardia, no lo deje entrar,
guardia,
porque es un ladrón

</td><td>

Guard, don't let him in,
guard,
because he's a thief!

</td></tr>
</table>

By contrast, the corresponding stanzas in Peret's version read:

<table>
<tr><td>

Yo soy un gitano fino,
Fino, fino, filipino,
con mucha *firicutancia*,
pero mucha *firicutancia*
que a mí me tratan como
a un vecino.

</td><td>

I am a fine Gypsy man,
Fine, fine, *filipino*,
with a lot of circumstance,
but so much circumstance,
that I'm treated like a
neighbour.

</td></tr>
<tr><td>

Guardia, no lo deje entrar, porque
porque es un ladrón.
Oiga guardia … No lo deje entrar
porque, porque, porque es
un ladrón.

</td><td>

Guard, don't let him in, guard,
because he's a thief!
Hey, guard, Don't let him in,
because, because, because
he's a thief!

</td></tr>
</table>

As we can see, both versions imagine a racialized speaker, whether Black or Roma, who imagines himself as "fine" or elegant, but who is not welcomed in certain spaces because he is judged to be a criminal. In both versions, the speaker's claim to elegance ironically contrasts with deliberately mispronounced or misused words, such as the various distortions of the word "circunstancia" ("circumstance") as well as, in Peret's version, the conversion of the word "filipino" into an empty signifier that rhymes with "fino." Yet there are also significant differences between the two versions. In the original song, the Black speaker states that he is treated "like a pig," which is consonant with the song's narrative of exclusion. In contrast, Peret's version says the speaker is treated "like a neighbour," even though the subsequent stanza suggests that he is constantly perceived as a thief. By highlighting the contradiction between the Roma's status as "neighbours" in Spanish society and the hegemonic perception of them as delinquents, Peret's version calls attention to what Teresa San Román has termed the "versatility of prejudice" enacted against the Roma, given that they are often celebrated when performing music or dance, but only as long as they are kept at a safe distance away from *payo* communities (81). In addition, although both versions feature the word "guardia," which can mean any kind of guard, the term acquires a strong association with policing in Peret's version, given the antagonistic relationship between the Francoist Guardia Civil and Spain's Roma community. In this way, Peret's version again accentuates the police's role in enforcing state-sanctioned racism.

Like "Cumaco San Juan," "El gitano Antón" also readapts a Latin American song about anti-Blackness to the context of anti-Roma racism in Spain. In this case, however, Peret's lyrical revision of the song is more extensive. Both songs narrate a story about a murder victim who is Black (in the original) or Roma (in Peret's version). After the murderer is arrested, a policeman, who is himself Black (in the original) or Roma (in Peret's version), asks the killer why he did it. In both cases, the murderer reveals that his motivation was racial hatred: in the original, he claims that the victim deserved to die "por ser tan bembón" ("for having such big lips"), while in Peret's version, the reason is "por ser tan caló" ("for being such a Gypsy"). At this point, however, the narratives diverge. In the Puerto Rican original, the Black policeman is intimidated by the killer. In response to the killer's admission, the Black policeman "recoge el bembe" ("hides his big lips"), suggesting that he is afraid that the killer will enact violence on him, too. The song ends by instructing its listeners to "Esconde la bemba que ahí viene el matón" ("Hide your lips for the killer is coming"). Bárbara Abadía-Rexach has convincingly argued that the Puerto Rican song's suggestion that Blacks should attempt to disguise their Blackness to avoid being victims of racial violence reveals a certain "pessimism" in which racism is depicted as "a structure of thought and behavior that inevitably passes from generation to generation and which can be excusable" (17).

Peret's version, by contrast, refuses to allow any deference to racist behaviour. Instead, in Peret's narrative, the Roma policeman is outraged by the killer's admission of racial hatred:

El gitanito sacó la pusky	The Roma policeman took out his gun
y le hizo, pam pam pam.	and went, bam bam bam!
¡Asesino, esa no es razón	Murderer, that's no reason
pa' mararlo; esa no es razón	to kill him, that's no reason
pa' mararlo, esa no es razón!	to kill him, that's no reason!

Unlike the Puerto Rican original, Peret's rendition of the song imagines how Spain's Roma can infiltrate the police, the institution long used to marginalize them, and serve payback to the racist *payo* killer. In this way, Peret's song expresses a solidarity with anti-Black racism in the Americas, but also rewrites the Puerto Rican original as an antiracist revenge fantasy. In doing so, Peret's version turns the emerging quinqui stereotype on its head: although it inhabits the stereotype of Roma violence, it also portrays the Roma as victims of *payo* racism rather than as a source of degeneracy in *payo* society.

As adaptations of Latin American songs about anti-Black racism, Peret's songs "Cumaco San Juan" and "El gitano Antón" offer a powerful critique of racism in diverse contexts while undermining late-Francoist myths of peace, wealth, and the absence of diversity or dissent. Their cosmopolitan outlook is strengthened by the broader, culturally hybrid sound of the rumba catalana, whose mixed influences from Spain, Latin America, and the Anglophone world contrasted with the vision of a monolithic, internally homogenous Spanish nation that much of the popular culture of late Francoism, such as Manolo Escobar's star image, promoted. At the same time, however, the antiracist critique of songs like "Cumaco San Juan" or "El gitano Antón" is marked by an undeniable ambivalence. After all, the extensive Latin American influences in Peret's music, which included rhythms, instrumentation, and lyrical adaptations of Caribbean songs, were easily marketed as "Spanish" enough to appeal to tourists who were eager to consume the "Spain Is Different" myth, as well as to consumers of *macho ibérico* comedies who were invested in late-Francoism's upward mobility rhetoric. Both of these groups clearly appreciated the danceability, liveliness, and cosmopolitanism of Peret's music, but may not have noticed the penetrating social critiques that many of his lyrics articulate.

The presumed compatibility of Peret's music with late-Francoist economic and ideological objectives is clearly exemplified in a scene in the musical comedy *El mesón del gitano* ("The Gypsy's tavern," dir. Antonio Román, 1969), another film in which Peret starred and performed numerous hits. This film, which reached almost 1.6 million viewers, includes a scene in which Peret performs "El gitano Antón" for a group of delighted English tourists in his flamenco venue. After singing "Happy Birthday" to an elderly woman in English, Peret performs the song by circulating amongst the seated tourists, who gleefully applaud, cheer, and dance, utterly oblivious to the song's dark narrative of racial vengeance. The camera keeps Peret at the centre of the frame in medium long shot, using tracking, panning, and long takes to construct him as a magnetic spectacle from which neither the fictional tourists nor the film's real viewers can avert their gaze. Yet even as the tourists gawk gleefully at Peret, that they clearly do not understand a single word of the song is emphasized by tidbits of dialogue in English heard at various moments during the scene. This becomes even clearer when one of the tourists, an older woman, jumps to her feet and begins to dance with the musicians using exaggerated, comical movements (figure 3.2). In this way,

Figure 3.2. An older tourist dances to the song "El gitano Antón" in *El mesón del gitano* (dir. Antonio Román, 1969).

the biting social commentary of "El gitano Antón" is disguised by the jovial rhythm and by the woman's farcical dancing. Rather than signalling transatlantic antiracist solidarity between Spain and the Caribbean, the song's Latin influences are commodified as little more than irresistible fun for tourist consumption. Recalling Lauren Postigo's characterization of Peret's music as "banal" and as "appropriate for partying," we can surmise that many Spanish listeners of the era would have also consumed Peret's music in a similarly hedonistic, socially disengaged manner. Put simply, many consumers heard and enjoyed Peret's music, but did not appreciate its polysemic quality because its lyrics were obscured by its rhythms.

Yet, even as *El mesón del gitano* heralds Peret's music as a pleasurable commodity for tourist consumption, the film's narrative, too, contains an easily overlooked critique of racism. The film narrates the story of how the philandering Peret becomes a love object for Lina (Dyanik Zurakowska), an interior decorator whom he hires to redesign his restaurant as a flamenco venue. Although Lina's character is Spanish, being portrayed by a Belgian actress with blond hair and blue eyes makes her look conspicuously white when juxtaposed with Peret's olive skin and jet-black hair. As such, their romance narrative draws on the *macho ibérico / sueca* formula that was omnipresent in comedy films of the era; yet, unlike these other narratives, the racial contrast between Peret and Lina is portrayed as transgressive and taboo. When Lina's mother Mara (Yvonne Bastién), who lives in London and is pale-skinned with red hair, finds out about their budding romance, she quickly travels to Madrid to express her staunch opposition to her daughter's involvement in an interracial relationship. Mara contrives a scheme in which she will lure the womanizing Peret into dating her and her daughter at the same time so that she can illustrate to Lina the fundamentally deceitful nature of the Roma. She also hatches a simultaneous plan for Peret's musical talents to be discovered by a powerful agent so that he will be sent off to tour the Americas. Eventually, Lina walks in on Peret and her mother kissing; yet, Lina reconciles with her mother, forgives Peret, and decides to keep seeing him anyway.

The film's happy ending is characterized by several contradictory implications. Its overarching narrative, in which interracial love triumphs over prejudice, seems to offer an optimistic tone about Roma-*payo* relationships, which were generally looked down on at the time.[12] Furthermore, although Mara sets out to demonstrate Peret's deceitful nature, it is she, rather than he, who ends up being the film's most deceitful character. By showcasing the deceptive capacity of *payos*, the film anticipates the searing social critique of one of Peret's later songs, "Quién me puede asegurar" ("Who can assure me?" 1978), the refrain of which repeatedly poses the question: "¿Quién me puede asegurar / que los gitanos engañan, y no lo hacen los demás?" ("Who can assure me / that the Roma are deceitful, but others are not?").

Furthermore, while the film alludes to the stereotype of Roma hypersexuality by portraying Peret as an incorrigible womanizer, such a quality was an inherent characteristic of the *macho ibérico* character mould and is also readily perceptible in similar roles played by *payo* actors like Manolo Escobar, Alfredo Landa, and José Luis López Vázquez. For all of these actors, the constant pursuit of sexually available women on screen was portrayed as comical, relatable, and fun, as well as a celebration of Spanish virility. Although *El mesón del gitano* does not refute the stereotype of Roma hypersexuality, it does call attention to the resemblance of Peret's characters to those of commercially dominant *payo* stars, who engaged in behaviours that were similar to those that supposedly justified the vilification and marginalization of the Roma. By reframing the stereotypes of hypersexuality and deceitfulness as common traits of Roma and *payos*, the film attempts to soften viewers' perception of the Roma in a manner that parallels Mara's eventual acceptance of her daughter's relationship. Like the cinematic Escobar, the film implies that the cinematic Peret may have committed excesses with women and occasionally ended up in jail, but he was far from being a *quinqui*.

In sum, despite their jovial quality and apolitical veneer, Peret's music and films reveal a concerted effort to challenge Francoist narratives from within the confines of the hegemonic pop culture industry. His multifaceted star image simultaneously offered a commodified, palatable vision of Roma identity to large *payo* audiences while also infusing traditionally Spanish rhythms with foreign influences, divorcing the Roma image from Andalusian tropes, calling attention to police racism, and celebrating Spain's racial and linguistic diversity. In this way, like his father's character in the song "El mig amic," Peret used his own particular blend of "grace" and "style" to commercially exploit the *macho ibérico* trope while also critiquing various forms of anti-Roma racism, even if many listeners and viewers didn't realize it at the time.

A Nightmare Come True: Ángel Fernández Franco as Gypsified *Payo*

Like Escobar and Peret, *quinqui* figures such as El Lute (Eleuterio Sánchez), El Vaquilla (Juan José Moreno Cuenca), and El Trompeta (Ángel Fernández Franco, known in films as El Torete), whose lives were transformed into legends by the press and the cinema between the 1960s and 1980s, represented a range of meanings to large and diverse audiences. However, to fully understand the *quinqui* media phenomenon, I argue that we must explore its connection to anti-Roma racism, especially in light of its frequent portrayal of *payo*-Roma racial mixing as a source of tragic outcomes. This theme is especially prevalent in the *Perros callejeros* trilogy, a highly successful collection of films made by José Antonio de la Loma, who is often referred to as the "one of the fathers" of *quinqui* cinema (Florido Berrocal 133). The star of the trilogy, Ángel Fernández Franco, embodied the trope of the *payo agitanado* – that is, the Gypsified *payo*, or a *payo* who had absorbed Roma cultural influences. As the next section demonstrates, Fernández Franco's on-screen persona may be read as a reemergence of Manolo Escobar's nightmare in *Un beso en el puerto*, which imagined how *payos* might be swallowed into the underworld of the Roma. Yet, in the *Perros callejeros* trilogy, the Gypsification of *payo* society was construed no longer as a nightmare, but as a reality, something that was especially evidenced by the resettlement of Roma communities in *payo* neighbourhoods during the late 1970s and 1980s.

The *quinqui* figure's media appeal was largely driven by his ability to embody teenage fantasies of rebellion and sexual freedom, as well as alternative paths to social mobility for Spain's most marginal classes. Yet, as Martín Cabrera has argued, this stigmatized media icon also embodied fears that Spain's racially mixed urban peripheries were contaminating its major population centres with degenerate behaviours like criminality and drug abuse (122). Tellingly, the *quinqui* media phenomenon was not the only symptom of Spanish fears of urban degradation during this period. Rather, between the late 1970s and throughout the 1980s, a period that overlapped with *quinqui* cinema's heyday, a wave of anti-Roma violence mushroomed throughout Spain due to government-sponsored efforts to relocate Roma communities out of deprived urban peripheries. As Río Ruiz explains, during these years, Roma communities were frequently resettled in areas that were termed "special districts" ("barriadas de tipología especial"), which were located on the edges of or in unused areas of *payo*-dominated, working-class neighbourhoods (43). Roma resettlement produced particular resentment among working-class *payo* residents, many of whom hoped that the spaces given to the Roma would have been used for urban revitalization projects (45). As Calvo Buezas has demonstrated, *payo* hostility towards their Roma neighbours produced "a repetitive rosary of violent and discriminatory events" between the late 1970s and the early 1990s (19). These included heated and sometimes violent protests by *payo* neighbourhood organizations in cities such as Murcia, Lugo, Madrid, Santander, Bilbao, Valencia, Oviedo, Valladolid, Barcelona, Logroño, Gerona, and Zaragoza, with several of these cities experiencing multiple conflicts.[13] The racial tensions between *payos* and Roma during this decade sometimes led to the burning of Roma dwellings, as in Jaén, Avilés, and Madrid between 1984 and 1987 (16–18). It also led to efforts to block the admission of Roma students to majority *payo* schools in Vicálvaro, Gijón, and the Murcia area (17). Several incidents received intense media coverage during their day, such as the "caso Hernani" of 1980, in which the City Council of the Basque town of Hernani voted to expel all Roma from its territory (15). Another major case was the so-called Batalla de San Cristóbal of Madrid in 1983, in which a protest of two thousand *payos* devolved into rock throwing and gunshots, requiring the intervention of 150 police officers (16). As Río Ruiz notes, a great deal of *payo* resistance to Roma resettlement was based on what he terms the "miedo a caer" – that is, a "fear of falling" to the level of the Roma, rather than maintaining a superior position over them (51).

That *quinqui* cinema blossomed against a backdrop of anti-Roma mobilization and violence throughout Spain raises a difficult question: to what degree might *quinqui* films, which strongly associated Roma cultural influence with urban degradation, have influenced this nation-wide push to keep Roma migrants out of *payo* neighbourhoods? To answer this question, I argue that we must analyse the popularity of the *quinqui* trope in light of Teresa San Román's observation about the "versatility of [anti-Roma] prejudice" (81). According to San Román, audiences were able to revere Roma entertainers such as singers and dancers only as long as the Roma communities that produced them were located "somewhere else" – in other words, as long as they were kept at a safe distance from *payo* living or workspaces (81). Her comment echoes Calvo Buezas' observation that "[s]patial domination is the basic orienting criterion in the construction of identities in Spain" (30). For, as Calvo Buezas illustrates, at the time his surveys were conducted, the factor that generated the most anti-Roma sentiment was the idea of *payos* and Roma sharing spaces together, such as schools, neighbourhoods, workplaces, or households (30). These ideas can help to clarify how, even though the *quinqui* media figure harboured powerful identifications, desires and cultural fantasies for large audiences, he also may have channeled and inflamed entrenched anxieties about a perceived breakdown of Roma / *payo* spatial segregation as real-life Roma communities moved to working-class *payo* neighbourhoods. Although audiences could celebrate the *quinqui* figure's rebelliousness, bravado, and recklessness when performed on-screen, they were far less prone to tolerate what they saw as the destabilizing elements of Roma behaviour, such as criminality, misogyny, and drug use, in their real-life neighbourhoods and cities.

The disjuncture between the popularity of *quinqui* stars who displayed Roma cultural influence and the proliferation of anti-Roma sentiment in the late 1970s and 1980s is especially evidenced by the character El Torete, who is constructed as a *payo agitanado* or "Gypsified payo" in the three *Perros callejeros* films: *Perros callejeros* (1977), *Perros callejeros II: Busca y captura* (1979), and *Los últimos golpes de El Torete* (1980). Although played by a real-life *payo* delinquent named Ángel Fernández Franco, the character El Torete was not primarily based on Fernández Franco's life, but rather, on that of Juan José Moreno Cuenca (alias El Vaquilla), a notorious criminal of Roma origin. As Whittaker explains, director de la Loma hoped to offer the starring role of the first film to Moreno Cuenca but was unable to do so because Moreno Cuenca was in prison and was denied temporary release to participate in the shooting (30). Hence, de la Loma chose Fernández Franco, Moreno Cuenca's close friend, as a substitute. Although Fernández Franco's real-life alias was "El Trompeta" ("The Trumpet"), de la Loma gave him a new cinematic alias, "El Torete" ("The little bull"), to highlight his function as a proxy of "El Vaquilla" ("The little cow") (31). Fernández Franco and

Moreno Cuenca had been friends long before de la Loma offered either one of them a role. Their friendship is chronicled in the second and third installments of the trilogy, which recount a litany of crimes they committed together and other misadventures that they shared. The second film even alludes to the frustration of El Vaquilla at not being able to play himself when his character, who is played by a professional actor named Bernard Seray, complains that he, rather than El Torete, should have enjoyed fame and fortune from the first movie since it was based on El Vaquilla's life. The real-life El Vaquilla would only be able to play himself in one film, *Yo, el Vaquilla* ("I, El Vaquilla," 1985), which de la Loma made separately from the trilogy, and which narrates El Vaquilla's journey from childhood to prison.

The diegetic blurring between the real lives and fictional characters of Moreno Cuenca and Fernández Franco allegorized the destabilization of the Roma / *payo* racial boundary that was imagined to be taking place on Spain's urban peripheries. In these films, the racial distinction between El Torete, a *payo*, and El Vaquilla, who was Roma, is almost completely eroded; after all, both on screen and in real life, Moreno Cuenca and Fernández Franco behaved similarly, spoke with a similar slang, lived in similar neighbourhoods, committed similar crimes, and even bore a physical resemblance to each other (figures 3.3 and 3.4). The disintegration of the racial boundary as a result of their entangled identities becomes even more pronounced when we consider that the fair-skinned, blond-haired Bernard Seray, who plays El Vaquilla in the second and third installments, hardly embodied a distinctively Roma look, despite his character's repeated affirmations of Roma identity.

The idea that *quinqui* characters like El Torete stirred social anxieties about Roma encroachment by resembling the Roma and imitating their behaviours becomes especially evident when we consider that El Torete bears nearly all of the dominant markers of Roma identity that Calvo Buezas signalled in *España racista*. In response to the question, "What distinguishes *payos* from the Roma?" notably, only 27.6 per cent of respondents highlighted corporeal markers like skin tone or hair colour as the principal marker of racial difference (392–3). Furthermore, even when respondents did choose skin colour as the most distinguishing trait, they overwhelmingly mentioned it *"alongside several other attributes"* such as speech, poverty, and customs (245, original emphasis). By contrast, behavioural or social qualities together comprised 72.4 per cent of responses, and so held primacy over bodily markers when distinguishing the Roma from *payos* (392–3). In this way, Calvo Buezas' findings illustrate a parallelism between social perceptions of the Roma in real life and their representation in cinema. We will recall, for example,

Figure 3.3. Ángel Fernández Franco with fellow cast member Grace Renat, pictured in *Perros callejeros 2: Busca y Captura* (dir. José Antonio de la Loma, 1979).

that popular film genres like folkloric musicals had long accentuated the prevalence of behaviour, costume, and speech over phenotypical markers as the most indicative characteristics of Roma identity. As a result, both in cinema and real life, the Roma / *payo* racial boundary was marked by a certain visual ambiguity that emphasized the possibility that someone like Ángel Fernández Franco, a light-skinned *payo* from a marginal neighbourhood, could *become like* the Roma without actually being Roma.

Fernández Franco's performances as El Torete in the *Perros callejeros* trilogy reflect a number of other Roma racial markers. For instance, Calvo Buezas' surveys further indicate that 25 per cent of respondents found qualities like poverty, filth, and living in impoverished neighbourhoods to be the most distinctive qualities of the Roma (394). Another 21 per cent responded that the Roma were identifiable as "thieves and lazy people," a response that reflected a perception of them as delinquents and social parasites (394). Finally, another 22 per cent said

Figure 3.4. Juan José Moreno Cuenca, pictured in *Yo, El Vaquilla* (dir. José Antonio de la Loma, 1985).

the Roma had a "different culture" that included attributes like speech, nomadism, and dancing (394). In addition, Calvo Buezas highlights both the use and sale of drugs as comparatively new stereotypes associated with the Roma during the 1980s, in contrast to the much older stereotypes of poverty and delinquency (298). These various markers illustrate how it would have been easy for audiences to read El Torete, a master thief from an impoverished neighbourhood who liberally used drugs, spoke with Roma-inflected slang, played a character based on a real-life Roma counterpart, and fell in love with Roma women, as demonstrating a high degree of Roma influence, despite not being Roma.

Yet, although the *payo* / Roma racial boundary is blurred by El Torete's proximity to Roma stereotypes, the *Perros callejeros* trilogy also works to re-establish and reinforce that racial boundary in other ways. For instance, the trilogy portrays El Torete as only *partially* contaminated by Roma savagery; after all, his many degenerate and antisocial behaviours are tempered by occasional expressions of loyalty, caretaking, falling in love, or other humanizing qualities. By contrast, the trilogy also contains several relentlessly cruel, unambiguously

Roma male villains whose characters lack redeeming qualities and who serve as a foil against which El Torete must define his identity. These Roma villains, which include El Esquinao and El Mosque in the first film, or Vicente, El Pijo, and Sebastián in the second, are all active participants in the trilogy's most grisly depictions of violence. The Roma villains' sadistic exploits, which include the castration of El Torete in the first film and several brutal rape scenes in the second, are more macabre than any of El Torete's misdeeds, which appear by contrast as teenage mischief gone awry. In addition to their depravity, de la Loma's Roma villains are also hopelessly anachronistic. Their incongruence with the modern world is not only evidenced by their use of horses as a mode of transportation, as Whittaker has observed, but also, and perhaps more dramatically, through their insistent enforcement of archaic gender norms like virginity tests, forced betrothals, and forced prostitution on their female family members (44). For these reasons, Florido Berrocal writes that de la Loma's Roma villains are construed as *others* within a *quinqui* world already marked by otherness (142). Their otherness exceeds that of El Torete, who is constructed as a fundamentally good-hearted youth who has fallen victim to unfortunate social circumstances.

By construing Roma men as villains, the first and second *Perros callejeros* films facilitate audiences' identification with El Torete, whose redeemable or human qualities stand out in juxtaposition with Roma depravity. At the same time, however, the presumed narrative opposition between El Torete and Roma villains is diluted by El Torete's sentimental entanglements with Roma women. In both the first and second films, El Torete unsuccessfully tries to save his Roma women lovers from their anachronistic culture. These interracial romance plots constitute what I call the "failed white saviour" narratives of the *Perros callejeros* trilogy. According to these narratives, El Torete is construed as just far enough outside of Roma identity to attempt to rescue Roma women from Roma men; yet, at the same time, as a *payo agitanado*, he is also too inextricably entangled with Roma identity to actually save anyone from it, including himself.

In the first film, *Perros callejeros*, a failed white saviour narrative emerges around El Torete's deep attraction to Isabel, a young Roma woman, who is fiercely guarded by her uncle El Esquinao, a formidable Roma patriarch, and her cousin El Mosque, to whom she is engaged. Over the course of the film, neither El Esquinao nor El Mosque ever show the slightest concern for Isabel's happiness or well-being. Instead, they repeatedly justify their callous application of cruel gender norms, such as her forced betrothal to El Mosque or the requirement that she undergo a virginity test, as necessary applications of "nuestra ley" ("our law.") By contrast, El Torete reaffirms his *payo* identity numerous times throughout this film and its sequels by using the expression "vuestra ley" ("your law") when speaking to Roma characters. Hoping to rescue Isabel from her cruel family, El Torete invites her to run away with him and enlists her help as a partner in his robbery schemes. However, when El Esquinao discovers that El Torete has taken Isabel's virginity, he has El Torete kidnapped and castrated in what is undoubtedly one of the trilogy's most harrowing scenes. Martín Cabrera has compellingly argued that the castration scene dramatizes the film's effort to contain the racialized excesses of El Torete's transgressive sexuality, noting that its setting amongst horse stables signals "a process of racist dehumanization" by portraying Torete as an "animal that must be subdued and tamed" (124).

The animalization of El Torete in the castration scene, however, is inverted in a subsequent scene in which the protagonist, still convalescing from his attack, ambushes El Esquinao and El Mosque and enacts vengeance on them. After spotting the Roma villains as they exit a building, El Torete slowly drives behind them through an empty parking lot. A point-of-view shot frames the two unsuspecting Roma victims through the windshield of El Torete's car in a manner that is reminiscent of a hunter watching his prey through a weapon's-eye view. When his victims realize they are being followed, El Torete quickly shoots and kills El Mosque; yet, rather than shooting El Esquinao, he chases after him in the car. A second point-of-view shot frames El Esquinao through the windshield as he runs away. His image becomes larger and larger in the windshield as Torete's car approaches, and he soon is trapped by a large wall. As El Torete slams the car into El Esquinao's body three times, a series of close-ups illustrate not only El Esquinao's face as he screams and groans, but also his knees and his chest, which break, buckle or cave as the car smashes them. A counterpoint to the castration scene, this scene serves to portray El Torete as, in essence, a mirror image of El Esquinao, as both characters compete to outperform each other's cruelty. The film's effort to depict El Torete as capable of embodying El Esquinao's ruthlessness epitomizes the film's larger narrative of failed white salvation by emphasizing that El Torete, quite simply, is not different enough from El Esquinao to be a white saviour. For even though El Torete achieves the satisfaction of revenge, El Torete himself also dies as his car tumbles over a ravine while trying to escape the police, thus preventing him from rescuing Isabel or her unborn baby. By any measure, El Torete's effort to overcome the degeneracy of his racially contaminated underworld ends in failure.

The narrative pattern of failed salvation that structures the first *Perros callejeros* film also unfolds in the second film, *Perros callejeros II: Busca y captura*. In this film, we learn that El Torete is, in fact, still alive, since he is shown watching the scene of his own death in a movie theatre at the film's beginning. As the plot develops, El Torete develops a fondness for Charo, a Roma sex worker whose pimp, a Roma character named El Pijo, is initially in prison; as a result, the plot of the film, like that of its prequel, revolves around El Torete's efforts to save a Roma woman from her degenerate family. The extreme depravity of Roma culture is especially pronounced in a scene in which Vicente, Charo's cousin who has stepped in to serve as her guardian during El Pijo's absence, rapes her when she questions his authority. This moment is construed as a legitimate application of Roma customs because Charo's older sister Gumer has recognized Vicente as trustworthy and has ordered Charo to obey him. As Vicente beats Charo, rips off her clothes, and rapes her to enforce his authority, Gumer, strangely, remains in the room. She responds to the brutal attack on her sister only by looking away and turning up the radio. The song playing is at that moment is "Para que no me olvides" ("So you don't forget me") by Los Chunguitos, a Roma group known for its urban *rumba* sound.

Like numerous other scenes of graphic sexual violence both in *quinqui* films and in other genres studied in this book, the spectacular cruelty of this scene invites audiences simultaneously to feel horror for the victim and to relish their own sadistic fantasies by projecting them onto racialized villains. In the scene of Charo's rape, a long take lingers on the two characters as Vicente forcibly exposes Charo's breasts while she screams and resists. In this way, the scene invites its audiences, which included a large base of adolescent males, to savour this moment as a lurid sexual fantasy. This is reinforced by the scene's alternation between neutral and high angles, which empower the viewer to watch the attack voyeuristically from an omniscient vantage point. The scene's function as a spectacle of Roma depravity is further accentuated by the background song, "Para que no me olvides." On one level, the song speaks through its lyrics, which emphasize the idea that Charo will never forget the memory of this terrible sexual assault. On another, as an urban *rumba*, it also speaks through its sound. Whittaker has argued that the *Perros callejeros* trilogy's abundant use of urban Roma music served a range of purposes, which included fomenting a "sense of acoustic community and solidarity" among the film's viewers (174), endowing the films' depiction of Roma peoples with "a degree of authenticity" (184), and enhancing the films' commercial success through cross-media promotion. In the scene of Charo's rape, however, this emblematically Roma musical style underscores the supposed "authenticity" of the Roma community's anachronistic, misogynist cultural norms. Like the rape scenes analysed in chapter 2, which depict white women being raped by Black Africans, the scene of Vicente's rape of Charo serves a dual purpose that can be described as "pornographic" and "propagandic" (Kitossa 32–5). While its pornographic dimension gratifies an assumed heterosexual male viewer by stimulating repressed fantasies, its propagandic function serves to exploit existing stereotypes of a marginalized community, in this case the Roma, in order to fortify the boundaries of the dominant *payo* society. By bestowing an aura of authenticity on the scene, the song implies that Roma life and culture are irrevocably marked by moral and cultural debasement. The film further drives this point home through two more almost unwatchable rape scenes that are committed by another one of Charo's relatives, Sebastián, an inmate in Barcelona's La Modelo prison: one against his male cellmate El Chino, and another involving the daughter of a policeman.

While these various rape scenes unequivocally construct Charo's Roma family as the paragon of degeneracy, it is also notable that, throughout the trilogy, El Torete's sexual behaviour is portrayed as *almost* just like that of the films' Roma villains. Although El Torete is never shown violently raping women, multiple scenes portray him as showing indifference or apathy to women's consent when trying to get them in bed. In the first film, for instance, when spending the night at the house of a woman named La Merche, Torete climbs into her bed naked despite her repeated demands that he leave her alone, and ultimately seduces her by falsely claiming to be a virgin. Later in the same film, in a scene in which Torete has driven Isabel to a secluded area, Isabel repeatedly asks him not to "hacerme aquello" ("do it to me") and he promises he won't; however, he does, in fact, begin to touch her and kiss her anyway, and ultimately impregnates her. In the second film, Torete, while being chased by police, rushes into the women's bathroom of a nightclub and forces a woman into a stall with him, where he proceeds to kiss her and touch her even though she says, "¡Quita!" ("Get off!"). In the third film, as Torete robs a house inhabited by an older couple and their adult son, the matronly woman desperately cries for help because she fears she will be raped. Her histrionics, however, are portrayed as comical, given the audience's awareness that El Torete would be unlikely to choose an older woman as a sexual partner. By implying that Torete's decision not to rape her is a matter of taste rather than sexual ethics, the film not only betrays the sexism and sex stereotyping of the time, but more important to this discussion, also trivializes the brutality of the trilogy's other rape scenes while implying that Torete would have been more than capable of raping a younger woman victim.

As we can see, the *Perros callejeros* trilogy is replete with instances in which Torete's irrepressible promiscuity leads him to disregard the line of consent with his numerous women partners. Although none of these instances is as violent as the rape scenes committed by Roma characters, El Torete's repeated expressions of indifference to the sexual autonomy of his partners undermine his ability to perform a salvific role for Roma women. Rather, these milder scenes of sexual assault mark El Torete's resemblance to the trilogy's Roma villains, even though it is clear that he is *payo*. Like that of the Roma villains, Torete's sexual behaviour is governed by a paranoid performance of masculinity in which sexual access to women's bodies becomes a measure of his ability to re-establish agency and control over his own life, which has been relegated to a profoundly marginal status. As a result, El Torete is simply *not different enough* from his Roma counterparts to embody a heroic role in contraposition to their degeneracy. For despite his supposed repudiation of patriarchal Roma laws, El Torete's own performances of masculinity are based on a similar value system in which women's voices about their own sexual agency are denied, discounted, or ignored.

In sum, while the *Perros callejeros* trilogy imagines Fernández Franco's character, El Torete, as a good-hearted *payo* surrounded by Roma villains, it also portrays him as irrevocably contaminated by their degeneracy through a number of strategies. In addition to the films' extensive reliance on Roma slang and music, El Torete is portrayed as matching Roma brutality and embodying Roma hypersexuality through numerous scenes in which he enacts revenge on his enemies or violates women's sexual consent. Through their tragic endings, these films call attention to El Torete's not being, quite simply, white enough to be a white saviour. Instead, his screen persona reactivates entrenched social anxieties that had surfaced in earlier films, such as those of Manolo Escobar, about the possibility that *payos* might fail to distinguish themselves from the Roma. In films like *Un beso en el puerto* and *Me has hecho perder el juicio*, Escobar's misadventures cause him to fall *almost* to the level of the Roma, but he is protected by the spatial segregation of being kept in a different jail cell. Furthermore, in *Un beso en el puerto*, Escobar's nightmare of becoming Roma and being overpowered by a Roma rival abruptly ends when he wakes up, still safely *payo*, still separated physically from other Roma criminals, and still able to walk free from the jail. By contrast, the *Perros callejeros* films suggest that the notion that *payos* might descend to the level of Roma degeneracy is no longer just a bad dream, but a reality. As traditional forms of spatial segregation between *payos* and Roma eroded, the intermingling of these groups on urban peripheries produced tragic figures like El Torete, whose absorption of Roma customs and behaviours leads him to inhabit a failed whiteness that prohibits him from rescuing himself or anyone else from the contagious degeneracy of the Roma. This helps us to understand why El Torete's star image as a *payo agitanado* could have achieved tremendous popularity with *payo* audiences while also fanning the flames of anti-Roma sentiment in real life. While his display of Roma influence thrilled audiences who admired his defiant rejection of *payo* bourgeois norms of propriety, it also exemplified how the already precarious *payo* / Roma boundary had been further eroded and undermined by Roma migration and resettlement. Consequently, while Fernández Franco's star image riveted audiences with fantasies of freedom and rebellion, it also underscored the disturbing fragility of the psychological safety net offered by the *payo* / Roma racial boundary.

Conclusion

This chapter has examined how the popular cinema of late Francoism and the Transition harnessed social anxieties about the permeability of the *payo* / Roma racial boundary. Despite a dominant narrative of upward racial and economic mobility, fears of Roma encroachment on urban areas seeped through a wide range of popular films of various genres, including those that starred Manolo Escobar, Peret, and Ángel Fernández Franco. The star personas of these male actors both drew on and revised earlier tropes of Roma identity, which privileged female protagonists, Andalusian settings, and happy endings. Instead, as the dictatorship aged and eventually gave way to democracy, Roma migration and resettlement generated fears that society's weakening ability to control the imagined degeneracy of this population might lead to the erosion of the nation's upward global trajectory. Although the *payo* / Roma racial boundary undoubtedly offered a "psychological wage" associated with not being Roma, the increasing presence of Roma communities in Spain's large metropolitan areas called attention to the permeability and volatility of that boundary and, consequently, to deep-seated fears that Spain's belonging in global whiteness could only ever be precarious at best.

Chapter 4

Whiteness under Siege: The Legacies of Francoist Comedy in Democratic Spain

A slapstick tale of misadventures stemming from the legalization of gambling after Franco's death, *Los bingueros* (dir. Mariano Ozores, 1979) was among the most successful Spanish films of the Transition. In one memorable scene, the *macho ibérico* characters Amadeo (Andrés Pajares) and Fermín (Fernando Esteso) accompany two female servers from the local bingo parlour, one of whom is Black, to their apartment. Although the men's intention is to hook up, they do not immediately realize that they have been lured into a trap. As the women partially undress them while giving them drugs – a process that involves numerous, rapid-fire jokes about the Black woman's skin colour – a knock on the door interrupts the encounter. The scantily clad Amadeo and Fermín are met by two strangers, a man and a woman, who claim that the woman is about to give birth. In reality, the strangers, a gay man and a trans woman, are friends of the bingo servers, and their arrival is part of a ruse to lure Amadeo and Fermín into a queer orgy. As the faux birth proceeds, the trans woman's genitalia is accidentally exposed. Outraged, the *machos ibéricos* plan their revenge: one of them grabs a basin of hot water and throws it all over the trans woman's groin as she screams in agony. The two men then escape the house, blurting insults as they leave.

Like many other Transition-era popular comedy films, this scene depicts racial and sexual otherness as intimately intertwined sources of degeneracy. According to the film's logic, post-Franco Spain, which was personified by the ne'er-do-well *machos ibéricos*, was being assailed and emasculated by a morally dissolute, multicultural modernity in the absence of Franco, whose death was portrayed as a catastrophic loss for the nation. Consequently, popular comedies offered audiences who were exhausted by change and sceptical about democracy the cathartic experience of punishing the culprits of the nation's decline. The formula was a success: *Los bingueros* attracted more than 1.5 million viewers in cinemas in its day, making it one of the most successful domestic films of 1979, and paving the way for its enduring status as a cult classic.[1] After its debut, Ozores, who had already forged a decades-long career in popular filmmaking during the Franco regime, directed eight more comedies featuring the Pajares / Esteso duo, as well as similar films with other stars. His cinematic recipe of integrating Francoist comedic tropes with current events, gratuitous female nudity, and thick layers of socially derisive humour shaped a majority of the forty films he made between 1975 and 1985, as well as films by other directors who imitated his style.

The persistence of Francoist-style comedy films in the post-Franco era stood in stark contrast with the objectives of the Miró law of 1983, which sought to erase the cinematic legacy of the dictatorship by only offering government subsidies to films that met stringent quality standards. Pilar Miró herself is said to have personally despised Ozores' films, which she allegedly disparaged as "cine para fontaneros" ("cinema for plumbers") (Arenas). Yet, despite the derision they faced from critics and activist groups, *comedias ozoristas*, as they have been called in Spanish, managed not only to resonate with audiences of the early democratic era, but to those of subsequent generations, too. These films have remained well known to younger viewers through their circulation on television, digital, and DVD formats, and retain a cult fanbase among many Spaniards who grew up with them as children (López Frías). They also remain influential in contemporary cinema by way of imitation and allusion, which is especially evident in Santiago Segura's franchises, *Torrente* (five films, 1998–2014) and *Padre no hay más que uno* (four films, 2019–24).[2] In addition to their enduring popularity with audiences, *comedias ozoristas* have achieved a certain critical reappraisal in recent years. For instance, Ozores won the lifetime achievement *Goya de Honor* in 2016, which led to several special screenings of his films in theatres. Ozores' impact on Spanish cinema was also the subject of extensive reflection in a recent televised docuseries called *Pajares and CIA*, which was released by Atresmedia in 2022.

Although the limited scholarly attention afforded to *comedias ozoristas* has examined their overt misogyny and homophobia, much remains to be said about their intense racism.[3] While the Black woman in *Los bingueros* is only a secondary character, in several other similar comedies of the early democratic period, racialized characters such as Blacks and Arabs were construed as villains, and were portrayed as contaminating the whiteness and patriarchal structure of Spanish society. In contrast to late-Francoist comedies, which depicted the working classes as upwardly mobile and therefore as becoming whiter, these post-Franco comedies portrayed white, working-class Spanish men as trapped in desperate economic circumstances, and consequently, as being surpassed on a global hierarchy by sinister, dark-skinned foreigners. These foreigners, in turn, were depicted as wealthier and more educated than Spaniards, as threats to the chastity of Spanish women, or, as we see in *Los bingueros*, as scheming to lure Spanish men into queerness.

The racism that saturates *comedias ozoristas* of the early democratic era was symptomatic of anxieties related to Spain's *other* transition: namely, its evolution from a nation of emigration to a nation of immigration, which overlapped with its political transition during the 1970s and early 1980s. Although most scholarly narratives mark the late 1980s or early 1990s as the beginning of what might be called the "era of immigration" in Spain, the first decade of democracy should be regarded as a crucial antecedent to that era. For, as we will see, Spain's journey towards European integration, which culminated in its admission to the European Union (previously known as the European Economic Community, or EEC) in 1986, was inseparable from fears of a looming avalanche or invasion of racialized others. These fears were palpable in a variety of cultural forms even during the years in which immigration to Spain from the Global South was still in its infancy, and found their most prominent expression in popular comedies, especially those directed by Ozores and his imitators. In this chapter, I argue that these *comedias ozoristas* contributed to Spain's Europeanization by propagating a "Fortress Europe" mentality – that is, the idea that Europe's borders needed to be fortified to protect it from immigration – even while immigration to Spain was still in its earliest phase. In doing so, these films primed large audiences to support or at least passively accept what was arguably the most transformative law of the decade: the *Ley de extranjería* ("Immigration Law") of 1985, a legal instrument whose intention was to expel unwanted immigrants, to assert Spain's belonging in Europe, and to stabilize Spain's volatile whiteness.

Although the aura of nostalgia that surrounds *comedias ozoristas* today has obscured their xenophobic legacy, I argue that their ability to stoke racial prejudice becomes apparent once again when we consider the use of very similar comedic formulas, especially the *macho ibérico* archetype, for unambiguously propagandic purposes, as has been frequently practised by Vox, contemporary Spain's most prominent anti-immigration party. The uncomfortable resemblance between the ostensibly apolitical racial humour of comedy films and the overtly political racial humour of Vox accentuates the capacity of popular films to massage audiences' receptiveness to racist political messaging. Despite racial humour in comedy films often being disguised as ironic, nostalgic, or family-oriented, the troubling similarities between *comedias ozoristas* and Vox's humorous propaganda reveal the insidious ability of racial humour to reassert the centrality of whiteness as the principal marker of national and European borders in a multiracial society.

What follows will first explore relevant context about immigration-related anxieties during the first decade of democracy and theorize the role of racial humour in constructing a European identity out of a volatile national whiteness. It will then analyse the representation of Blacks and Arabs in a representative selection of Ozores' Transition-era comedies, as well as the influence of *comedias ozoristas* on Spanish cinema today. Finally, we will explore the resemblance that *comedias ozoristas* share with contemporary xenophobic discourses.

The *Other* Transition: Becoming "Fortress Europe"

The argument that cheaply produced, formulaically scripted, and unabashedly bigoted popular comedy films somehow contributed to Spain's integration into Europe may seem surprising for a number of reasons. The field of Spanish film studies has long described a tension between the "Nuevo cine español" ("New Spanish cinema," or NCE) and "Viejo cine español" ("Old Spanish Cinema," or VCE) from the 1960s onward, in which the former followed European trends or appealed to European audiences, while the latter remained firmly rooted in domestic film traditions and rarely found success outside Spain's borders (Triana-Toribio, *Spanish National Cinema* 70–84). Ozores' comedies fall squarely in the VCE category, which marks them as an unlikely source of Europeanizing influences. Furthermore, Ozores' films epitomized the cultural polarization that marked the early years of the Transition, often referred to in Spanish as the *destape*. As Jordi Marí has demonstrated, this period witnessed a sharp ideological conflict between those who viewed the permissive culture of the *destape* years as "a sign of tolerance, democracy and liberty," on one hand, and those who clamoured against sexual liberalization and social change as "unequivocal symptoms of ... [and] betrayal to the fundamental principles of the Fatherland" on the other (245). Although Ozores' films participated in the culture of gratuitous eroticism that saturated many cultural forms during this period, they did so for the express purpose of channeling nostalgia for Spanish men's traditional position as patriarchs.

Even in their day, Ozores' films were perceived as anachronistic or retrograde to many viewers due to their overt misogyny and homophobia, which stood in stark opposition to the flourishing of feminist and gay activism and the emergence of a vibrant queer culture during the first decade of democracy.[4] The conservatism of his films came fully into relief when, as Alejandro Melero has observed, they were shown side by side in the same theatres as a veritable plethora of Spanish films that affirmed or re-evaluated previously taboo sexualities and gender identities[5] (*Placeres ocultos* 46). The idea that Ozores' films were backward-looking even by the standards of their own time becomes even more conspicuous when we consider that, while these films clung to Franco-era attitudes towards women and gays, the legal framework that once reinforced and protected such attitudes was eroding. This was evidenced by the reform of the *Ley de peligrosidad y rehabilitación social* ("Law of social dangerousness and rehabilitation"), a hardline Franco-era law whose articles condemning homosexuality were eliminated in 1979, as well as by the legalization of divorce in 1981 and the partial legalization of abortion in 1985.

Despite the reticence of Ozores' films to accept the fast-moving social changes of the Transition, I argue that they nonetheless buttressed the nation's journey towards Europeanization because of their role in promoting a "Fortress Europe" mentality. The term "Fortress Europe" is often used to describe an idea of Europe as characterized by "a high degree of internal mobility with an impermeable external shell" (Rumford 160), which, in turn, "[erects] racial, ethnic and religious boundaries" between those understood as European and those who are not (Castan Pinos 4). Spain's journey towards becoming part of "Fortress Europe" began in the 1970s, the decade that witnessed its transition to democracy as well as its evolution from being a producer of emigration to a recipient of immigration. As discussed in chapter 1, in the 1960s and early 1970s, about three million Spaniards emigrated to Northern Europe in search of jobs (Richardson 68). However, this wave of emigration came to a screeching halt in 1973, when a global economic recession was triggered by "the decision of the oil producers' cartel OPEC (Organisation of Petroleum-Exporting Countries) ... to treble the price of crude oil on international markets" (Harrison 3, original parenthesis). The repercussions of the petroleum crisis were felt all over the world, but its effects were especially acute in Spain, where rapid economic growth that had lasted for more than a decade came to a sudden end. In addition to limiting Spain's access to petroleum, the crisis decimated the critical economic lifeline of emigration by causing Northern European countries such as France, Germany, and Belgium to sharply reduce their recruitment of Southern European labour. These problems gave rise to a long-term spike in unemployment that lasted until the mid-1980s. As Preston notes, the economic suffering generated by this crisis contributed significantly to a feeling of disenchantment with democratization among Spain's working classes, many of whom had hoped the Transition to democracy might serve as "a panacea for all of Spain's ills" (Preston location 3305). Preston also observes that right wing media aimed to exploit this disillusionment by promoting a false narrative that Francoism had created prosperity while democracy had triggered economic decline, a narrative that was perpetuated in Ozores' popular comedies (Preston location 3292–8).

The decline in emigration caused by the oil crisis occurred at a time when the number of foreigners moving to Spain was increasing steadily. As Antonio Izquierdo Escribano illustrates, Spain's foreign-born population increased from about 60,000 to about 160,000 over the course of the 1960s; while growth continued during the 1970s, it slowed as a result of the recession, but accelerated again in the 1980s, increasing to about 242,000 by 1985 and 335,000 by 1987 (30). Although the majority of foreigners in Spain during the 1960s, 1970s, and early 80s were well-off European sunseekers and retirees, a consistent trickle of low wage labourers from Latin America and Africa grew from about 1980 onward (López de Lera 234). Between 1986 and 1991, the overall number of foreigners in Spain accelerated dramatically, as did the percentage of foreigners who were low-wage labourers (233). As immigration from the Global South became more visible, it began to make a noticeable imprint on Spanish cultural production. Silvia Bermúdez, for example, has demonstrated that popular music from the mid-1980s onward frequently engaged with themes of immigration, especially with regard to Black African, Latin American, and North African migrants (*Rocking the Boat* 15–17). Likewise, a sizeable corpus of Spanish immigration cinema is usually narrated as having emerged in 1990 with Montxo Armenáriz's film *Las cartas de Alou* ("Letters from Alou"), which chronicles the tribulations of an undocumented Senegalese migrant in Spain (Santaolalla 120). Jeffrey Coleman has analysed a comparable trajectory in theatre, as the year 1991 marked the publication of the first Spanish play to feature a thematic focus on immigration from the Global South, Ignacio de Moral's *La mirada del hombre oscuro* ("The dark man's gaze").

Significantly, however, the cultural impact of immigration from the Global South can be traced further back than the late 1980s or early 1990s; in other words, well before immigration actually began to produce visible shifts in the demographic landscape. For instance, as Alberto Elena has demonstrated, the first Spanish film to address North African immigration was a documentary short called *Viaje a la explotación* ("Journey to exploitation"), which was made in 1974, while the Franco regime was still in power ("Representaciones" 60). Made by an underground, anti-Francoist film collective called the Grupo de Hospitalet, it chronicled the experiences of Moroccan labourers in Barcelona who had endured perilous conditions to arrive to Spain and who continued to suffer exploitative labour conditions. Latin American migration was also registered by the comedy film *Zorrita Martínez* (dir. Vicente Escrivà, 1975), which is about a Venezuelan singer who must get married in order to legalize her presence in Spain. Likewise, in August 1976, the illustrated magazine *Blanco y Negro* published an article called "¡Marroquíes avizor!" ("The Moroccans are coming!"), which linked the end of Spanish imperialism in Africa to a looming influx of immigration. In this article, journalist Rubio Gómez-Caminero expressed alarm that an already visible presence of several thousand Indian and Moroccan labourers in the Canary Islands would soon metastasize into a full-blown invasion following the decolonization of the Spanish Sahara. The author was especially perturbed by the nightmarish thought that "Los hindúes ya se nos han metido hasta en el club de tenis" ("The Indians have already infiltrated the tennis club"), a comment which reveals an assumption that socially exclusive spaces should only be accessible to those with white skin (qtd. in Goytisolo 104). As Raquel Vega-Durán has observed, the piece was accompanied by "a drawing of a grasping and threatening hand that stretched from Morocco and tried to grab hold of the Canary Islands" (xi).

In a response to "¡Marroquíes avizor!" written one month later, the prolific novelist and social commentator Juan Goytisolo observed that Gómez-Caminero's xenophobic tone should sound strikingly familiar to anyone who had lived in France, given that country's widespread media rhetoric about North African and Black migrants as stealing French jobs, as living in squalor, or as rapists who relied on crime and drugs to survive (105). Goytisolo's view that Spain was adopting or imitating the anti-immigrant rhetoric of nearby European countries turned out to be prescient, given that Spain's ongoing efforts to join the European Economic Community (EEC) would require it to pass a harsh, new immigration law to appease its European neighbours. On 26 July 1977, the newly democratic Spanish government formally requested accession to the European Economic Community ("Spain and the European Union"). By 1981, the Spanish parliament had attempted to pass its first *Ley de extranjería* or Immigration Law in an effort to assuage European fears that Spain's admission would open Europe's southern border to an unwanted influx of immigrants (Tornos 9; Orgaz Alonso 6; Sainz de la Peña 124). Although the 1981 *Ley de extranjería* was tabled due to the dissolution of Parliament caused by the snap elections of 1982, another version of the law was passed through an expedited process in January 1985, one year before Spain's accession to the EEC, which occurred on 1

January 1986 (Sainz de la Peña 129; "Spain and the European Union").
The year 1985 also witnessed the signing of the Schengen Agreement by
five European countries, thus offering free movement to their citizens
across national borders; Spain would become a signatory to this agreement in 1992.

That the birth of the Schengen agreement and the passing of Spain's
Ley de extranjería occurred in the same year illustrates that Spain's journey towards overcoming its previous image as an "Africa of Europe"
was inseparable from becoming part of "Fortress Europe." The *Ley de
extranjería* of 1985 was an especially important step in the fortification
of Spain's borders, as it completely overhauled previous immigration
laws that have been described as "erratic" (Santamaría Ibeas 496) and
"very generous to recognize the rights of foreigners" (Sainz de la Peña
123). One of its most distinctive provisions was to create three tiers of
foreigners: first, the citizens of EEC countries, who enjoyed rights comparable to Spanish citizens; second, the citizens of countries with which
Spain shared historical ties, such as its former colonies; and third, the
citizens of any other state, who enjoyed the least rights of all (Santamaría Ibea 500). In practice, however, the differences between the last two
groups were minimal, and were not nearly as consequential as the distinction between European and non-European citizenship (Santamaría
Ibea 500). The legal stratification of European and non-European migrants greatly shaped the law's most important function, which was to
differentiate between legal and illegal migrants, and to provide a legal
framework for expelling the latter or denying them entry (Sainz de la
Peña 129).

The harshness of the *Ley de extranjería* of 1985 was criticized by various labour unions and Catholic groups, and also provoked legal challenges to its constitutionality (Orgaz Alonso 6–7). Although the law
included a six-month window for undocumented immigrants to apply for regularization, in practice, only about 25 to 50 per cent of these
were actually able to obtain the required documentation to do so, a
number that dropped to 20 per cent in the case of Moroccans (Sainz
de la Peña 132–3). The law's passage caused especially intense fallout
in Ceuta and Melilla, Spanish enclave cities on the African continent
surrounded by Morocco, where large, historically rooted, yet undocumented Muslim populations suddenly found themselves subject to
deportation. This sparked a wave of protests, clashes with police, and
business closures in both cities between 1985 and 1988, when a special process for granting nationality to Muslim residents was finalized
(Rubiano Segovia 246–9). Given their status as marking Europe's only
land border with the African continent, Ceuta and Melilla have since

become known as "visual embodiments of Fortress Europe," as they have been surrounded by border fences since the mid-1990s whose express purpose is to deter migration (Castan Pinos 3). These border walls have been increasingly fortified and militarized over the years, usually with large amounts of EU funding, despite migrants' attempts to climb over the fences or to swim around them, resulting in a plethora of illegal pushbacks and deaths.[6]

The legal construction of a "Fortress Europe" in the 1980s by way of the *Ley de extranjería* and the Schengen agreement was matched by a symbolic fortification of Spanish and European borders in various forms of media. As Diego López de Lera notes, the representation of immigration in Spain in mass media during the 1980s was highly "distorted": despite Spain's receiving far fewer migrants than other Western European countries such as France, Britain, or Germany, media narratives routinely suggested that Spain, too, was being subjected to an "avalanche" of immigration on par with these other countries (239). This illustrates how immigration anxieties preceded the realities of immigration in Spain, as many Spaniards likely perceived their immigration to be numerically comparable with that of other countries even when it was not. Similarly, he notes, mass media often portrayed all immigrants as an undifferentiated cluster of foreigners, and tended to emphasize narratives about how marginal immigrant communities were creating social problems (240). As Bermúdez has shown, these patterns were echoed in popular music, where depictions of immigrants were frequently governed by strategies of "racial containment" that imagined immigrants as "coloured" or racialized in contrast to Spanish whiteness (*Rocking the Boat* 56). Coleman, too, has argued that from the 1990s onward, theatre constructed immigrants as a "fictionalized enemy" that is envisioned as "inimical and antithetical to Spanish society" (5).

Given the volatility of Spain's whiteness, which had been imagined as rising and falling in different moments across history, the construction of a "Fortress Europe" in both the law and in cultural production in the 1980s offered an opportunity to stabilize the racial boundaries of Spanish identity by reinforcing the nation's whiteness. Ozores' *destape* comedies performed exactly this function, as much of their humour revolves around a defence of Spain's whiteness from the contamination of racial foreigners. Although these films were produced in a period in which immigration to Spain from the Global South was still in an early stage, they nonetheless promoted the notion that Arabs and Blacks were hiding around every corner; had stolen Spanish men's opportunities for jobs or marriage; were threatening the moral, racial, and economic integrity of the nation; and were surpassing Spaniards on a global hierarchy. Unlike much cultural production after 1990, which depicted both Arabs and sub-Saharan Africans predominantly as poor labourers, Ozores' films portrayed these groups as wealthy and educated in contrast to economically depressed Spaniards, whose circumstances were limited by unemployment, scarcity, and economic recession. By enacting a symbolic expulsion of unwanted, racialized foreigners in same the years as Spain was advocating for admission to "Fortress Europe," these films primed their viewers to imagine a Spain in which the mass expulsion of dark-skinned outsiders could become a reality, a wish that would not take long to come true.

At the same time, given that *comedias ozoristas* are often forgiven for their flaws today because of their nostalgic value, it is especially important to consider the role of humour in fortifying a white racial identity. As sociologist Raúl Pérez has argued in his recent book *The Souls of White Jokes*, racial humour "holds significant affiliative power" due to its ability to "contribute to social alignment, building solidarity, and maintaining and reproduce a shared worldview" (26). Yet, he notes, "while a key function of social humor is in drawing some people closer together, an equally significant aspect is the capacity of humor to keep us apart" (26). Specifically, he notes, although humour has long enabled whites "to derive amusement, pleasure and solidarity from laughing at non-whites" (9), it also achieves its power by "appear[ing] as something other than it is – harmless and delightful rather than socially destructive" (21). Pérez further argues that the ability of racial humour to disguise itself as innocent fun has proven to be a useful resource for promoting white nationalist ideologies in a variety of contexts, ranging from the United States to Nazi Germany (50–84). After all, the ability of humour to portray itself as unserious, ironic, or polysemic enables proponents of far-right ideologies to attract new adherents by portraying racist content as "just jokes" (13). Such a strategy, he writes, enables humour to serve as a "veil" that obscures the true intentions of such content, which is to strengthen "white supremacist affect, ideology and rhetoric" (84).

Although Ozores' comedies never claimed any overt political objectives, a closer analysis reveals striking similarities between their comedic formulas and some of the rhetorical strategies of Vox, contemporary Spain's far-right, anti-immigration party. The visual and rhetorical parallelisms between Ozores' style of comedy, which many Spaniards grew up watching on television with their families, on the one hand, and overtly xenophobic propaganda of recent years, on the other, invites reflection about the ways in which these films might continue to prime audiences to receive or accept racist messages today. To demonstrate this resemblance, we must first closely examine a representative sampling of racial humour in Ozores' Transition-era comedies, especially pertaining to Blacks and Arabs.

A Xenophobic "Melting Pot": Screening Racial Difference

Ozores' *destape* comedies were all about the economic desperation of working-class, white Spanish men. In these films, it was common to see *macho ibérico* characters waiting in the unemployment line, as in *Los bingueros*; squatting at a friend's house, as in *Yo hice a Roque III* ("I made Rocky III," 1980)[7]; facing dispossession of their property, as in *Los energéticos* ("The energetic ones," 1979); or inventing duplicitous schemes to get by, as in *Los liantes* ("The troublemakers," 1981). Furthermore, in contrast to late-Francoist comedies, which portrayed their protagonists as achieving happy endings like wealth or marriage, democratic comedies depicted their *machos ibéricos* as returning to highly similar conditions as when they started. For these reasons, post-Franco *destape* comedies obsessively portrayed their economically stagnant, yet socially fast-changing society as subject to both figurative and literal "blackening." This blackening was imagined in moral terms due to shifting norms around gender and sexuality, as well as in demographic terms, due to fears of a looming immigrant invasion.

In Ozores' comedies, the "blackening" of Spanish society was personified by highly caricatured Arab and Black characters. A noticeable pattern that can be traced throughout his films, as well as in films by other directors who imitated his style, is the superimposition of the historical figure of the "Moor," a term long used to describe Muslim inhabitants of medieval Spain, onto the contemporary Arab. In films ranging from Pajares / Esteso collaborations like *Los liantes* and *Los energéticos*, to historical parodies of medieval or early modern times like *Cristóbal Colón, de oficio... descubridor* ("Christopher Columbus, discoverer by trade" 1982) and *El Cid cabreador* ("El Cid the piss-off," dir. Angelino Fons, 1983), Arab and Moorish characters were portrayed as virtually interchangeable, regardless of whether the film was set in a historical or contemporary era, or whether the Arabs in question were of Iberian, North African, or Middle Eastern origin. These characters were generally construed as wealthy, male villains who were scheming to deprive Spaniards of what little they had, whether in films with a contemporary setting like *Los liantes* and *Los energéticos*, or in films with a historical setting like *Cristóbal Colón*.[8] They were also imagined as threats to Spanish masculinity, whether by stealing Spanish women, as in *Los liantes*; by baiting Spanish men into queerness, as in *Los energéticos*; or by their own effeminacy, as in *Cristóbal Colón* and *El Cid Cabreador*. Likewise, the Arab or Arab-inspired characters in Pajares / Esteso collaborations, in historical parodies, or in other Ozores comedies like *Es peligroso casarse a los 60* ("It's dangerous to get married at age 60," 1981), all made use of similar costumes and props such as turbans, flowing robes, and hookahs, and constantly alluded to the Arabs' possession of large harems of women. These "screen Arabs" were overwhelmingly played by white Spanish actors who, in several instances, used makeup to darken their skin, as Antonio Ozores did in *Los energéticos* and *Es peligroso*. Furthermore, abundant verbal allusions in several of these films linked their "screen Arabs" to recent or contemporary events, such as Spain's colonial humiliations in North Africa, the petroleum crisis, or the growth of Moroccan immigrant communities in Spain.

Despite being made at an early stage of immigration to Spain, these Transition-era films are fully demonstrative of Daniela Flesler's arguments in her landmark book *The Return of the Moor*, which focuses primarily on the period after Spain's admission to the EEC in 1986. In that book, Flesler argued that "both historical and fictional 'Moors' coexist in the same symbolic paradigm in the Spanish cultural imaginary" (4) while also demonstrating that "contemporary Moroccan immigrants ... often become conceptually collapsed into this category of the imaginary and threatening 'Moor'" (4). Yet Ozores' *destape* comedies also demonstrate that, in the years that led up to Spain's admission to the EEC, the menacing ghost of the historical "Moor" was summoned to perform more work than *only* to articulate immigration panic. Instead, it simultaneously served as the brunt of frustrations about the petroleum crisis, which was seen as the product of malevolent Arab machinations, as well as being considered responsible for the loss of Francoism's upward mobility narratives, which was acutely felt given the severance of Spanish emigration northward as an economic lifeline and that policy's resulting rise in unemployment.

At the same time, the anti-Arab racism of these films converged and overlapped with anti-Black racism, which was articulated through a comparable range of tropes. For instance, the films *Es peligroso casarse a los 60* and *La Lola nos lleva al huerto* ("Lola is taking advantage of us," 1984) overtly voiced immigration panic by depicting foreign, highly educated Black men – a medical student and an architecture student, respectively – as setting permanent roots in Spain and as marrying or having relationships with Spanish women. Curiously, *Es peligroso* also draws on tropes reminiscent of the "screen Arabs" of other films to portray its Black characters. In this film, a handsome Black African prince named Yusuf (Helder Sánchez) wins the heart of a Spanish woman,

Juanita (Adriana Ozores), but his family members, some of whom are played by Spanish actors in blackface, are portrayed as performing Arab tropes such as wearing turbans, smoking hookahs, possessing harems, and the like. *Los energéticos* also merges anti-Black and anti-Arab racism by featuring two villains, an Arab sheikh and a Black American femme-fatale spy, who scheme to dispossess Pajares' and Esteso's characters of their land and alternately emasculate them in a litany of ways.

An especially noteworthy aspect of the representation of Arabs and Blacks in several of these films is their ability to oscillate between hyper-straightness and queerness. In *Los energéticos*, for example, the Arab and Black villains are both marked by queerness. On one hand, the Sheikh's dialogues with the *machos ibéricos* are saturated with desire and sexual innuendo. On the other hand, the character Carla, a Black femme fatale spy, was played by noted transgender actress Ajita Wilson, which offers the film multiple opportunities to emphasize her gender ambiguity. Similar patterns unfold in *La Lola nos lleva al huerto*, in which Pajares' and Esteso's characters compete for the affection of a white Spanish woman, with each one believing he is the father of her child. However, at the end of the film, the baby is born Black, and it is discovered that his father is a Black character named Porfirio (Charles Emanuel), whose markedly effeminate gestures and intonation insinuate his queerness. On one level, the queering of racialized foreigners in early democratic comedies reflected the subgenre's relentless denigration of homosexuals of any background as sick, predatory, or contagious (Melero, "Hormones and Silk" 1464–70). Yet, unlike a majority of white Spanish gay characters in popular comedies, racialized characters such as Arabs and Blacks were never *strictly* gay. Despite their queer leanings, Arab male characters were portrayed as possessing vast harems of women; Black men were portrayed as capable of marrying Spanish women and fathering interracial children; and Black women, despite their deceitfulness or gender ambiguity, were still portrayed as pornographically alluring to the *machos ibéricos*. In these films, the ambivalent sexualities of Black and Arab characters were imagined as constituting a *double* threat: their queerness suggested an erosion of Spanish masculinity or patriarchal dominance, while their straightness often implied an erosion of Spain's whiteness by highlighting their capacity for reproduction.

The imaginary link that early democratic comedies posited between dark skin and queerness was not new in Spanish cinema; it had already surfaced in late-Francoist films like *¡Vivan los novios!* (dir. Luis García Berlanga, 1970), in which a repressed *macho ibérico* played by José Luis López Vázquez finds himself pursuing a queer Black cross-dresser, as well as *Ligue story* (dir. Alfonso Paso, 1972), which depicted hippie culture as a breeding ground of both interracial and gay sex (see chapter 1). Yet democratic era films went beyond their Francoist predecessors by frequently giving racialized characters more prominent roles as named villains rather than as unnamed background characters. The increased prominence and visibility of these characters illustrates the intensification of anxieties about Spain's transition into a receiving society of immigration, which these films portrayed as a consequence of the moral degeneracy hearkened by the loss of Francoism. By representing Arabs and Blacks as morally dissolute, dark-skinned outsiders in the years that preceded Spain's entrance into Fortress Europe, Ozores' films constituted a xenophobic "melting pot" of racism, homophobia, and misogyny that would be continually consumed by Spanish audiences in subsequent years and decades.

A closer look at several emblematic Ozores films, such as *Los energéticos* (1979), *Es peligroso casarse a los 60* (1981) and *La Lola nos lleva al huerto* (1984), will help illustrate the above arguments. *Los energéticos* narrates the story of two *machos ibéricos*, Floro Belloto (Esteso) and Agapito Mondongo (Pajares), who must try to stop outsiders from expropriating their family properties for the construction of a nuclear plant. Concretely, they are caught between the machinations of Americans, who want to build the plant; Arabs, who oppose the plant because it will create competition with their petroleum; and the local Spanish government, which is portrayed as eager to sell out its citizens to the highest bidder. The film's main villains, an Arab leader named the Sheikh Muley (Antonio Ozores) and a Black American spy Carla (Ajita Wilson), illustrate the subgenre's paranoid imaginary of racialized sexual deviancy, which served to fortify a sense of besieged whiteness in the years that led up to Spain's entrance into Fortress Europe.

The role of the Sheikh Muley in the film is, primarily, to emasculate Belloto and Mondongo by displaying his unlimited access to women's bodies while constantly trying to entrap the Spaniards in queer sexual situations. Upon cajoling the *machos ibéricos* to find his large Arab encampment, which just happens to be established in an open field near their small town in rural Spain, the Sheikh astonishes them with outrageous luxuries such as limousines, helicopters, lavish decorations, and a large harem. Once inside the Sheikh's tent, the *machos ibéricos* are granted time alone with the women of the harem – a situation so overwhelmingly delightful that the two men later describe all of their previous sexual experiences as "gilipolladas" ("bullshit"). Yet this performance of straightness is punctuated by a litany of jokes about the three men having sex each other in various combinations. At one point, when the *machos ibéricos* are bickering because one slept with the other's sister, the Sheikh resolves the dispute by suggesting that the aggrieved Belloto should rape the culprit, Mondongo, a threat that Belloto reiterates insistently for the rest of the film. In a later scene, the Sheikh takes the two *machos ibéricos* to the sauna of an upscale hotel in Mallorca, where he attempts to hide them from the Americans' persuasion tactics. Cramped in a tight medium long shot, the three men, nearly naked and with their bodies touching, are unaware that Carla, the Black American spy, has locked the door and turned up the heat to trap them. As the men sweat profusely, gasp for air, and resort to slapstick antics to try to escape, the Sheikh stupidly declares that it is time to leave. In response, Mondongo announces, "¡Maricón el último!" ("Last one's a fag!"), but when none of them is able to escape, the scene suggests that they are all, indeed, queer. This idea is further buttressed by the space of the sauna itself, as saunas were a staple of an increasingly visible and socially accepted gay male subculture that flourished during the Transition years (Guasch 121–6). Yet another implication of queer desire between Spaniards and Arabs occurs near the film's end, when the Sheikh and one of his male henchmen agree to let the *machos ibéricos* live despite having tried to kill them. Realizing he will never see them again, the Sheikh, who is visually enlarged by a low angle point-of-view shot that reflects the perspective of the *machos ibéricos*, tells his minion, "Es una lástima, porque el pequeño tiene unos ojitos tan prometedores. En fin. ¡Vámonos, cariño!" (It's a shame, because the little one has such promising eyes. Anyways, let's go, honey!") The Sheikh's underling pauses for a moment, before glaring at the *machos ibéricos* and flipping his shoulder in a decidedly feminine manner. This sequence unsubtly accentuates the menacing quality of Arab sexuality, which, it is implied, would happily ensnare Spanish men into its web of perverse degeneracy.

Taken together, these various scenes form a blatant pattern in which the *machos ibéricos* are pushed to the brink of queer sexual encounters by a perverse Arab masculinity. At the same time, however, the Sheikh was played by Antonio Ozores, the brother of the director Mariano and a frequent supporting actor in Pajares / Esteso films, which would have undoubtedly softened the protagonists' humiliation for audiences. Ozores was a familiar face in popular comedies of both Francoism and the Transition and his role as the Sheikh in *Los energéticos* was not the only one in which he played a campy racial stereotype; he also dons Orientalist drag in the much earlier film *Los económicamente débiles* (dir. Pedro Lazaga, 1960), which I examine in chapter 1, and, as we will see in this chapter, in the later film *Es peligroso casarse a los 60* (1981). Ozores' familiarity within the filmic universe of popular comedy, and his recurring portrayals of racial stereotypes, would have lightened the tone of his otherwise cruel manipulation of the *machos ibéricos* in *Los energéticos*. In this way, his role as the Sheikh simultaneously embodies not only the racialized threat of a *Reconquista* in reverse, but also a desire to return to the comforting stability of Francoist patriarchy despite the regime's demise. His ambivalent role in *Los energéticos* as a racialized villain with a friendly face highlights his role in fortifying a white masculinity that was seen as threatened by sinister foreign machinations. In *Los energéticos*, as in many other films, the protagonists' brushes with homosexuality – especially with another man who is gendered as hypermasculine yet racialized as an enemy of Spain – produced a comedic thrill for audiences by illustrating the resilience of white, Spanish masculinity despite the innumerable assaults of an increasingly unfamiliar world. As such, these films not only comforted change-weary viewers by scapegoating foreigners and queers, but also by recycling familiar faces of Francoist cinema. This latter strategy, as we will see, became key to the subsequent erasure or dismissal of these films' bigotry and racism as they obtained cult status in later decades.

The film's other villain, the Black American spy named Carla, forms an interesting counterpoint to the Sheikh in *Los energéticos*. Like the stereotyped Arabs, Wilson's character inhabits a foreignness that is portrayed as sexualized yet threatening. Known to Spanish audiences as the star of European sexploitation movies like *The Nude Princess* (dir. Cesare Canevari, 1976) and *Black Aphrodite* (dir. Pavlos Filippou, 1977), Wilson's on-screen appeal was that of an exotic sex goddess; furthermore, as an African-American who had achieved fame in European cinema, she also exemplified a certain "Black mobility and cosmopolitanism" (Richardson 198). Although her transgender status was not publicly known during her lifetime (Richardson 193), her gender ambiguity was an important part of her star persona, as numerous films that she starred in emphasized her ability to move between genders.[9] Although *Los energéticos* does not explicitly mark Wilson's character as transgender, it nonetheless masculinizes her by using low angle point-of-view shots to make her appear larger or by using neutral angles to underscore her height with respect to the *machos ibéricos*. The film's efforts to masculinize her while also accentuating her sex appeal help to construe her character as an embodiment of perverse desire for the *machos ibéricos*, whom she simultaneously titillates and emasculates throughout the film by way of her pornographic exoticism.

The film's oscillating depiction of Carla as an object of desire and as the epitome of racialized sexual degeneracy is evident throughout the film. In her first appearance, she converses with her white boss about

Figure 4.1. Two *machos ibéricos* (Andrés Pajares and Fernando Esteso) are
kidnapped by a Black spy (Ajita Wilson) in *Los energéticos* (dir. Mariano
Ozores, 1979),

how to extract the bumbling Spaniards from the Sheikh's influence;
when her boss observes that "Los castellanos son como toros" ("The
Spanish are like bulls"), she responds in a sinister, impassive tone:
"No parecen difíciles" ("They don't look difficult") and "Habrá que
ablandarlos" ("We'll have to make them soft"). Her castrating power
is further emphasized in a series of subsequent scenes that depict her
abduction of the protagonists. After trapping them in the sauna with
the Sheikh, she humiliates them once again when she interrupts their
efforts to flirt with naked women in the hotel pool. In this scene, an
imperious, barely clothed Carla, filmed in a low angle medium shot
that visually magnifies her while accentuating her breasts, ambushes
the unsuspecting *machos ibéricos* by summoning divers armed with bay-
onets to surround them in the pool's waters, a scenario that bluntly
accentuates her phallic power and the feminization of the Spanish
protagonists. Ordering the Spaniards to follow her, she forces them
aboard a motorboat and takes them to an undisclosed location. A subsequent scene set on the boat shows Carla and the *machos ibéricos* on
the boat, where she stands impassively as the men joke about her bare
breasts (see figure 4.1). Framed by a neutral angle medium shot, the
sequence alludes to Wilson's gender ambivalence by portraying Carla

as physically towering over the *machos ibéricos*, who appear infantilized by comparison.

Although erotic fantasies about Black women had already become commonplace in European erotic cinema before the release of *Los energéticos* – not only by Wilson's previous films, but also by other erotic films like *Emmanuelle nera* ("Black Emmanuelle, dir. Bitto Albertini, 1975) – Carla's association with fantasies of sexual domination in *Los energéticos* is perhaps most notable of all because of what *doesn't* happen. Despite being alone with the *machos ibéricos* in a state of partial undress in numerous scenes, there is no physical sexual contact between Carla and the male protagonists, an uncommon circumstance in these comedies, which routinely depicted the *machos ibéricos* as aggressively touching, kissing or grabbing naked women, including Black women. In Pajares' memoirs, we learn that a scene of a passionate kiss between Mondongo and Carla was filmed but not included in the final film because Pajares insisted that it be cut upon hearing a rumor that Wilson was transgender (location 880–1). This detail is important because it calls attention to the assumption that interracial sexuality was only seen as titillating as long as it reinforced white masculine power. The kissing scene, we can imagine, was probably conceived to offer the *machos ibéricos* the chance to reassert their virility by conquering Carla sexually, perhaps in a manner akin to *Ligue story* (1972), in which the *macho ibérico* protagonist beats and then subdues a belligerent, masculine Black woman (see chapter 1). Yet, in an uncanny instance of life imitating fiction, Wilson's perceived ability to lure the *machos ibéricos* into queerness beyond the diegetic confines of the film was considered too unnerving to be shown on screen.

By repeatedly emphasizing Carla's racial otherness, gender aberrancy, and malevolent sexual power, *Los energéticos* implies an associative link between these characteristics and her plot function as an instrument of foreign meddling in Spanish affairs. Like the scene from *Los bingueros* discussed at the beginning of the chapter, in which a highly sexualized Black woman almost beguiles the *machos ibéricos* into a sexual encounter with her transgender friend, Wilson's character in *Los energéticos* highlights how the erotic allure of Black femininity, which is contaminated by perversely masculine qualities, ultimately constitutes a beautiful, yet deceptive trap. A counterpoint to the Sheikh's character, which fluctuates between scapegoating Arabs and idealizing Francoism's patriarchal past, Wilson's character construes androgyny and racial otherness as emblems of a degenerate modernity; in doing so, it encourages its viewers to retreat into a jingoistic, protective armour of white masculinity, an invitation that mirrored Spain's journey towards admission to Fortress Europe during those years.

Anxieties about an imminent "blackening" of Spanish society become even more palpable in *Es peligroso casarse a los 60*, a narrative about an old-fashioned Spanish patriarch (Paco Martínez Soria) who must confront his racism when his daughter falls in love with a Black African man. An adaptation of a Hollywood film of the civil rights era called *Guess Who's Coming to Dinner* (dir. Stanley Kramer, 1967), *Es peligroso* is one of the earliest feature-length films made in democratic Spain whose narrative focuses on immigration. Even so, it has received little attention in studies of Spanish immigration cinema – perhaps because of its unabashed trafficking in overtly racist humour – which sets it apart from much-analysed social dramas about immigration of the 1990s. While this film does not portray its racialized protagonists as inclined to queerness, as other films do, it does interweave its anxieties about an avalanche of immigration with deeply conflicted memories about Spain's colonial relationship with Africa or, more specifically, Equatorial Guinea, a country to which it insistently alludes but disguises with a fictional name.

The film's title, which underscores the perils of marrying in old age, refers to the decision of Mariano, an older, rustic bachelor who runs a successful tourism company in Madrid, to marry a middle-aged woman named Gloria (Julita Martínez) in hopes of fathering his first child. Although Gloria is initially not able to conceive, Mariano accidentally discovers that he has an adolescent daughter who lives in a rural town, the product of a casual sexual encounter from his youth. The daughter, Juanita (Adriana Ozores), is brought to live with the couple, but her uncouth, masculine demeanour requires her to be domesticated and feminized. A few years later, the rebellious Juanita falls in love with Yusuf (Helder Sánchez), a handsome Black medical student who turns out to be a wealthy prince from a fictional African country called Tajima. Even though Yusuf is rich, attractive, and educated, Juanita and her mother realize that introducing him to Mariano will be a delicate affair, given his intense anti-Black racism. Eventually, the royal African family flies to Spain to meet the Spanish family. Accompanied by a cadre of gun-toting guards, the royal family exemplify a coarse mixture of Arab and sub-Saharan African stereotypes, and their imbecilic demeanour – especially that of the king, who is played by Antonio Ozores in blackface – contrasts sharply with their son's refinement and urbanity. However, shortly after the African royal family's arrival, their political rivals in Tajima take advantage of their absence to seize control of the government, thus engulfing the tiny country in chaos and preventing the royal family's return. Mariano is consequently forced to offer all of his new African relatives jobs in his tourism company. The film's alarmist depiction of the inevitable blackening of Spanish society, which is especially emphasized by the fear-mongering notion that Blacks are moving to Spain *en masse* and must be given jobs in Spanish companies, is further reinforced by the film's incessant deluge of racist jokes about Black skin, which populate its dialogues from start to finish. Yet, despite stirring up a plethora of racial paranoias, the film ends on a presumably more hopeful note by depicting the aging Gloria as finally managing to conceive Mariano's child. This final detail allows the film to maintain a tenuous optimism in the preservation of Spanish society's future whiteness.

The interlocking anxieties about racial contamination and reverse colonization that surface in *Es peligroso* converge in the character of Yusuf, the Black Prince Charming who portends the nation's irreversible transformation. On the one hand, Yusuf's ability to feminize Juanita, the unruly Spanish *paleta*, as well as his notable resemblance to Sidney Poitier, the Oscar-winning actor who plays his homologous character in the Hollywood original, construe him as both straight and morally upstanding, the antithesis of sexually ambiguous villains like Carla or the Sheikh Muley in *Los energéticos*. On the other hand, the underlying deceptiveness of his allure is conveyed by his utterly ridiculous family, whose asinine behaviour negates every positive quality that Yusuf otherwise demonstrates. Ozores' portrayal of the king is especially noteworthy in this regard: in addition to recycling several tropes from his Arab impersonations, such as wearing a turban and constantly smoking a hookah, his character speaks only in gibberish that masquerades as an African language, and wears garishly unconvincing black make-up (see figure 4.2).

The ominous quality of the African family's racial difference becomes especially evident in the scene in which the African family meets Mariano, the Spanish patriarch, for the first time. As the royal family's armed entourage enters Mariano's house, Mariano, who has no idea that his daughter's chosen partner is Black, drops to the floor in fear, assuming that his house is being attacked by burglars. Yet, when he looks up from the floor, a low angle point-of-view shot shows his view of the handsome Yusuf, his father the king, a heavily armed Black guard, all of whom are looking down on Mariano (figure 4.3). This shot, which sutures the viewer to Mariano's perspective, bluntly conveys fears of a sudden invasion of Blacks, whose menacing qualities are emphasized by the king's freakish make-up, the guard's rifle, and the low angle, which visually enlarges all of them. The idea that such ominous figures might unexpectedly become incorporated into one's family is construed as especially terrifying, so much so that the film never mentions the conception or birth of the young couple's interracial children at all.

Figure 4.2. Antonio Ozores with Paco Martínez Soria and an uncredited actress in *Es peligroso casarse a los 60* (dir. Mariano Ozores, 1981).

Figure 4.3. African royals and guards in *Es peligroso casarse a los 60* (dir. Mariano Ozores, 1981).

Instead, the closing scenes pivot to the more comforting narrative of the birth of a white child to an aging white mother, as if to alleviate the unpalatable prospect of the birth of interracial children. In this way, despite being a film of the democratic era, *Es peligroso* reinforces a pattern I observe in chapter 2, in which late-Francoist popular cinema hid interracial children from view by keeping them off screen or portraying them as white.

Like other films discussed in this chapter, *Es peligroso* uses racial humour to fortify a white masculine identity in a manner that paralleled Spain's ambition to become part of Fortress Europe. It is especially revealing that the film's release in 1981 coincided with the first attempt to pass a *Ley de Extranjería*, even though that law would ultimately not be passed until 1985. However, this film also demonstrates the ways in which racial humour can be haunted by painful memories, in this case, those that pertain to the end of Spanish colonialism in Africa. This becomes especially clear when we consider the ambivalent role of Spain's problematic, unresolved memory of its African empire, which derives from the unmistakable resemblance between Tajima, the fictional African country described in *Es peligroso*, and the real-life Equatorial Guinea. For example, depicting the dashing Prince Yusuf as an African medical student who speaks impeccable Spanish evokes a long history of elite Equatorial Guineans studying at Spanish universities, a phenomenon that had been occurring since at least the 1960s and which had produced a sizable diaspora in Spain by the time this film was made.[10] Secondly, at one point, Prince Yusuf astounds Juanita's family by revealing that his family was not always royal; instead, he explains, "eligieron [a mi padre] hace diez años cuando mi país se declaró independiente" ("my father was elected ten years ago when my country became independent"). This account clearly alludes to postcolonial turmoil in Equatorial Guinea: after obtaining independence in 1968 (about thirteen years before the film's release), its newly elected president, Francisco Macías Nguema, seized control of the government as a dictator, thus becoming a kind of "king" despite having previously been "elected," as the fictional Yusuf explains. The parallelisms become even more apparent at the end of the film, when the royal family's adversaries enact a coup d'état and force them to abdicate power. These events mirror the 1979 coup d'état that marked the overthrow of the Macías regime and its replacement with that of Teodoro Obiang Nguema. The onset of this dictatorship, which occurred only two years before the release of *Es peligroso*, also produced a significant influx of Equatorial Guineans living in Spain, which would have given weight to the film's anxiety about the blackening of Spanish society.[11]

Even though the political events referenced in the movie are not difficult to identify, it is revealing that they are not explicitly associated with the real-life Equatorial Guinea. The film's indirect, yet transparent allusions to Equatorial Guinea's history reproduce the late-Franco era's policy of *materia reservada* (classified information), in which all information about Equatorial Guinea was censored from the press because the Franco regime found its political troubles embarrassing. Even though that policy was lifted in 1976, and even though this film was made several years later, in 1981, the film's reluctance to call Equatorial Guinea by its name suggests a lingering feeling of colonial shame, one that somehow justified perpetuating or reviving the defunct *materia reservada* policy. Despite the genre's reliance on thrilling audiences with spectacles of the *macho ibéricos'* resilience in a rapidly changing society, there was no thrill, it seems, to be produced from the still-fresh memory of imperial decline. Instead, the film's ambivalent memory of this embarrassment is symptomatic of a phenomenon that Ann Laura Stoler has termed "colonial aphasia." Arguing against the oft-invoked idea of colonial amnesia, which suggests that memories of colonialism in former metropoles have been forgotten, Stoler contends that such memories can be better described in terms of a "dismembering, a difficulty speaking, a difficulty generating a vocabulary that associates appropriate words and concepts with appropriate things" (125). The film's oblique treatment of Equatorial Guinea's postcolonial aftermath perfectly fits this description. Far from being forgotten, Spain's relationship with its former colony is remembered very clearly in this film; yet, for those who remained attached to Francoism's myths of imperial resurgence, its memory was still too painful to be discussed openly.

The entanglement of anti-immigrant sentiment and colonial memory is similarly perceptible in *La Lola nos lleva al huerto* (1984), a film in which the *machos ibéricos* are disappointed to learn that a Black man, rather than one of them, is the biological father of their mutual lover's newborn child. A diatribe against the dissolution of the institution of marriage, the film portrays Lola, a single, yet promiscuous expectant mother, as a beautiful opportunist who takes advantage of the generosity of the *machos ibéricos* Ataulfo (Pajares) and Paco (Esteso) as each one tries to prove his worth as a suitable father. Their efforts, however, are frustrated when Lola escapes to a commune that is home to a strange religious cult led by an eloquent hustler named Barati Rama, who agrees to take care of Lola while she is pregnant and to adopt her baby once it is born. When Ataulfo and Paco arrive at the commune searching for Lola, they are blocked by a bizarre Black cult member, Porfirio Rebolledo (Charles Emanuel). A close friend of Lola's who first

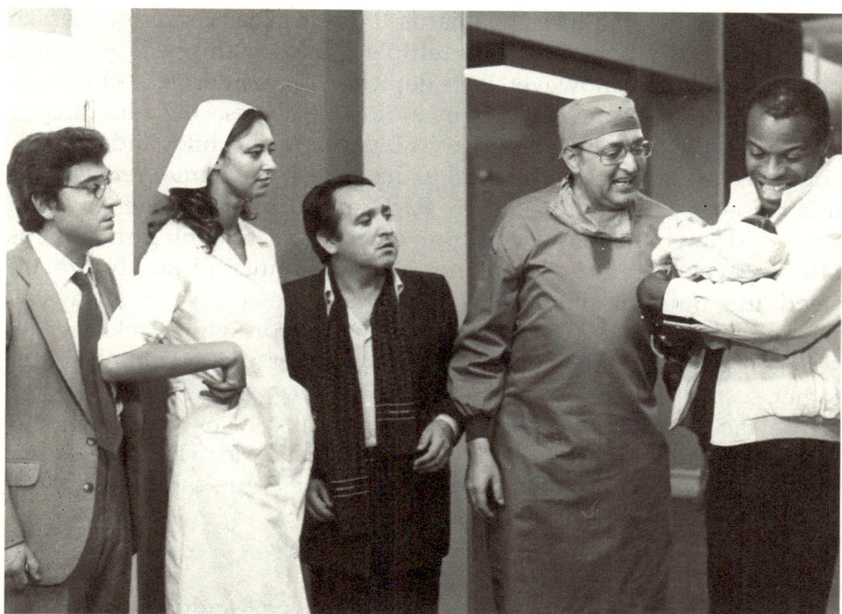

Figure 4.4. A Black character is recognized as the father of a newborn child in *La Lola nos lleva al huerto* (dir. Mariano Ozores, 1984).

introduced her to the sinister cult, Porfirio is an architecture student who speaks with a marked Caribbean accent, a detail that exemplifies, once again, the genre's obsession with reverse colonization. Furthermore, as mentioned previously, Porfirio possesses a markedly effeminate demeanour that affects his gestures and speech, a detail which, in the conventions of the subgenre, unmistakably associates him with queerness. Although Porfirio tries to coerce the *machos ibéricos* into joining the cult, they ultimately escape when Lola refuses to leave. Porfirio's character then disappears until the end of the film, when he shows up at the hospital just as Lola's child is born and is recognized as the true father of the dark-skinned, interracial newborn (figure 4.4).

As its plot indicates, this film rehashes many of the patterns we have already identified in the *destape* comedy's engagement with racial humour, especially its depiction of a deceitful, sexually ambiguous Black character who offends the *machos ibéricos*' fragile virility. As in *Los energéticos* and *Es peligroso*, this Black character is imagined as a herald of an ominous, multicultural future: a highly educated, postcolonial invader, it is he who lures Spaniards to the sinister commune, which is conspicuously populated by multiple Black worshippers. A unique quality of this film, however, is its depiction of an interracial child: unlike many films that preceded it, including *Es peligroso*, this film directly showcases the birth in Spain of a visibly interracial child, and even includes a close-up shot of the child to drive the point home. Yet, because this close-up is accompanied by background music of stereotypical African drums, the audience is prevented from imagining the film as offering even a tenuous acceptance of Spain's multicultural future. Instead, this music implies that the interracial newborn will always be marked as foreign due to its racial contamination with Blackness, despite its being born in Spain to a Spanish mother and a Latin American father.

The racialization of the child as irrevocably Black and foreign is further reiterated by the film's closing moments, in which the disappointed *machos ibéricos* share the following dialogue as they walk out of the hospital:

ATAULFO:	Es un niño muy rico.
PACO:	Y muy negro. Claro, que él no tiene la culpa de nada.
ATAULFO:	¿Qué vas a hacer ahora?
PACO:	Yo, apuntarme al Ku Klux Klan.
ATAULFO:	Yo voy a casa a romper un disco que tengo de Antonio Machín.[12]

(ATAULFO:	He's a very beautiful child.
PACO:	And very Black. Of course, it's not his fault.
ATAULFO:	What are you going to do now?
PACO:	I'm going to join the Ku Klux Klan.
ATAULFO:	I am going to go home to break a record I have of Antonio Machín.)

As this dialogue indicates, the *machos ibéricos* are not primarily disturbed because the child turned out to be someone else's, but because it turned out to be Black. Their closing jokes reinforce this point by illustrating their desire to enact revenge not only on Porfirio, but on Black people throughout the world, whether by joining a well-known American white supremacist organization or by destroying the work of a prominent Afro-Cuban musician. The intersection of US and Spanish imperial racism is particularly notable in this dialogue, which implies that Spaniards should import American models of racial violence to address the invasion of Spain by its former colonies that Porfirio, as an

Afro-Latin character, embodies. Although *La Lola ...* may offer one of Spanish cinema's earliest representations of an interracial child born in Spain, it is clear that the film's intention in doing so is to encourage its viewers to take refuge in a defensive masculinity that vents its frustrations through white supremacist rhetoric.

Curiously, however, this closing dialogue is not the film's only allusion to American racial violence. Another such reference occurs earlier in the film, when Porfirio and several other cult members are trying to convince Ataulfo and Paco to join the sect. When the *machos ibéricos* politely decline, Porfirio insists, explaining that they will especially enjoy the initiation rite: "Esto es muy divertido. Se os mete en un barril de miel. Luego, se os empluma. Después, se os arrastra por un hormiguero, y si pasáis la prueba, sois miembros de la secta" ("This is a lot of fun. First we put you in a barrel of honey. Then we feather you. Afterwards, we drag you through an ant colony, and if you pass the test, you are members of the sect"). As Porfirio speaks, he and his accomplices, some of whom are Black, carry ropes that they twirl menacingly in the direction of Ataulfo and Paco. Understanding that they are not being given a choice, Paco responds, "¡Que te emplumen a ti!" ("Go get feathered yourself!") in an affected Caribbean accent; the *machos ibéricos* then run for the gate while the multiracial cadre of sect members chases after them, continuing to spin the ropes menacingly as if to lasso or hang them. In addition to reiterating the subgenre's association between multiculturalism and emasculation, this scene's depiction of a racially diverse group of attackers chasing *machos ibéricos* with ropes is reminiscent of American depictions of lynching – which, as we saw in chapter 2, also made their way into Spanish cinema in films like *Bienvenido, Padre Murray* (dir. Ramón Torrado, 1964) – but with a reversal of racial roles. Here, is it not whites chasing Blacks, but Blacks chasing whites; furthermore, the scene's inversion of the racial hierarchy intersects with a range of other perverse distortions such as a Latin American chasing Spaniards, effeminate men chasing virile ones, and cult members chasing Catholics.

As we have seen, the Ozores films *Los energéticos, Es peligroso casarse a los 60*, and *La Lola nos lleva al huerto* exemplify a number of recurring patterns in the representation of Black and Arab characters in the democratic *destape* comedy. Although many of the characteristics attributed to these racialized characters, such as deceptiveness, hypersexuality, an inclination to queerness, or excessive wealth, had circulated in earlier films of the Franco era, the increased prominence of these characters as villains during the first decade of democracy illustrates the intensification of immigration-related anxieties as

Spain transitioned into a receiving nation of immigration. While the cinematic link between dark skin and queerness suggested a simultaneous moral and demographic "blackening" of Spanish society, the emergence of colonial memory in films like *Es peligroso* and *La Lola* illustrates the extent to which even in its earliest days, immigration to Spain was haunted by the still painful memory of Spain's imperial disintegration under Francoism. It is also notable that Spanish cinema would not offer much to challenge these widely consumed, Transition-era depictions of immigration until the 1990s. Yet, it is equally important to illustrate not only the impact these films had on audiences of their era, but also on those of subsequent decades due to the films' continued circulation and subsequent influence on Spanish cinema, as is evident in the next section.

(In)Visible Racisms: The Afterlives of the *Comedia Ozorista*

Despite their poor production value and reliance on bigoted humour, many of Ozores' Transition-era films have remained familiar to Spanish audiences of later decades through TV and video formats and through their palpable influence on later Spanish cinema. In the 1990s, award-winning festival dramas like *Ay, Carmela* (dir. Carlos Saura, 1990) and the much-analysed immigration film *Bwana* (dir. Imanol Uribe, 1996) starred Andrés Pajares in roles that spotlighted his talent for physical humour, thus drawing on the star image he had crafted with Ozores in the 1970s and 80s. In the same decade, the impact of Ozores' comedies travelled beyond Spain's borders, as the Hollywood director Mel Brooks allegedly plagiarized numerous gags from Ozores' *Cristóbal Colón, de oficio … descubridor* (1982) in a historical parody of his own, *Robin Hood: Men in Tights* (1993) (López Frías). In 2016, Ozores was awarded the lifetime achievement *Goya de Honor*, which generated special theatre screenings of his films by way of "crowdfunding."[13] That same year, a young director attempted to remake *Los bingueros* as a narrative of Spanish youths' economic desperation during the 2008 to 2014 economic crisis.[14] In 2022, the five-episode docuseries *Pajares and CIA* explored the enduring resonance of Ozores' collaborations with Pajares and Esteso.

The persistent popularity and influence of Ozores' films is also evident through their acquisition of cult status. Although definitions of the term "cult" are debated, the word generally refers to the ways in which films, especially those of past eras, can develop long-lasting, devoted fanbases, even if only niche ones, who attribute special significance to them. As López Frías has observed, Ozores' Transition-era films have developed a particular fanbase among the so-called *Generación EGB*,[15] a term used to describe a generation of Spaniards who celebrate cultural memorabilia of the 1970s and 1980s, the decades that marked their school years. To make sense of this generation's interest in reclaiming the films of their youth, it is helpful to consider Ernest Mathijs and Xavier Mendik's arguments about why certain films obtain cult status. For instance, Mathijs and Mendik argue that the "badness" or lack of aesthetic quality of certain films allows audiences to interpret them as embodying a certain "otherness" or "opposition to the 'norm' or mainstream" (2). This argument is perfectly applicable to Ozores' comedies, whose humour can feel both countercultural because of its outdated, slapstick quality, yet whose thematic focus on the economic marginalization of working-class protagonists echoes the experiences of younger viewers who "struggle to make it to the end of the month" (López Frías). Likewise, *comedias ozoristas* also demonstrate a pronounced capacity for what Mathijs and Menik call "transgression," that is, the films' penchant for "obliterat[ing] ... the barriers of good and bad" (2). This trait is especially evident in the comedies' complete disregard for contemporary standards surrounding the expression of racist, sexist, or homophobic attitudes, which, of course, have shifted dramatically since the late 1970s or early 1980s. For example, Iago Fernández, a writer for Vice.com, described the experience of attending a special screening of *Los bingueros* at Madrid's Golem theatre in 2016 as "un oasis de la corrección política" ("an oasis from political correctness"). This phrase accentuates the sensations of pleasure or relief that can accompany unrestricted indulgence in taboo humour, which makes the films feel enjoyably transgressive to some viewers. Furthermore, like many other cult films, Ozores' comedies are also saturated with nostalgia, that is, "a yearning for an idealized past" (Mathijs and Menik 2–3). The nostalgic value of these films emerges both within the films themselves, which express a patent longing for the absent Franco regime, as well as among viewers who remember having grown up watching them on television with their families. For example, in his interview for the *Pajares and CIA* docuseries, the famous comic actor Javier Cámara stated that Pajares / Esteso films were the ones "que veías con tu padre que estaba fumando en el sofá y con tu mamá que estaba haciendo punto" ("that you watched on your couch with your dad smoking a cigarette and your mom knitting"). Likewise, filmmaker David Trueba, who was also interviewed for the series, underscored the films' nostalgic quality by commenting that "A través de Pajares y Esteso veíamos a nuestros propios padres y abuelos" ("Through Pajares and Esteso we saw our own parents and grandparents.")

Yet, while *comedias ozoristas* clearly offer a range of pleasures and meanings to present-day audiences, their contemporary relevance is often discussed in a way that erases, obscures, or quietly forgives their unabashed bigotry, especially with regard to race. This was especially apparent at the 2016 Goya Awards, in which Ozores was presented with his Lifetime Achievement award. This ceremony cloaked Ozores' cinematic legacy in an aura of nostalgia by portraying the physically fragile, white-haired Ozores, who was ninety years old at the time, as an innocuous, grandfatherly patriarch of Spanish cinema. For instance, it is significant that Ozores was introduced on stage and was handed his trophy by his nieces Emma and Adriana Ozores, both of whom are actors who appeared in several of their uncle's films. By emphasizing Ozores' warm relationship with recognizable female actors from his own family, the ceremony emphasized the familiarity and domesticity of his films, thus inviting nostalgic recollections of them such as those expressed by Cámara and Trueba. Likewise, both the Spanish Film Academy's press release about the award and Ozores' speech at the ceremony explicitly referenced a litany of Franco-era actors who starred in his films, such as Alfredo Landa, López Vázquez, Pajares and Esteso, Concha Velasco, Gracita Morales, and others ("Y el Goya de Honor es para ..."). The faces and voices of these period-specific stars, whom Duncan Wheeler has referred to as the "lifelong actors" of Spanish popular cinema, are often experienced nostalgically by viewers, including younger ones, because they "have accompanied [Spanish audiences] their whole lives" and "frequently maintain continuity ... across different circumstances and across different media" (153). The nostalgic celebration of Ozores' collaborations with past stars was visually reinforced by the camerawork of the televised ceremony. As Ozores gave his acceptance speech, the low angle shot that framed him was punctuated by several shots of A-list actors of Spanish cinema looking on at him admiringly, including Penélope Cruz, Javier Bardem, Ricardo Darín, Pedro Casablanc, and others. In this way, the camera established a connection between Spanish cinema's present-day "lifelong actors" and those of the previous eras, all while visually magnifying Ozores through the low angle.

In contrast to the 2016 Goya Awards, the *Pajares and CIA* docuseries of 2022 makes a serious attempt to counterbalance nostalgic views of Ozores' comedies with other perspectives that acknowledge and confront the films' overt prejudices. To this end, an especially important contribution of the series is its effort to highlight the perspectives of women commentators, including those of women who worked on the films as well as women viewers of today. For instance, the series features recurring interview segments with Carolina Iglesias, a contemporary comedian, screenwriter, and activist. In the second episode, Iglesias states that "Me cuesta mucho reírme, sinceramente" ("I sincerely find it hard to laugh") at the plethora of jokes in Pajares / Esteso comedies that denigrate women or LGBT people. She also notes that the nostalgic halo that surrounds these films has obscured their hurtful qualities "porque se vuelven como algo 'pop' o algo 'kitsch'" ("because they turn into 'pop' or 'kitsch'"). Yet the limitations of the series' perspective become evident when, immediately after one of Iglesias' segments, a snippet from the Pajares / Esteso film *Los chulos* (1981) is shown. In this clip, a Black woman is shown in close-up imploring, "No, ¡por favor!" ("Please, don't!"), when suddenly the hand of Esteso, still in close-up, slaps her across the face, producing a hyperbolically loud "thwack" sound as she grimaces and falls over. Although the docuseries problematizes the misogyny of such humour, it completely overlooks the racism of it, which is further reinforced by the absence of interviews featuring nonwhite commentators or viewers.

In addition to dismissing or overlooking the racism of Ozores' comedies, both the 2016 Goya ceremony and the *Pajares and CIA* docuseries feature limited or no discussion of what is arguably the most conspicuous evidence of Ozores' present-day cinematic legacy, namely, the blockbuster-level success of Santiago Segura's two franchises, *Torrente* and *Padre no hay más que uno*. These franchises follow Ozores' lead by featuring *macho ibérico* protagonists whose misadventures are interwoven with racist, sexist, and homophobic slapstick humour. Furthermore, like Ozores' comedies, Segura's films offer contemporary audiences an opportunity to nostalgically remember the popular cinema of late Francoism and the Transition. As Núria Triana-Toribio has shown, there are numerous parallelisms between the Torrente character, an obese, corrupt, misogynist, and unabashedly racist ex-cop who is played by Segura himself, and Alfredo Landa's incarnations of working-class masculinity in the 1970s, ranging from the unexceptional physique to the receding hairline to the shameless objectification of women ("Santiago Segura" 150–5). The *Torrente* films also feature numerous appearances by myriad actors of late Francoism and the Transition, including not only Pajares and Esteso in the fourth and fifth films, but also Chus Lampreave in the first and fifth, José Luis López Vázquez in the second, and José Sacristán in the fourth. The *Torrente* films offer an especially prominent position of honour to Tony Leblanc, a Franco-era actor who starred in several films studied in chapter 1, including Ozores' early classic *Los económicamente débiles* (1960). Leblanc played significant supporting roles in the first four

Torrente films after a professional hiatus of more than two decades; he died in 2012, two years before the fifth film's debut. As Barry Jordan has observed, Leblanc's place of privilege in the *Torrente* films constitutes a deliberate effort to forge "a type of counter-cultural, filmic *memoria histórica* of the national cinema" (295). This argument is equally applicable to the *Padre no hay más que uno* films, whose comedic premise of a large, chaotic family driven by a battle between the sexes is evocative of numerous Franco-era comedies, such as *La gran familia* ("The Big Family," dir. Fernando Palacios, 1962). The title of the franchise, which refers to a popular Spanish refrain about the uniqueness of fatherhood, is also reminiscent of the Pajares / Esteso comedy *Padre no hay más que dos* ("Father there are only two," dir. Mariano Ozores, 1982). Likewise, the first of the *Padre* films, released in 2019, features bumbling male characters nicknamed "Pajares" and "Esteso."

In addition to their numerous intertextual connections to comedy films of late Francoism and the Transition, Segura's franchises also recycle many of Ozores' comedic formulas, including their reliance on jokes about women, or queer or racialized characters who threaten the male protagonist's virility or racial purity. Although countless examples could demonstrate the point, one scene that is especially reminiscent of Ozores' post-Franco comedies occurs in *Torrente 4: Crisis letal* (2011). In this scene, Torrente, having fallen victim to the economic ravages of the economic crisis of 2008 to 2014, finds himself taking a shower in prison. The scene is introduced by a long shot that reveals two rows of communal showers with naked male prisoners standing under them, a clear majority of whom are Black. A cut leads to a medium-close up of a huge, Black male prisoner making kissing faces at Torrente, who is showering next to him. Torrente is shown first gazing towards the Black man's face; yet, as he looks downward, his eyes suddenly bulge with shock. This detail calls attention to the stereotype of Black men's oversized genitalia, which are alluded to but not shown. To save himself from imminent rape, Torrente drops his soap, slides it towards the person next to him, and walks away. The Black man, crazed with desire, stares lustfully at the other white prisoner's anus, which is framed by a close-up point-of-view shot that resembles pornography due to its highly explicit nature. In the subsequent shot, we hear a piercing scream as Torrente escapes the shower area. This scene recycles one of Ozores' most tried-and-true formulas: namely, the racialized villain who almost contaminates the *macho ibérico* with queerness. It is especially evocative of the sauna scene in *Los energéticos*, in which numerous gay jokes emerge when Pajares' and Esteso's characters are trapped, nearly naked, in a sauna with an Arab Sheikh. The *Torrente* movies feature a litany of comparable racist and homophobic gags that target not only Blacks, but also Latin Americans, Asians, Arabs, and the Roma.

The brazen racism of the highly lucrative *Torrente* films has largely been read as part and parcel of the franchise's effort to deploy a "deeply Spanish" sense of humour (Jordan 291), such as that derived from Spanish black comedy or *esperpento* traditions, as a means "to liberate those inner drives which are normally held in check by repressive forms of socialization" (303). In this way, the *Torrente* films play a similar function today as Ozores' comedies, which also offer contemporary viewers the opportunity to experience what Iago Fernández termed an "oasis from political correctness." Significantly, however, the supposed "liberation" from repressive social strictures that these films offer requires a denial or minimization of the dangerous potential of their indulgence in racial humour. For example, in response to multiple critics' accusations that the first *Torrente* film was excessively bigoted, Segura claimed that "El protagonista es un facha, pero la película para nada. Al revés, arremete contra todo esto y se ve todo con ironía" ("The protagonista is fascist, but the film isn't at all. On the contrary, it decries all of this and looks at everything with irony") (qtd. in Jordan 294). Segura's claim implies that the films' ironic, parodical tone invites viewers to laugh harder at the asinine Torrente than at any of his socially marginalized victims. In this way, irony is meant to serve as a distancing mechanism through which viewers can feel superior to Torrente and to racialized characters at the same time, thus preserving the idea that neither the viewer nor the films they are watching are actually reinforcing racism. These psychological relief mechanisms are overlaid with nostalgia, as the *Torrente* films' abundant allusions to earlier popular cinema hark back to an era in which comparable racial comedy formulas were widely used but were considered unremarkable and harmless.

Like the *Torrente* movies, the *Padre no hay más que uno* films also disguise their racism but do so by associating racist humour with the intimacy of the domestic sphere and the innocence of childhood. In these latter films, Segura's lead character once again embodies an inept, retrograde masculinity, but this time, he is an overwhelmed father who struggles to maintain control over his unruly family, especially when forced to perform women's traditional roles like caring for children or keeping up with housework. Yet, in contrast to the *Torrente* franchise, in which racist vitriol cascades from the mouth of an overweight ex-cop, in the *Padre no hay más que uno* films, it is predominantly, although not exclusively, the family's children who produce a flagrant array of racist utterances. Tellingly, many of the children's racist jokes revolve around the premise of losing racial whiteness, a formula that echoes the paranoias of racial contamination and inversion that course through Ozores' Transition-era comedies. In the first *Padre* film, two of the children cry and whine when their father tells them they can't become Black and threaten to disrupt their mother's much-needed vacation to demand her permission to do so. A similar joke emerges in the second film when the little boy, after having been told that sexual reproduction is like planting seeds in the ground, asks if eating chia seeds will make an unborn baby Black due to the seeds' dark colour. Comparable jokes about racial transformation are applied to those of Asian descent. In the first film, an extended dialogue occurs between a little boy and his uncle about whether or not being bitten by a Chinese person will make someone become Chinese. This latter joke is connected to a recurring gag in which the neighbours' adopted son, who was born in China, is repeatedly referred to with denigrating names like "Contratado" ("Rented") and whose white mother, in the second film, threatens to return him to the land of his birth.

The infantilization of racism in the *Padre no hay más que uno* films calls attention to the franchise's genealogical relationship with another strand of racial humour in Spanish cinema. In particular, these films are reminiscent of Marisol musicals discussed in chapter 2 – namely, *Tómbola* ("The raffle," dir. Luis Lucia, 1962) and *Marisol rumbo a Río* ("Marisol goes to Río," dir. Fernando Palacios, 1963). These two films also infantilize racism by spotlighting Marisol's hierarchical relationship with her Black sidekick, who was played by Equatorial Guinean actress Jöelle Rivero. Yet, while Rivero's self-deprecating humour concentrated on jokes about Black people turning white, in the *Padre no hay más que uno* films, the jokes work the other way around, focusing on whites turning Black or Asian. Even so, both filmic corpuses function as vehicles of anxieties about the volatility of whiteness. In Marisol's era, the preoccupation was about moving past the "Africa of Europe" stereotype and ascending into racial whiteness; by contrast, in the twenty-first century, children's jokes about racial transformation function as a "safe space" for viewers to entertain fears that Spain's hard-won whiteness might be erased or lost as Spanish society becomes increasingly multiracial.

By reducing racism to family-friendly play, the *Padre* films, like the *Torrente* films before them, grant audiences permission to laugh at jokes that, outside the filmic universe, could easily be read as unacceptably aggressive, ignorant, or hurtful. Yet, despite the use of distancing mechanisms like nostalgia, irony, or infantilization to disguise the impact of racism, I argue that we must be attuned to the ways in which the humour of both past and present *comedias ozoristas* possess a significant "affiliative power," especially with regard to race (R. Pérez 26). In other words, as Carolina Iglesias reminds us in *Pajares and CIA*, we must be attentive to the ways in which claims about these films' nostalgic, ironic, or liberating qualities obscure the question of who, exactly, is being invited to laugh. After all, the humour of these films assumes and reinforces a white, heterosexual, cisgendered male gaze, while excluding, stigmatizing, or caricaturing the gaze of other viewers who do not belong to those categories. As Pérez argues, the dangerous potential of racial humour stems precisely from its ability to portray itself as "harmless and delightful rather than socially destructive" (21). The shape-shifting quality of racial humour, he argues, has historically enabled it to sweeten, soften, or normalize real-life racial ideologies while disguising itself as "just jokes" (13). For this reason, despite the variety of reasons for which racism in these films has been dismissed, minimized, or ignored, it is worth observing the uncanny resemblance that several of these films share with contemporary far right political humour, especially that which is generated by Vox, Spain's extreme right-wing party.

Racial Humour as Political Weapon: The Case of Vox

An important question to ask is to what extent past and present *comedias ozoristas* may contribute to normalizing racist ideologies by echoing or reinforcing the messages of more overtly propagandistic racial humour, which, as in popular films, often disguises itself as inoffensive play. This is especially evident in the ways in which some of Vox's most prominent members, such as Santiago Abascal, its leader, or Bertrand N'dongo, a naturalized Spaniard of Cameroonian origin who refers to himself online as "el negro de Vox" ("The Black guy from Vox"), have appropriated the *macho ibérico* trope on social media to advance Vox's anti-immigration agenda.

The idea that Abascal's portrayal of himself on social media is reminiscent of a modern day *macho ibérico* has been echoed by numerous online commentators (Rodríguez Veiga; Ruiz-Castillo). This idea emerges from his performance of what Nicholas Manganas calls Abascal's "Iberian swagger," that is, his comically hyperbolic performances of masculinity (4). An especially notable example of the comical reception of Abascal's performances of masculinity can be found in his recurring social media pictures that accentuate his chiseled physique while he works out or parades on the beach. In response to these images, an article from the online newspaper *El Cierre Digital* mocked Abascal as "an 'involuntary' LGBT icon" by suggesting that several photos on his Instagram page, such as one that shows him shirtless emerging from the waters of a beach, are highly reminiscent of gay erotica (González). Yet some of Abascal's pictures clearly suggest that they were deliberately intended to be received as humorous. For example, in one Instagram photograph from 2 September 2017, Abascal is seated on a rock over an expansive landscape, his muscular legs bared to the upper thigh, while pointing directly at his erect nipples poking through his skin-tight shirt as he smiles mischievously. Given that one of Vox's central ideological tenets is the rejection of nontraditional sexualities and family structures, this gesture reveals a contradictory, yet unmistakably humorous confluence of both overt homoeroticism and homophobia, a detail that echoes many popular Spanish comedies, from *Los bingueros* to *Torrente*. That Abascal posted this picture alongside many other images of himself performing serious political activities suggests a certain awareness of the power of humour to further Vox's xenophobic message. After all, beyond its silliness, this image also portrays Abascal as dominating or conquering a vast landscape while calling attention to his exaggerated virility. In this way, the photo echoes several *comedias ozoristas* that we have analysed by subtly yet humorously accentuating the supposed need of white men to reclaim their presumably lost power, while nonetheless disguising this message with a playful, jocular tone.

Abascal's self-objectifying images on social media recall a long genealogy of non-humorous iconographies of masculinity, especially visual images used by Fascist authoritarian dictators like Italy's Benito Mussolini. As Richard Dyer reminds us, Mussolini routinely appeared in photography in various states of undress in order to establish a link between his muscular physique, his virility, and his political power, thus portraying himself as "the supreme hero figure of the regime" (171). Like Abascal's social media pictures, Mussolini's self-objectifying images were intimately related to the cinema, as "Mussolini drew his gestures from silent screen heroes" (171). Likewise, Mussolini's hypermasculine image was subsequently replicated in Italian post-Fascist peplum cinema, a popular genre of action film whose abundant images of scantily clad musclemen and bodybuilders, Dyer argues, offered working-class audiences the chance to "work through" the contradictory legacies of Fascism (176). The hypermasculine quality of these and other images of white musclemen in twentieth-century global visual culture was inextricably linked to discourses of racial superiority, given that they insinuated "an assertion of the value and even superiority of the white male body" – especially for working-class males, who may have seen themselves as embodying an "underachieving" masculinity (147). Yet, in contrast with the predominantly earnest depictions of white male physiques that Dyer analyses, Abascal's social media photographs convey an intentionally humorous twist, evincing an awareness of the ability of humour to cause his images to go viral, and therefore, to attract more viewers to Vox's propaganda.

The ability of Abascal's humorous *macho ibérico* persona to effect real-world consequences became especially clear in November 2018, roughly one month before the Andalusian regional elections in which the party achieved a watershed electoral victory by capturing twelve parliamentary seats. In anticipation of the election, Abascal released a tweet that read, "La Reconquista comenzará en tierras andaluzas" ("The Reconquest will begin in Andalusian lands"). It was accompanied by a video that depicted Abascal and several other men riding on horses against a barren landscape, accompanied by music from the cinematic trilogy *The Lord of the Rings*. In particular, Abascal's dark green and brown attire invited immediate comparisons with Aragorn, the character from *The Lord of the Rings* who is known for ascending from his role as a member of the Rangers of the North, a border patrol, to become King of Gondor. As the tweet gained viral attention, it generated a litany of parodies from various commentators, who ridiculed it by accentuating its reliance on a range of tropes derived from popular cinema and television, such as its exaggerated masculinity, its reductive binary of good and evil, and its exploitation of ethnic and religious oppositions to fabricate an epic narrative.[16] The video provoked not only derision, but also outrage. Viggo Mortensen, the actor who plays Aragorn in *The Lord of the Rings* movies, was so perturbed by Abascal's politicization of his character that he published a stern rebuke of it in *El País* ("La torpeza política y mediática de Vox").

Notably, Abascal's video draws not only on his image as a *macho ibérico*, but also on another comedic formula that is prevalent in *comedias ozoristas*, namely, the idea of highly caricatured Arabs as enacting a reverse *Reconquista* on the supposedly degenerate society of early democratic Spain. Although the video does not directly depict any Arabs or Moorish characters, it clearly summons a racial imaginary in which mythical "screen Arabs" from any time or place are imagined as stealing Spanish jobs, emasculating Spanish men, or contaminating Spanish society with their vaguely defined degeneracy. Although the allusions to *Lord of the Rings* suggest an intention to portray Vox's anti-immigration crusade as akin to an epic film, many viewers found the video hilarious, which could have easily led them to conjure images of a comical battle between Christians and Moors, such as those depicted in historical parodies like *Juana la loca ... de vez en cuando* (dir. Mariano Ozores, 1981) or *El Cid Cabreador* (dir. Angelino Fons, 1983). Yet, despite the amusement that Abascal's video generated – or, more probably, because of it – it is indisputable that the video successfully achieved a propagandistic aim. For indeed, the laughter that the video provoked, which was most likely intentionally designed to cause it to go viral, appears to have contributed to the party's landmark victory one month later. We can only wonder how many viewers were introduced to the video – and therefore, to the racist message of Vox – by way of the laughter of others who shared it, or perhaps even by their own laughter. By blurring the line of "laughing at" Abascal or "laughing with" him, the response to the video calls attention to the shape-shifting power of racial humour, which can make a figure like Abascal look ridiculous while simultaneously fortifying racially exclusive ideas of national identity.

Since the watershed electoral victory of 2018, Vox has continually relied on humour to recruit adherents to its openly anti-immigration, anti-feminist agenda. We might also consider the case of Bertrand N'Dongo, the self-styled "negro de Vox." N'Dongo first gained notoriety in 2019 for his online persona as a Black immigrant who made controversial anti-immigration and anti-feminist videos, often with an overtly humorous bent. Although his online persona was not originally affiliated with Vox, his popularity, especially on Twitter (now X), where at the time of writing, he has more than 70,000 followers, led him to be named as an adviser to Rocío Monasterio, the leader of Vox Madrid, from 2019 to 2021. As if to recycle Abascal's 2018 strategy, in April 2019, just days before the general election in which Vox would enter the Congress of Deputies for the first time by winning 10.3 per cent of the national vote, N'Dongo released a humorous rap music video on Youtube in collaboration with performance artist Sofía Rincón called "Superfacha" ("Superfascist"). In this video, he and Rincón portrayed themselves as superheroes who, wearing the Spanish flag as a cape, were immune to accusations of being called "fachas" ("fascists") by progressives. Using laser beams and fireballs, they could also instantly transform leftists into passionate right-wing crusaders. One of its most memorable moments occurs when N'dongo ironically rescues Rincón, who has been wounded in her battle with a leftist, by feeding her Spanish *tortilla de patatas* (potato omelette). The video instantly went viral, obtaining 18,000 views within twelve hours ("El rap viral 'Superfacha'").

Like Abascal's earlier "Andalusian Reconquest" video, "Superfacha" comically reworks the conventions of various popular cultural forms, such as hip-hop music and the superhero film. Also like Abascal's video, the humour of "Superfacha" has an overtly kitsch quality that illustrates its desire to be read as an *españolada*. This term refers to a genealogy of Spanish cultural production that, like *macho ibérico* comedies of past and present, aims to represent a national essence despite often evincing an ironic self-awareness of its humble quality. The music video's intention of being read as an *españolada* is evidenced not only by the omnipresent images of the Spanish flag and its colours, but also by N'dongo's gesture of rescuing Rincón by feeding her *tortilla de patatas*. Despite its overt absurdity, the idea of a Black male immigrant rescuing a white female Spaniard with the tropes of her national culture construes N'dongo as an exceptional immigrant, one whose patriotism and loyalty to the cause of defending the "true Spain" legitimizes his presence in the country, even as the video demonizes white progressives, and by extension, the mass of unexceptional immigrants with whom they claim to empathize. Furthermore, the video reinforces the *machismo* of traditional *españoladas* in a number of ways. For instance, the gender politics of the rescue scene, in which a woman is predictably saved from harm by a man, rehearse the anti-feminist orientation of Vox, which defends traditional family and gender structures as an essential part of its platform. In essence, this video construes N'Dongo as a Black *macho ibérico* by showcasing his embodiment of Spanish nationalism and masculinity despite his Blackness, reinforcing his supposed exceptionalism in comparison to the rest of Spain's immigrant population.

Another example of N'Dongo's appropriations of comic formulas that are reminiscent of Spanish popular cinema can be found in a Twitter (now X) video dated 5 January 2023. In this video, which has garnered about 200,000 views at the time of writing, N'Dongo dressed up as King Baltasar, one of the traditional three Magi who has historically been depicted as Black in Western art. He then filmed himself leaving coal outside a government building as a backhanded Christmas gift for Pedro Sánchez, the Prime Minister from the left-leaning PSOE party. N'dongo's performance of the Baltasar character was clearly intended to stoke controversy not only by the effort to insult Sánchez, but also by invoking the blackface performance tradition with which the Baltasar character has long been associated. N'dongo's intention for his performance to be read as a kind of blackface despite his own Blackness is especially emphasized by his mockery of his own skin colour, which occurs when he describes the coal he leaves for Sánchez as "más negro que yo" ("blacker than me"). This double-entendre about Black skin is an oft-repeated tactic for N'dongo, whose Youtube channel is similarly titled "La cosa está muy negra" ("The situation is very black"). By inviting viewers to laugh at his Blackness, N'dongo invites white viewers to see him as a projection of their own racial anxieties and fantasies, thus "providing a relational model" against which to celebrate their own "common whiteness" (Roediger 117–18). In addition, Ndongo's campy, multicolored costume, which includes a large, billowy, gold turban, further adds to this effect by echoing the longstanding conflation of Arab and Black stereotypes in a variety of traditional cultural forms, including popular cinema. We might recall, for example, films like *Los económicamente débiles* (dir. Mariano Ozores, 1960) or *Es peligroso casarse a los 60* (dir. Mariano Ozores, 1981), both of which feature scenes in which blackface make-up is combined with Arab-inspired props or costumes like turbans and hookahs. By harnessing these historically entrenched comic tropes of Spanish culture in a self-consciously kitsch manner, N'dongo's performance of the King Baltasar character evinces his desire, once again, to construe his social media image as that of an exceptional Black immigrant. Crucially, however, the exceptionalism he performs emerges not only from his right-leaning politics, but also, and perhaps more importantly, from his willingness to indulge, rather than challenge, white viewers' racist fantasies about nonwhites.

As the prominent antiracist activist Moha Gerehou has explained, Vox's interest in appropriating a figure like N'Dongo for its cause stems from his ability to allow the party to "blanquear su discurso" ("whitewash its discourse"), that is, to allow it to deny or deflect accusations of racism by showcasing the party's openness to Black adherents (225). More specifically, we might say that N'Dongo's videos serve Vox's agenda by allowing its adherents to ventriloquize their racist beliefs on a Black clown, which results in making N'dongo the butt of his own jokes. By serving as a mouthpiece of white racial anxieties while offering white adherents of Vox a shield against accusations of racism, N'dongo's performances perform a role comparable with many Spanish comedies, such as those discussed in this chapter, which also offer an assumed white viewer a "safe space" to release racial resentments, prejudices, or frustrations that they might otherwise feel obligated to repress. Unlike N'dongo's performances, of course, comedy films such as those made by Ozores or Segura do not claim any overt political intentions. Even so, they nonetheless serve to banalize, normalize, or naturalize racist humour – for example, with jokes about white children becoming Black, white men being raped by Black men in prison, or portrayals of Spain as subject to a reverse *Reconquista* by invading Arabs, and the like – by framing them as innocent amusement, as self-parody, or as nostalgia for earlier periods of Spanish culture. This banalization of racist discourse, in turn, can predispose audiences to be receptive to more explicitly political forms of racial humour, such as that of Abascal or N'dongo, and this risks amplifying the racist political aims of a far-right party like Vox.

Conclusion

In this chapter, we have seen how Francoist comedy traditions were adapted and repurposed to serve as channels of white racial resentment both during and after what I call Spain's *other* transition, that is, its metamorphosis from a producer of emigration to a receiver of immigration. Although Ozores comedies like *Los bingueros, Los energéticos, Es peligroso casarse a los 60*, or *La Lola nos lleva al huerto* were made during the first decade of democracy when the "era of immigration" to Spain was still in a very early phase, they nonetheless stoked fears of an imminent immigrant invasion through their highly caricatured, stigmatizing depictions of Arabs and Blacks. These xenophobic depictions symbolically reinforced Spain's evolution from an "Africa of Europe" to a member of "Fortress Europe" as Spain moved towards European integration during the late 1970s and early 1980s. As we have seen, the xenophobia that these films exude mirrored European anxieties about Spain's potential to serve as a gateway of unwanted immigration. In this way, it is not surprising that these films coincided temporally with Spain's efforts to pass the harsh *Ley de extranjería* of 1985, whose aim was to fortify Europe's southern border against an influx of immigrants.

Despite their unabashed racism, misogyny, and homophobia, the *comedia ozorista* subgenre has continued to resonate with younger Spanish audiences over the decades, who often remember these films nostalgically or identify with their portrayals of economic hardship. These films have also inspired other contemporary directors like Santiago Segura, who has reanimated the conventions of both late-Franco and post-Franco *macho ibérico* comedies through his *Torrente* and *Padre no hay más que uno* franchises. On one level, the effort of past and present *comedias ozoristas* to offer their assumed white audiences a temporary reprieve from the strictures of politically correct discourse may seem forgivable, understandable, or perhaps even socially beneficial. However, the deleterious potential of such humour becomes evident when we consider the ways in which comparable varieties of racial humour, especially the reappropriation of the *macho ibérico* figure, have been used as promotional material by anti-immigration parties like Vox. The resemblance between nonpolitical and overtly political racial humour calls attention to the capacity of humour to soften the edges of racist political messaging, thus making such messages look familiar, palatable, traditional, or even harmless. It is thus necessary to consider the ways in which humour, despite its ideological ambivalence or its capacity for multiple meanings, can serve a similar function as a legal mechanism like the *Ley de extranjería* or a physical structure like the border walls of Ceuta and Melilla: namely, to fortify national and European boundaries, thus marking anyone perceived as nonwhite as perpetually non-Spanish and non-European.

Conclusion

Like many of the films of late Francoism and the Transition discussed in this book, contemporary Spanish cinema evinces a range of anxieties and desires related to whiteness. For instance, a plethora of films continue to rehearse the myth of benevolent empire, wherein Spain imagines itself as destined to rescue racialized peoples from their own savagery. At the same time, anxieties about the volatility of whiteness – that is, the ease with which it can be lost after having been gained – also permeate a number of contemporary Spanish films, especially those that imagine the nation as returning to its previous condition as an "Africa of Europe." Yet, despite Spanish cinema's persistent concerns about embodying or surrendering whiteness, a growing body of cinema also aims to decentre the white gaze and the myth of European belonging in a variety of ways, such as by revealing their harmful consequences upon racialized bodies, or by experimenting with new techniques to construct an alternative gaze.

Chapter 2 showed how the popular cinema of late Francoism and the Transition constructed a mythology of imperial benevolence that stymied the development of a more authentic memory of colonial violence and its aftermath. In the democratic era, the memory of the African empire has remained marginal, as only a scarce number of films have centred their narratives on the African colonial past, and most of these have achieved limited commercial success.[1] A notable exception is *Palmeras en la nieve* ("Palm trees in the snow," dir. Fernando González Molina, 2015), a historical drama about a white Spanish woman who attempts to uncover long forgotten details about her father's life as a settler in colonial Guinea. This film, which was made with a budget of 10 million euros, grossed a total of about 18 million euros and reached almost three million viewers in cinemas.[2] A high budget, commercially successful film about the African empire that achieved a large viewership, this stands out in the panorama of post-Franco Spanish cinema, and arguably marked a significant moment in the construction of a popular colonial memory in Spain.

However, as Gonzalo Álvarez Chillida has shown, the ability of *Palmeras* to serve as a vehicle of memory is of limited value due to its glaring historical inaccuracies. Although the film's errors are indeed abundant,[3] one of the most conspicuous, he writes, is its complete erasure of the presence of Spanish missionary activity in its Guinean colony ("Palmeras" 253–5). This omission, in his view, serves to disguise Spain's "ethnocidal" destruction of precolonial Guinean cultures while accentuating Guinean exoticism and difference for cinematic effect (255). Yet, despite the film's refusal to portray the religious colonization of the territory, it is arguable that *Palmeras* remains structured by a "missionary imaginary" that resembles that of late-Francoist films. As Celia Martínez-Sáez has argued, *Palmeras* couches its salvific portrayal of Spanish colonialism in the interracial romance narrative at the film's centre, which occurs between the Spanish settler Kilian (Mario Casas) and a Guinean woman named Bisila (Berta Vázquez). For Martínez Sáez, this romance narrative serves as a metaphor for colonialism itself by establishing a parallelism between the colonial conquest of African territory and Kilian's sexual conquest of Bisila, a damsel-in-distress figure who must be protected from anachronistic, misogynistic Guinean sexual norms (29–35). In this way, the missionary imaginary of late Francoism pervades *Palmeras* despite the absence of priests and nuns: in this film, the old narrative of salvation by evangelization is grafted onto a narrative of salvation by romance. By spectacularizing the racial and cultural difference of Guineans and by emphasizing Spain's role as a saviour, this film, like many others that came before it, reflects and reinforces a white gaze.

Narratives of white salvation have continued to populate Spanish screens in a variety of other genres that do not explicitly focus on colonialism. In the case of comedy, we might recall several recent films starring Carmen Machi, including *Thi Mai, rumbo a Vietnam* ("Thi Mai, journey to Vietnam," dir. Patricia Ferreira, 2017), *Lo nunca visto* ("A remarkable tale," dir. Marina Seresesky, 2019) and *Llenos de gracia* ("Full of grace," dir. Roberto Bueso, 2022). In all of these films, Machi's roles repeatedly enact the assumption that white Spaniards must rescue racialized peoples, whether by adopting a Vietnamese child in *Thi Mai*; by offering shelter to disoriented, highly caricatured Black Africans in a remote town in *Lo nunca visto*; or by playing a nun who must rescue an orphanage that is home to several Black children in *Llenos de gracia*. A notable pattern in all of these films is their intention of adding

complexity to the "white saviour" myth by portraying Machi's characters or communities as also needing to be "saved" by racialized peoples in order to resist processes of death, loss, or decay. In *Thi Mai*, an
older woman's desire to adopt is an attempt to compensate for her own
daughter's death; in *Lo nunca visto*, Black immigrants are seen as the
key to repopulating the otherwise dying village; and in *Llenos de gracia*,
the visibly dilapidated orphanage is hindered by its closed-minded,
old-fashioned staff, whom Machi's character must challenge or defy in
myriad ways. The pattern that emerges from these films is one in which
Spain is imagined as an old, moribund, or decaying society – perhaps
a reference to its exceptionally low birth rate and anxieties about population decline[4] – and that it can only be rejuvenated by immigration
from the Global South. Yet this idea is inseparable from an effort to first
construe racial minorities as being indebted to the generosity, altruism,
or heroism of Machi's characters. While the idea that racialized peoples
owe something to Spanish society in return for rescuing them may constitute a new variation of the "benevolent empire" myth, it does little to
reshape the racial power dynamics in which whiteness is imagined as
the core of Spanish identity.

Perhaps one of the most striking examples of a well-intentioned film
to rehearse the trope of the white saviour is *Carmen y Lola* ("Carmen
and Lola," dir. Arantxa Echevarría, 2018), which recounts how two
Roma adolescent girls fall in love with each other and face extreme
hostility, rejection, and cruelty from their community. This film, which
was made by a *paya* feminist director, was aimed primarily at festival
audiences, but nonetheless attracted considerable attention by winning
two Goya awards, including one for Echevarría for best new director.
In many ways, its depiction of the Roma is reminiscent of that of earlier
popular film traditions, especially in its abundant portrayal of Roma
music and dance to showcase the exoticism of its subjects, as well as in
its emphasis on antiquated, patriarchal norms as distinctively Romani
cultural traits. Yet, beyond its lack of originality, the film generated a
tremendous controversy that centred on questions about intersectionality and the role of white feminists in participating in the struggles of
racialized women. The director, Echevarría, has been quoted as justi-
fying the need to make *Carmen y Lola* because, in her view, "O cuenta
una paya la situación de una mujer gitana o no la cuenta nadie" ("either a *paya* must tell the story of Roma women or no one will tell it
at all") (qtd. in Kali). Likewise, it has also been reported that during
pre-production, Echevarría received feedback on her film's indulgent
recycling of stereotypes from well-known Roma filmmaker José Heredia
Moreno, director of *El amor y la ira: cartografía del acoso antigitano* ("Love

and wrath: cartography of anti-Roma harassment", 2015), but Echevarría refused to incorporate any of his suggestions (Kali). These factors incensed members of the organization *Asociación Gitanas Feministas por la Diversidad* ("*Association of Roma Feminists for Diversity*"), who released a statement decrying *Carmen y Lola* as "otra producción más de super-héroes, solo que esta vez la superpaya está detrás de la cámara y no-sotras somos las exóticas, las sensuales, las oprimidas y las manipuladas a las que viene a rescatar de nuestro pueblo de salvajes y villanos" ("yet another superhero movie, except this time the super-*paya* is behind the camera and we are the exotic, sensual, oppressed, and manipulated women whom she comes to rescue from our culture of savages and villains") ("Vetadas Gitanas Feministas"). In a response to this statement, Echevarría defended her film by claiming to speak from a position of universal sisterhood, declaring that: "antes de directora de cine, soy mujer … Creo que somos hermanas, más allá de las razas o los credos. Creo que las mujeres debemos de luchar juntas en este camino de empoderamiento femenino" ("More than a film director, I'm a woman … I believe we are sisters, beyond races or creeds. I believe that women should fight together in the path of female empowerment") (qtd. in "Carmen y Lola: Una película sobre el amor"). The tensions between Echevarría and *Gitanas Feministas* escalated to the point that Echevarría refused to participate in a roundtable with members of the association at the Pamplona International Festival of Cinema and Women, causing *Carmen y Lola* to be taken off the festival's program (Miguel Trula).

Echevarría's use of the rhetoric of sisterhood to defend her film from accusations of racism is especially remarkable. The idea of "sisterhood," a term once commonplace in second-wave feminist discourse, has long been interrogated by feminists of colour like Audré Lorde and bell hooks, who have argued that it masks multiple forms of stratification, privilege, and inequality among women (Oyewumi 1–2). Yet even if we recognize, for a moment, the good intentions that underlay Echevarría's claims of promoting a feminist sisterhood, it is surprising that she would refuse to participate in a public discussion of her film with her supposed "sisters," the members of *Gitanas Feministas*. This contradiction evinces Echevarría's anxiety about the precarious relationship between the illusion of sisterhood and the naming of whiteness. After all, Echevarría's vision of sisterhood, in which she constructs herself as bravely telling a story for those who cannot speak for themselves, can only function if she speaks from a horizontal position of power with her marginalized subjects. To be labelled a "white woman" director, as *Gitanas Feministas* essentially called her, accentuates the verticality of her position of privilege compared with Roma women. As such, the naming of Echevarría's whiteness threatened to erode the legitimacy of her emerging cinematic identity as spokesperson for nonwhite women. This is a role that she clearly intends to continue to play, considering that her subsequent film, the bluntly titled *Chinas* ("Chinese women"), which debuted in October 2023, addresses the experiences of young adolescent women of Chinese descent growing up in Spain. Of course, there are many ways in which Echevarría could have made a version of *Carmen y Lola* while recognizing the implications of her social position. For instance, she might have shown more willingness to question her assumptions about Roma women's lack of agency or demonstrated a more collaborative spirit with Roma women's organizations and Roma filmmakers. Instead, Echevarría's claims of "sisterhood" bear an uncanny resemblance to the "sisterly" disposition of the well-meaning missionary nuns of late-Francoist cinema, such as those that appear in *Cristo negro* ("Black Christ," dir. Ramón Torrado, 1963), *Encrucijada para una monja* ("A nun at the crossroads," dir. Julio Buchs, 1967), or *Esa mujer* ("That woman," dir. Mario Camus, 1969). Like *Carmen y Lola*, these films attempted to obscure Spanish racism by promoting narratives about cinematic "sisters" whose selfless efforts to civilize savages were met with undeserved cruelty.

Intertwined with these abundant narratives of white salvation are historically entrenched concerns that Spain's hard-won journey towards whiteness might be easily reversed at any moment, reverting it back into an "Africa of Europe." These apprehensions are especially evident in cinema of the economic crisis of 2008 to 2014. During these years, a global economic crisis heavily impacted Spain, sparking a dramatic rise in unemployment, a significant drop in GDP, a soaring public debt, and the emergence of social movements rooted in anti-austerity sentiment such as 15-M (A. Bermudez and Brey 83–5). Significantly, these years witnessed a temporary reversal of a phenomenon that I have referred to as Spain's *other* Transition: namely, its evolution from a producer of emigration into a recipient of immigration. In 2012, net emigration from Spain exceeded net immigration for the first time since the 1970s, something which signalled the deterioration of economic opportunities and quality of life for native-born Spaniards and immigrants alike (Ortega-Rivera et al. 2). Consequently, films of these years were marked by a recurring pattern in which Spaniards were depicted as losing their privileged global stature and instead falling to the level of racialized peoples from other parts of the world, especially the Global South.

A prominent example of the racial reversal trope in crisis cinema can be found in the animated film *Españistán* ("Spainistan," dir. Aleix Saló, 2011). Intended as promotional material for an eponymous graphic novel, this short film, which accumulated three million views on You-tube within one month of its release, offers a concise explanation of the economic and legal factors that contributed to the crisis (Aranda). As its title suggests, the film dramatizes Spain's economic suffering by portraying it as a descent into a third world hellscape. Although the film is narrated primarily in Spanish, its occasional use of English-language terms such as "Spanish dream" and "Spanish way of life" calls attention to the hollow, illusory nature of Spaniards' supposed belonging in a Global North associated with anglophone cultural influence. This becomes especially evident in the final lines of the voiceover narration, which state: "Descubrimos, de pronto, que éramos pobres, y lo que es peor, que nunca habíamos dejado de serlo. Y que quizá esto ya no era España, sino Españistán" ("We discovered, suddenly, that we were poor, and even worse, that we had never stopped being poor. And that perhaps this was no longer Spain, but Spainistan"). As these words are spoken, a soundtrack of Arabic-sounding music emerges, and continues for another twenty seconds. By linking economic conditions in Spain to a loss of membership in the Global North and a consequent descent into "Arabness," the title, the narration, and the soundtrack jointly imply a link between Spain's loss of economic stature and its loss of whiteness. The crisis, it is suggested, essentially caused Spain to degenerate back into its previous stature as an "Africa of Europe," or maybe even revealed that it had never stopped being one at all.

Similar apprehensions about a loss of whiteness during the crisis years undergird a number of other films of various genres, ranging from the documentary *En tierra extraña* ("In a foreign land," dir. Icíar Bollaín, 2014), to the lighthearted comedy *Perdiendo el norte* ("Off course," dir. Nacho Velilla, 2015), to the satirical mockumentary *Selfie* (dir. Víctor García León, 2017). All of these films portray Spaniards as, essentially, descending to the level of immigrants from the Global South. In *En tierra extraña*, which features interviews with Spanish emigrants who were forced to move to Scotland to evade economic hardship, several interviewees repeatedly compare themselves with immigrants from Africa and Latin America. For instance, one Spanish woman states that "Somos exactamente lo mismo [que ellos], pero en Edimburgo" ("We are exactly the same [as them], but in Edinburgh"); likewise, another man declares that "me veo súper reflejado" ("I feel very identified") with Latin American migrants due to his own experience of displacement and poverty. The film itself reinforces these assertions when it intersperses one of its interviews with decontexualized images of African migrants crossing the border walls of Ceuta and Melilla. As Mary Kate Donovan has noted, the film's various comparisons between Spaniards and Global-South migrants "[gesture] toward the possibility of shared experience as producing solidarity" ("Memory" 555). However, she notes, these analogies are also "overly simplistic" (555), given that they "[obfuscate] the situations from which various migrant groups emerge and the conditions that produce their suffering, including race, class and citizenship" (557).

The portrayal of the crisis as a moment in which Spaniards have been transformed back into racialized others also surfaces in *Perdiendo el norte*, which comically narrates the tribulations of in young Spanish emigrants in Germany. *Perdiendo* attempts to draw solidarity with Spanish migrants of today by comparing them with their forbears who emigrated to Germany during late Francoism. It invites this comparison through its myriad allusions to the late-Francoist classic, *Vente a Alemania, Pepe* ("Come to Germany, Pepe," dir. Pedro Lazaga, 1971).[5] However, *Perdiendo* also dramatizes the humiliation of its Spanish protagonists by depicting them as occupying a social rung that is closer to Turks, a racialized migrant community with a large population in Germany, than to native-born Germans. By showcasing the comic fallout of a situation in which Spaniards with university degrees must live in a Turkish neighbourhood and work at a kebab restaurant under a tyrannical Turkish boss, the film implies that its protagonists "are now living similarly to how they had perhaps formerly perceived immigrants in Spain" (Britland, "La crisis" 31). In other words, one of the film's primary jokes revolves around a premise of racial reversal, in which Spaniards who imagined themselves as destined to enjoy privileges of being European find themselves confronting their longstanding status as, essentially, "Africans of Europe."

The satirical mockumentary *Selfie* follows a formula that is comparable with that of *Perdiendo* by narrating how Bosco, the sheltered, bigoted son of a government minister, finds himself in a range of humiliating situations after his father is sent to prison for corruption. Abandoned by his family and without the protection of his wealth, Bosco finds himself first having to spend a night at the house of his family's Latin American housekeeper, and later moving to Lavapiés, a neighbourhood long associated with immigration in Spain's cultural imaginary, where he must live with a Black African roommate. Bosco's interactions with these immigrant characters are marked by cringeworthy ignorance, selfishness, and racism, such as when he asks his roommate, who is from South Africa, if he came to Spain in a *patera* (makeshift boat). The film clearly intends for us to view these moments with a certain critical distance due to its multiple strategies of self-reflexivity and irony, which Joanne Britland has analysed in detail ("El *Selfie*"). Even so, in both *Perdiendo* and *Selfie*, racialized characters serve primarily as foils through which to measure the depth of the Spanish protagonists' loss of privilege. While such a comedic formula may have served a cathartic or therapeutic function for Spanish viewers who were grappling with severe economic hardship at the time, it nonetheless evinces an effort to elicit pity for Spaniards who have lost their traditional place of superiority over other groups, especially racialized ones. In doing so, this comedic formula evinces a desire to restore a pre-crisis racial hierarchy in which Spaniards might see themselves once again as unambiguously belonging to an empowered, prosperous Global North.

Through its abundant narratives of both white salvation and the loss of whiteness, contemporary Spanish cinema continues to accentuate how whiteness, as a mythology of racial superiority, has proven enduring, yet illusory; pervasive, yet precarious; and entrenched, yet volatile. Indeed, Afro-Spanish actor Malcolm Treviño-Sitté expressed frustration with Spanish cinema's privileging of white gazes at the 2024 Goya Awards when, having taken the stage to present the award for Best Art Direction alongside actress Toni Acosta, he spontaneously protested: "¡Más diversidad racial en el cine español! ¡Y sin perdón!" ("More racial diversity in Spanish cinema! And no apologies!"). Despite the large amount of work that remains to decentre the hegemonic white gaze in Spanish cinema, a range of emerging filmmakers, both white and non-white, have made significant inroads in this regard. Although it is beyond the scope of this book to analyse their work in detail, filmmakers such as Xavi Artigas, Xapo Ortega, Rubén H. Bermúdez, Pablo Vega, and others have produced a body of work that interrogates, confronts, revises, reframes, or simply disengages from the tropes and patterns of racial representation outlined in this book. We might consider, for example, how several documentaries made by white Catalan filmmakers Xavi Artigas and Xapo Ortega, including *Ciutat morta* ("Dead city," 2014), *Tarajal* (2016) and *Idrissa: Chronicle of an Ordinary Death* (2018) have all cast a spotlight on the violent and even lethal consequences for immigrants and racialized Spaniards that emerge from the hegemonic white gaze of Spain's state institutions, ranging from the police, to the criminal justice system, to immigrant detainment centres. Similarly, we might consider how *A todos nos gusta el plátano* ("We all like plantain," 2021), the debut film of Afro-Spanish director Rubén H. Bermúdez, contrasts the generalization embedded in its title with a fragmentary, kaleidoscopic portrayal of the daily lives of several Afro-Spanish youth. By using footage that its subjects filmed themselves, the film accentuates the youths' role as viewing subjects in their own right, while also underscoring the plurality of Afro-Spanish experiences, gazes, and identities. Likewise, we might also consider the short film *Proud Roma* (2022), made by Romani filmmaker Pablo Vega, in which a Romani woman's emotionally gripping monologue demands a revalorization of diverse Romani identities and histories, while also accentuating the importance of cross-racial solidarity. As Spanish cinema continues to reflect a greater degree of diasporic, intercultural, and antiracist perspectives, the soil in which the roots of whiteness have invisibly thrived will continue to be loosened, thus paving the way for new ways of looking, being, and coexisting to flourish.

Notes

Introduction

1 In this book, I capitalize the English word "Black" when referring to
   racialized communities who adopt this term as a way of countering
   the historical denigration of this community and as a way of signalling
   equivalent respect to them as other minority groups whose names are
   usually capitalized ("Asian-Americans," "Latinos," "Native Americans,"
   "Jews," etc.) In Spanish, I leave the word "negro" and its variants in lower
   case because in Spanish, the names of both majority and minority groups,
   whether these are defined in ethnic, racial, national, or religious terms, are
   generally written in lower case.
2 All translations are mine unless otherwise noted. Throughout this book,
   quotations from primary sources, such films, novels, autobiographies, or
   songs, are cited in the original language, followed by English translation.
   By contrast, quotations from secondary sources like academic books,
   academic articles, news articles, and the like are cited only in English
   translation if they were written in a language other than English.
3 Although it is difficult to estimate the Black population of Spain during
   this time period, it is generally undisputed that it remained very small
   until the 1990s. Donato Ndongo Bidyogo, a major Equatorial Guinean
   writer who spent many years exiled in Spain from the 1960s onward,
   describes Spain's Black community during the 1960s as both "scarce"
   and geographically scattered, consisting only of small populations of
   "Equatorial Guineans, most of them students; Cubans who fled the
   revolution of Fidel Castro … and, lastly, African-Americans at the military
   bases of Torrejón, Rota and Zaragoza." Although the population of
   Equatorial Guinean exiles increased after the country's independence in
   1968 due to the brutality of its dictator, Francisco Macías Nguema, this
   community remained statistically small, amounting only to about 6,000 in
   1978 (Fraguas).

4 This is evidenced by several academic studies that have addressed the long-lasting cultural influence of these advertisements, including articles by Diana Palardy, Silvia Espinosa i Maribet, and Elena Añaños et al.

5 In this book, I use the terms "Roma" or "Romani" as preferred English-language equivalents for communities who refer to themselves in Spanish as "gitanos" or "romaníes." Although the English word "Gypsy" was once in popular use, it is increasingly considered unacceptable, and I reserve this word for stereotypical representations of Roma characters in literature, theatre, and film (i.e., the "screen Gypsy.") I distinguish between these terms intentionally to accentuate the vast distance that separates hegemonic fictions about bohemian, musical Gypsies from the realities of exclusion and exploitation that have long characterized Roma life in Spain. Likewise, I use the Spanish word *payo* to refer to non-Roma Spaniards who belong to the dominant racial majority.

6 Most cultural studies scholarship on immigration in Spain marks the late 1980s or early 1990s as the moment in which immigration began to produce visible changes in Spain's demographic landscape. This is reflected in studies by Flesler, Santaolalla, Ballesteros, S. Bermúdez, Coleman, and Murray (*Home away from Home*).

7 A genealogy of Spanish films that depict immigration empathetically is usually narrativized as emerging in 1990 with Montxo Armendáriz's *Las cartas de Alou,* and would continue throughout the decade with films like *Bwana* (dir. Imanol Uribe, 1996), *Taxi* (dir. Carlos Saura, 1996), *Cosas que dejé en La Habana* (dir. Manuel Gutiérrez Aragón, 1997), and *Flores de otro mundo* (dir. Icíar Bollaín, 1999), among others, as well as an ever growing number of twenty-first century films.

8 For specific studies on each of these groups, see Roediger for Irish Americans, Brodkin for Jewish Americans, or Guglielmo for Italian Americans.

9 In a 2016 article, Ulrike Vieten and Scott Poynting observed a dramatic growth in far-right racist political movements in a variety of countries in the 2010s, including the United Kingdom, France, Australia, Germany, Austria, Greece, and the Netherlands, among others (533–6). Likewise, in a 2019 study, Cas Mudde further observed that far-right parties had also come to dominate several governments, including those of Brazil, Poland, and Hungary, and had made significant gains in countries such as Italy, Bulgaria, and Slovakia, among others (2–5).

10 Examples of whiteness studies scholarship that demonstrate a transnational purview that extends beyond the Anglophone world include a number of edited volumes, including: *Working through Whiteness* (ed. Cynthia Levine-Rasky, 2002); *Postcolonial Whiteness* (ed. Alfred J. López, 2005); *At Home and Abroad* (ed. LaVinia Delois Jennings, 2009); *Unveiling*

Whiteness in the Twenty-First Century (ed. Veronica Watson et al., 2015); and *Routledge Handbook of Critical Studies in Whiteness* (ed. Shona Hunter and Christi Van der Westhuizen, 2022).

11 For a representative sampling of this work, see monograph studies published by Daniela Flesler, Isabel Santaolalla, Isolina Ballesteros, Raquel Vega-Durán, Silvia Bermúdez, N. Michelle Murray *(Home away from Home)*, and Jeffrey Coleman, as well as articles and books-in-progress by Mary Kate Donovan and Catalina Iannone.

12 Studies of race in nineteenth or twentieth century Spanish culture include monographs by Susan Martin-Márquez, Joshua Goode, Eva Woods-Peiró, Lisa Surwillo, and Julia Chang, as well as the edited volume *Unsettling Colonialism* (ed. Akiko Tsuchiya and N. Michelle Murray) and a special issue of *Transmodernity* on "Hispanic and Lusophone Whiteness Studies."

13 See monograph studies by Tatjana Pavlović, Sally Faulkner, Justin Crumbaugh, Jorge Pérez (*Confessional Cinema*), Tom Whittaker, and Francisco Fernández de Alba. Of these, only Crumbaugh and Pérez dedicate some attention to questions of race, but it is not their main focus.

14 Although empirical data about film audiences from this period is scarce and incomplete, Manuel Palacios Arranz's 2005 *El público cinematográfico en España* ("The cinema public in Spain") attempts to reconstruct the profiles of Spanish film audiences during late Francoism. His research indicates that in the 1960s, more men attended cinemas than women, as 59 per cent of men said they attended films regularly compared with 52 per cent of women (10). He also notes that over the course of the decade, the percentage of film viewers based in major cities like Madrid, Barcelona, or Valencia increased dramatically, based on rural to urban migration patterns (14–16). These immigrant viewers, he argues, likely propelled the increase in viewership in domestic films, such as *macho ibérico* comedies, despite the overall decline in film viewership due to the advent of television (16–18). Furthermore, Palacio Arranz's list of the most successful domestic films between 1966–1975 includes a pronounced majority of films that can be described *macho ibérico* comedies, many of which dealt with themes of rural to urban migration (17–18). Coupled with the genre's thematic focus on male protagonists, this data bolsters the likelihood that audiences of *macho ibérico* comedies were predominantly, although not exclusively, made up of working-class immigrant men.

15 A shorter, preliminary version of this chapter was previously published as the article: "'Spain is (not so) different': Whitening Spain through Late Francoist Comedy" in *Transmodernity*, vol. 8, no. 2, 2018, pp. 91–109.

16 The full titles of the *Torrente* films are: *Torrente, el brazo tonto de la ley* ("Torrente, the dumb arm of the law," 1998); *Torrente 2: Misión en Marbella*

("Torrente 2: Mission in Marbella," 2001); *Torrente 3: El Protector* ("Torrente 3: The protector," 2005); *Torrente 4: Crisis letal* ("Torrente 4: Lethal crisis," 2011); and *Torrente 5: Operación Eurovegas* ("Torrente 5: Operation Eurovegas," 2014). The full titles of the *Padre* films are: *Padre no hay más que uno* ("Father there is only one," 2019); *Padre no hay más que uno 2: La llegada de la suegra* ("Father there is only one 2: The arrival of mother-in-law," 2020); *Padre no hay más que uno 3* ("Father there is only one 3," 2022); and *Padre no hay más que uno 4* ("Father there is only one 4," 2024).

1 The Wages of Whiteness in Late-Francoist Comedies

1 Other popular comedies that depict Northern European emigration include *París bien vale una moza* (dir. Pedro Lazaga, 1972), which is studied in this chapter, as well as *Lo verde empieza en los Pirineos* (dir. Vicente Escrivá, 1973) and *Préstame quince días* (dir. Fernando Merino, 1971). A non-comedic example from the so-called Tercera vía ("third way" or middlebrow cinema) is *Españolas en París* (dir. Roberto Bodegas, 1972). Collectively, these are very few films to address the subject considering that three million Spaniards emigrated to Northern Europe during the 1960s and 1970s.

2 Although examples abound, the opening scene of *Manolo, la nuit* (dir. Mariano Ozores, 1973) follows a similar formula. In this opening scene, Landa's character struts by a gaggle of *suecas* on the beach; inexplicably, his physically mediocre body, balding head with dark hair, and unexceptional facial features attract the interest of *suecas* despite the abundance of pale-skinned, athletic, blonde male tourists from Northern Europe.

3 In this chapter, I cite two volumes that were edited by Huerta Floriano and Pérez Morán: *El "cine de barrio" tardofranquista* and *El cine popular del tardofranquismo*. Despite their distinct titles, these two volumes are the fruit of a single multiyear study of late-Francoist popular cinema that was funded by Spain's now defunct Ministry of Science and Innovation and that was conducted in collaboration with numerous scholars between 2009 and 2012.

4 Because box office statistics were only collected from 1965 onward, exact numbers are not available for *Los económicamente débiles*, although Valeria Camporesi ranks it as one of the most successful domestic films of 1960–1 (123). Box office figures are available for all the other films on the online database *Catálogo de cine español*, which is operated by ICAA (Instituto de la Cinematografía y de las Artes Audiovisuales). The total number of viewers for each of these comedies was as follows: 1,082,360 for *París bien vale una moza*; 2,801,393 for *Las que tienen que servir*; 1,454,324 for *Una vez al año ser hippy no hace daño*; 1,325,191 for *El alma se serena*; and 1,328,813 for

Ligue story. As Manuel Palacio Arranz has noted, *Las que tienen que servir* ranked among the top-grossing domestic films during the period from 1966 to 1970 (17).

5 Richardson writes: "From 1959 to 1973 Spaniards saw the most pronounced period of growth in their country's history. In the early 1960s Spain was removed from the U.N. list of developing nations; within a decade Spain had become a world leader in the production of energy, automobiles and other industrial goods. Foreign investment during the decade blossomed from \$40 to \$697 million. Personal income skyrocketed from \$290 per capita in 1955 to \$497 in 1965 to \$2,486 a decade later … Universal education also became the norm with the number of university students quintupling from 1960 to 1975, marked by a steady increase in the numbers of female students" (66).

6 Scholars have observed a pronounced decline in cinema viewership beginning in the late 1960s that would continue through at least the 1980s (Palacio Arranz 19–22, Camporesi 75–7). This shift is widely attributed to competition from television, although Palacio Arranz also theorizes that a diversification of leisure options in general during this period would have also contributed to the decline of cinema viewership (30–2). Even so, both scholars' work attests to the enduring ability of some domestic popular genres, especially comedy, to attract large audiences despite this decline (Palacio Arranz 16–18, Camporesi 93–4). For more discussion of popular comedy after Franco's death, see chapter 4.

7 Although *Los económicamente débiles* does not feature the *macho ibérico / sueca* narrative, it shares numerous characteristics with films that did. These include: a thematic focus on working-class men; an upward mobility narrative; a reliance on *paleto* humour; as well as several cast and crew members whose careers would later be indelibly tied to *landismo*-style comedies, including its director Pedro Lazaga and actors such as José Luis López Vázquez and Antonio Ozores.

8 Rosalía Cornejo-Parriego and Louie Dean Valencia García have respectively examined the coverage of the American civil rights movement in *Triunfo* and *Cuadernos para el diálogo*, both of which were left-leaning Spanish cultural magazines that were widely distributed and read during the late-Franco era. Valencia García notes that the coverage of US civil rights in *Cuadernos* prompted reflection about potential parallelisms between strategies of resistance in the United States and those that might be enacted against Francoism in Spain (135). Cornejo-Parriego suggests that *Triunfo*'s coverage was motivated by a similar objective of promoting empathy with the civil rights movement; however, the magazine impeded its own objectives by spectacularizing and eroticizing the bodies of the American Black subjects it portrayed (158).

9 Although this law applied to all forms of sexual immorality, in practice, it applied primarily to relationships between Spanish men and Guinean women, given the scarcity of Spanish women in the colony (113–14). Nerín notes that while a number of men were punished under the law, interracial relations between Spanish men and Guinean women continued even after the law's passage. Furthermore, although marriage between Spanish men and Guinean women was theoretically legal, the dominant anti-miscegenation sentiment made it extremely rare (115–16).

2 Imperial Death

1 Spain acquired the territories that comprise present-day Equatorial Guinea from Portugal under the terms of the Treaty of El Pardo in 1778. It obtained control over present-day Ifni in 1860, after it was ceded by Morocco. Similarly, it acquired the Sahara Colony in 1884 as a consequence of the Conference of Berlin. Finally, it obtained the Moroccan Protectorate following a treaty signed with France in 1912. However, in all of these cases, it did not develop significant attempts to establish a significant colonial infrastructure in these colonies until the twentieth century.

2 As Gustau Nerín notes, in the early years of the twentieth century, support for colonialism in Africa was primarily driven by the military but was generally detested by the wider populace, who viewed it as a "useless waste of lives" (19). Popular opposition to African colonial endeavours became particularly acute during the Rif Wars, and was a significant motivating factor in the ascent to power of Primo de Rivera in 1923 (19).

3 Lusotropicalism was an ideological pillar of the Salazar dictatorship in Portugal; as Stucki writes, "It was based on a distorted interpretation and political exploitation" of the work of Brazilian intellectual Gilberto Freyre, who had "developed ideas regarding miscegenation as a positive factor in the former Portuguese colony of Brazil and beyond" ("Hard side" 143). Similarly, Hispanotropicalism also drew on the theory of *Hispanidad* proposed by Ramiro de Maeztu, which defended Spain's status as a *madre patria* of the Hispanic world. Finally, Nerín associates the theory's reliance on Regenerationism specifically with Joaquín Costa, a nineteenth-century Spanish intellectual who argued that Spain's geographical proximity and historical racial ties with Morocco made it better suited to colonize Africa than other European powers (Nerín 14–15).

4 Racial make-up on white actors had a long history in Spanish cinema before and after *Fray Escoba*. It was used in missionary films such as *Misión blanca* (1946) and *La manigua sin Dios* (1949), both of which featured the Spanish actor Jorge Mistral made up as a "Tarzan look-alike with oiled torso" despite the films' respective settings in eighteenth-century Paraguay and twentieth-century Spanish Guinea (Labanyi,

"Internalisations" 33). It was also used in the 1927 and 1951 versions of the musical melodrama *El negro que tenía el alma blanca* ("The Black man with a white soul"), a rare example of another film to feature a Black main character. At the beginning of the 1960s, the use of racial make-up was still widespread. It was used in *Rosa de Lima* to "indigenize" several Spanish actors (Pérez *Confessional Cinema* 52). Furthermore, a number of comedy films analysed in this book, including ones made both before and after Franco's death, also demonstrate the widespread use of racial makeup on white actors (see chapters 1 and 4).

5 As Rosalía Cornejo-Parriego and Louie Dean Valencia-García have shown, the US civil rights movement, including descriptions of racial violence, received ample coverage and discussion in publications such as *Triunfo* and *Cuadernos para el diálogo*, among others.

6 Lumumba was a Pan-African politician who led Congo to independence from Belgium in 1960 and served as its first prime minister. However, he was deposed and assassinated in early 1961 after he relied on Soviet help to quash the post-independence Katanga separatist movements. This was seen as problematic by Western powers, who saw Congo as a pawn in the larger Cold-War conflict. The Simbas were Lumumba's disillusioned followers.

7 On the horrors of the Macías regime, Michael Ugarte writes: "Almost as if he were imitating the early patterns of the Franco regime, by 1972 Macías had taken complete control of the government, outlawed all political parties except one (PUNT – Punto Único Nacional de Trabajadores), and assumed the title of president for life ... The Macías government was responsible for state-sponsored terror: mass executions, the exit of up to one-third of the entire population, imprisonment of thousands of citizens, pilferage, ignorance and neglect of rising malnutrition and infirmity that many citizens were forced to endure. The country's infrastructure ... fell into ruin. Even Catholicism came under attack, thus putting an end to formal education. The economy collapsed; skilled citizens and foreigners left for relatively less draconian places such as Cameroon, Gabon and Nigeria" (25, original parenthesis).

8 Examples of Jess Franco films that followed variations of this formula include *Voodoo Passion* (Switzerland, 1977), *White Cannibal Queen* (Spain, Italy, and France, 1980), *Cannibal Terror* (Spain and France, 1981) and *Macumba Sexual* (Spain, 1983).

3 From Andalusian Gypsies to *Urban Quinquis*

1 As explained in the introduction, throughout this book I use the word "Gypsy" to refer only to stereotypical representations of Roma characters in literature, theatre, and film (i.e., the "screen Gypsy.") I use the word

"Roma" as a preferred English-language equivalent for communities who refer to themselves in Spanish as "gitanos" or "romaníes." Likewise, I use the Spanish word *payo* to refer to non-Roma Spaniards who belong to the dominant racial majority.

2   The *mercheros* are a distinct, traditionally nomadic ethnic group who are often confused with the Roma and have sometimes been referred to as "gitanos blancos" ("white Gypsies") (Barranco Nadal 18). Although García-Egocheaga argues that only *mercheros* were associated with the terms *quinqui* and *quincallero*, Pérez-Rodríguez has compellingly demonstrated a significant semantic overlap between the terms *quinqui/quincallero* and *gitano* (Roma) in a range of case studies from the twentieth century Spanish press.

3   The films of José Antonio de la Loma, a foundational figure of *quinqui* cinema, especially thematize *payo*-Roma relations. For instance, *Perros callejeros* (1977) and *Perros callejeros II: Busca y captura* (1979) revolve around *payo*-Roma sexual relationships, while *Los últimos golpes de El Torete* (1980) and *Perras callejeras* (1985) centre *payo*-Roma criminal friendships. Likewise *Yo, El Vaquilla* (1985) centres its narrative on a Roma protagonist as well as many of his Roma family members. Roma storylines are less pronounced in the films of Eloy de la Iglesia, except arguably for *Colegas* (1982), which stars Antonio and Rosario Flores, the children of folkloric actress and dancer Lola Flores. Even so, *quinqui* films by de la Iglesia, de la Loma, and other directors were saturated in Roma slang and Roma music, something that is discussed at length in chapters 4 and 5 of Tom Whittaker's book *The Spanish Quinqui Film: Delinquency, Sound, Sensation*.

4   This is evidenced by the 1954 version of *Morena clara* (dir. Luis Lucia), a folkloric musical starring Lola Flores, whose opening sequence narrates the Roma's origin in ancient Egypt.

5   Woods Peiró notes that almost all major stars of the folkloric genre were white or *paya* women who played Gypsy roles without being Roma themselves. Of these, the most significant exceptions were Pastora Imperio, Carmen Amaya, and Lola Flores, the last of whom was only one quarter of Roma descent (135).

6   As Rothea notes, this law was originally passed under the Second Republic, but was one of a handful of laws that the dictatorship maintained, as it served as an effective "weapon against anyone considered a social or political deviant during the dictatorship" (14).

7   Eva Woods Peiró notes that most stars of the folkloric genre were known to be able to pass equally as Roma or *paya*. For instance, the iconic folkloric star Imperio Argentina "embodied the somatic normativity of an Iberian variant of Hispanic whiteness, a white face with dark-brown to black hair" (27). Likewise, Raquel Meller, another folkloric star, "could equally

be Italian, as much as French, Portuguese or Argentine" (Díaz de Quijano qtd. in Woods-Peiró 75). In *quinqui* films, Roma characters were sometimes played by darker-skinned characters like Frank Braña (El Esquinao in *Perros callejeros*), but were just as often played by fair-skinned, blond-haired actors like Nadia Windel (Isabel in *Perros callejeros*) and Bernard Seray (El Vaquilla in *Perros callejeros II* and *Los últimos golpes de El Torete*). In all of these cases, make-up was not used to darken the skin of actors with a light complexion.

8 Throughout this book, I cite or analyse a range of examples of Francoist and early post-Franco cinema in which Black, Arab, and Indigenous characters were played by Spanish actors in dark makeup. Some of these include: *Misión blanca* (1946), *La manigua sin dios* (1949), *El negro que tenía el alma blanca* (1951), *Los económicamente débiles* (1960), *Los energéticos* (1979), and *Es peligroso casarse a los 60* (1981).

9 The life of "El Lute" was portrayed in later *quinqui* films like *El Lute: Camina o revienta* ("El Lute: Run for your life," dir. Vicente Aranda, 1987) and *El Lute II: Mañana seré libre* ("El Lute II: Tomorrow I'll be free," dir. Vicente Aranda, 1988).

10 The story was widely reported in news media of the time. A summary of the events can be found in the article "Detención de banda de estafadores a la Seguridad Social francesa" ("Arrest of gang that scammed French Social Security," *La vanguardia española*, 3 March 1970).

11 "El cumaco de San Juan" was originally written by Francisco Delfín Pacheco and performed by Alfredo Sadel. "El negrito bembón" was originally written by Bobby Capó and performed by Ismael Rivera.

12 Although there is no study about interracial *payo*-Roma relationships from the 1970s, Calvo Buezas' surveys on teachers and students from the 1980s indicated that, during the latter decade, 48 per cent of teenage students responded that they would be unwilling to marry a Roma person, while 64.9 per cent of their teachers indicated the same attitude (78). In addition, 69.4 per cent of teachers said they would not want their child to marry a Roma person (78). Considering that anti-Roma prejudice was shared by both students and teachers despite their generational difference, we can safely assume that these attitudes were prevalent in the 1970s as well.

13 Calvo Buezas enumerates all of these conflicts in greater detail in *España racista*, pp. 15–19.

4 Whiteness under Siege

1 All statistics about film viewership cited in this chapter come from the database of Spanish cinema operated by the Ministry of Culture and Sport (https://infoicaa.mecd.es/CatalogoICAA/es-es).

2 The full titles of the *Torrente* films are: *Torrente, el brazo tonto de la ley*
   ("Torrente, the dumb arm of the law," 1998); *Torrente 2: Misión en Marbella*
   ("Torrente 2: Mission in Marbella," 2001); *Torrente 3: El protector* ("Torrente
   3: The protector," 2005); *Torrente 4: Crisis letal* ("Torrente 4: Lethal
   crisis," 2011); and *Torrente 5: Operación Eurovegas* ("Torrente 5: Operation
   Eurovegas," 2014). The full titles of the *Padre* films are: *Padre no hay más que
   uno* ("Father there is only one," 2019); *Padre no hay más que uno 2: La llegada
   de la suegra* ("Father There is only one 2: The arrival of mother-in-law,"
   2020); *Padre no hay más que uno 3* ("Father there is only one 3," 2022); and
   Padre no hay más que uno 4 ("Father there is only one 4," 2024).
3 The handful of studies that have analysed these films include the articles
   "Comedia subgenérica" and "Las comedias de Mariano Ozores" by
   Miguel Ángel Huerta Floriano and Ernesto Pérez Morán, the article
   "Hormones and Silk" by Alejandro Melero, and the chapter "La comedia
   de mariquitas" from Melero's book *Placeres ocultos* (pp. 142–80). All
   of these studies dedicate significantly more attention to the films'
   homophobia and misogyny than to their engagement with racial issues.
4 The surge in feminist activism during the Transition is evidenced by the
   formation of a plethora of associations like the *Frente de Liberación de la
   Mujer* ("Women's Liberation Front") in 1976 and the *Organización Feminista
   Revolucionaria* ("Revolutionary Feminist Organization") in 1977, among
   others (S. Bermúdez et al. 416–19). It is also evidenced by a proliferation
   of feminist publications, ranging from the magazine *Vindicación Feminista*
   ("Feminist Vindication," 1976–8) to Lidia Falcón's double-volume work
   La razón feminista ("Feminist reason," 1981–2) (Bermúdez et al. 418–19).
   Likewise, queer activism also expanded dramatically during these years
   through the work of gay activist associations like *Movimiento Español de
   Liberación Homosexual* (Spanish Movement for Homosexual Liberation,
   1972–7) or *Front d'Alliberament Gai de Catalunya* (Gay Liberation Front
   of Catalonia) (1975–present), among others (Melero, *Placeres ocultos*
   37–46). In addition to activism, queer culture obtained a high degree of
   visibility during this period due to the celebration of the first Gay Pride
   events in Barcelona in 1978 and Madrid in 1979. It was also evident in the
   widespread practice of *travesti* or cross-dressing culture, which has been
   discussed in studies by Iñaki Estella and Valeria Vegas.
5 In the wake of Franco's death, many films openly addressed alternative
   gender and sexual identities such as transgenderism, cross-dressing, and
   both male and female homosexuality. Under Francoism, these subjects
   had been considered taboo and were alluded to only obliquely, if at all.
   Some of the most prominent Transition-era films to address these topics
   include: films by Eloy de la Iglesia such as *Placeres ocultos* ("Hidden
   pleasures," 1977) and *El diputado* ("The deputy," 1978), which address
   male homosexuality; *Me siento extraña* ("I feel strange," dir. Enrique

Martí Maqueda, 1977), one of the first Spanish films to represent a lesbian love story; *Cambio de sexo* (dir. Vicente Aranda, 1977), an exploration of transgenderism that starred prominent trans actress Bibiana Fernández; and *Ocaña: retrat intermitent* ("Ocaña: An intermittent portrait, dir. Ventura Pons, 1978), a documentary that discusses the cross-dressing performance art of José Pérez Ocaña. Although some of these films sensationalized their subject matter in various ways, their intention of deepening society's understanding about these previously taboo subjects sets them apart from Ozores' comedies, which aimed to stigmatize sexual and gender deviance as a source of humour.

6 For further information on this subject, see the following studies: Polly Pallister-Wilkins, "The Tensions on the Ceuta and Melilla Border Fences;" and Iker Barbero and Mariona Illamola-Dausà, "Deportations without the Right to Complaint: Cases from Spain." In addition, the documentary *Tarajal* (dir. Xavi Artigas and Xapo Ortega, 2016) offers an in-depth exploration of a 2014 incident at Tarajal beach near Ceuta, in which an illegal pushback attempt by the Guardia Civil, which included the use of rubber bullets, resulted in the drowning deaths of fourteen African migrants.

7 In this section of the chapter, all the films I cite were directed by Ozores unless otherwise noted.

8 Because a majority of these films featured male protagonists, they devote significantly more attention to male Arab or Moorish characters, who were usually villains, than to female ones. A noticeable exception is the historical parody *Juana la loca ... de vez en cuando* ("Joan the Mad ... sometimes," dir. José Ramón Larraz, 1983), which ridicules the historical figure of Joan the Mad by portraying her as hysterically vengeful against her Moorish rival Zoraida.

9 Many of Wilson's films highlighted her gender ambivalence without outing her as transgender. For instance, in the Italian sexploitation thriller *Eva Man* (dir. Antonio D'Agostino, 1980), Wilson's character helps rescue an intersex friend who has been kidnapped for her artificially enhanced sexual powers – a role which strongly accentuates Wilson's own gender ambiguity. Similarly, in *Macumba sexual* (dir. Jess Franco, 1983), Wilson's character, an African goddess who sexually enslaves men and women alike, possesses conspicuously masculine and feminine traits.

10 Although it is difficult to estimate precise figures, the visibility of Equatorial Guinean students in Spain from the 1960s onward is a well-known phenomenon that has been documented by Ndongo-Bidyogo and many others.

11 Yolanda Aixelà-Cabré notes that the ascent to power of both the Macías and Obiang regimes produced significant waves of migration to Spain that numbered at least in the thousands. She also notes that scholars have

estimated that approximately 100,000 emigrated from Equatorial Guinea between the 1970s and the 1990s, with Spain serving as the largest home of Equatorial Guinea's diaspora.

12 Antonio Machín (1903–1977) was an Afro-Cuban musician born to a Cuban mother and Spanish father; he settled in Madrid in the 1930s and lived there until his death. The allusion to him in *La Lola* … draws on his Blackness, his Cuban identity, and his status as an immigrant to construe him as a real-life embodiment of the fictional Porfirio.

13 As López Frías explains, this is a process by which fans use an online platform to gather interest in special theatre screenings of old films; a film is shown if a minimum number of viewers commits to buying tickets.

14 José Manuel Serrano Cueto's attempted remake, *Yo quise hacer Los Bingueros 2*, ended up as a documentary short rather than a feature length fiction film due to lack of financing.

15 The acronym "EGB" refers to *Educación General Básica* ("Basic General Education"), a term used to describe educational standards in Spain that were in effect between 1970 and 1990.

16 An article published in *El Mundo* gathered several of the most amusing parodies of Vox's tweet from Twitter ("Santi Abascal 'reconquista' Andalucía a caballo"). In many of these parodies, the music from *The Lord of the Rings* that was originally used to accompany Vox's video was replaced with music from various other popular film and television programs. Some of these included: *Curro Jiménez*, a Spanish television series from the 1970s that portrayed nineteenth century Andalusian banditry; the American Western series *Bonanza* of the 1950s and 1960s; and the theme from the spaghetti western *The Good, the Bad, and the Ugly* (dir. Sergio Leone, 1966); among others.

Conclusion

1 Other than *Palmeras en la nieve* ("Palm trees in the snow," dir. Fernando González Molina, 2015), fiction films that have addressed the African empire between 1975 and the present include: *Los baúles del retorno* ("Return luggage," dir. María Miró, 1995); *Lejos de África* ("Far from Africa," dir. Cecilia Bartolomé, 1996); and *La marcha verde* ("The green march," dir. José Luis García Sánchez, 2002). Feature-length documentary films to address the African empire from the same period include: *Hijos de las nubes, la última colonia* ("Children of the clouds, the last colony" dir. Álvaro Longoria, 2012), which won the 2012 Goya award for Best Documentary; *África 815* (dir. Pilar Monsell, 2014); *El escritor de un país sin librerías* ("The writer from a country with no bookstores," dir. Marc Serena, 2019); and *Memorias de ultramar* ("Memories from overseas,"

dir. Carmen Bellas and Alberto Berzosa, 2021). As the database of the Filmoteca Española indicates, all of these films achieved limited audiences in theatres, numbering about 25,000 viewers or less.

2 As in previous chapters, box office statistics come from the database of the Filmoteca Española unless otherwise noted.

3 As Álvarez Chillida notes, some of the film's most prominent historical errors include its gross oversimplification of colonial Guinea's ethnic makeup (253), its exaggerated, chronologically incorrect portrayal of anti-white violence committed by Blacks (256–7), and its portrayal of certain spaces as welcoming to Blacks that historically were segregated (256).

4 As González-Leonardo et al. have noted, although the population of Spain grew between 2000 and 2020 by 17 per cent, this growth is undergirded by notable tendencies towards depopulation, as about 63 per cent of Spanish municipalities experienced population decline during those same years. Likewise, they note that Spain has been projected by the United Nations to undergo population decline on a national scale from 2022. Valentina Romei further notes that Spain and other Southern European countries such as Portugal, Greece, and Italy "are among the top-ten world economies with the lowest number of births per woman."

5 For a complete discussion and analysis of these allusions, see Ana Mejón and Rubén Romero Santos's article "Perdiendo el norte: Una brújula para la crisis."

Film and Television References

A todos nos gusta el plátano. Directed by Rubén H. Bermúdez, 16 de Febrero Films, 2021.

África 815. Directed by Pilar Monsell, Proxemica Films, 2014.

Agítese antes de usarla. Directed by Mariano Ozores, Ízaro Films, 1983.

Alba de América. Directed by Juan de Orduña, CIFESA, 1951.

El alma se serena. Directed by José Luis Sáenz de Heredia, Chapalo Films, 1970.

Amor a todo gas. Directed by Ramón Torrado, PICASA, 1969.

Amor brujo. Directed by Francisco Rovira Beleta, Exclusivas Floralva Producción, 1967.

El amor y la ira: Cartografía del acoso antigitano. Directed by José Heredia Moreno. YouTube: Published on 17 May 2015. https://www.youtube .com/watch?v=jsWcYE3De0A&ab_channel=Jos%C3%A9Heredia

¡Ay, Carmela! Directed by Carlos Saura, Iberoamericana Films Internacional, 1990.

Balarrasa. Directed by José Antonio Nieves Conde, Aspa Producciones Cinematográficas, 1951.

Battle of Algiers. Directed by Gillo Pontecorvo, Casbah Films, 1966.

Los baúles del retorno. Directed by María Miró, Figaro Films, 1995.

Un beso en el puerto. Directed by Ramón Torrado, Arturo González Producciones Cinematográficas, 1965.

Bienvenido, Mr. Marshall. Directed by Luis García Berlanga, UNINCI, 1953.

Bienvenido, Padre Murray. Directed by Ramón Torrado, Copercines, 1964.

Los bingueros. Directed by Mariano Ozores, Ízaro Films, 1979.

The Birth of a Nation. Directed by David W. Griffith, Epoch Producing Corporation, 1915.

Black Aphrodite. Directed by Pavlos Filippou, Andromeda International
 Films, 1977.
Blanc i negre. Directed by Jan Baca and Toni Garriga, Central del Curt,
 1974.
Bonanza. Created by David Dotort and Fred Hamilton, NBC, 1959–73.
Bwana. Directed by Imanol Uribe, CARTEL, 1996.
Cambio de sexo. Directed by Vicente Aranda, Morgana Films, 1977.
Carmen y Lola. Directed by Arantxa Echevarría, HBO Max, 2018.
Las cartas de Alou. Directed by Montxo Armendáriz, Elías Querejeta
 Producciones Cinematográficas, 1990.
Los chulos. Directed by Mariano Ozores, Bermúdez de Castro, 1981.
El Cid. Directed by Anthony Mann, Samuel Bronston Productions,
 1961.
El Cid Cabreador. Directed by Angelino Fons, José Frade Producciones
 Cinematográfica, 1983.
Cine de barrio. Directed by Francisco Quintanar, Sebastián Junyent,
 José Manuel Parada, and Machús Osinaga, Televisión Española,
 1995–present.
La ciudad no es para mí. Directed by Pedro Lazaga, Pedro Masó
 Producciones Cinematográficas, 1966.
Ciutat morta. Directed by Xavier Artigas and Xapo Ortega,
 Metromuster, 2014.
Colegas. Directed by Eloy de la Iglesia, Ópalo Films, 1982.
Con el viento solano. Directed by Mario Camus, Pro Artis Ibérica, 1966.
Cosas que dejé en La Habana. Directed by Manuel Gutiérrez Aragón,
 Canal+ España, 1997.
Cristo negro. Directed by Ramón Torrado, Copercines, 1963.
Cristóbal Colón, de oficio … descubridor. Directed by Mariano Ozores,
 Constan Films, 1982.
Una cruz en el infierno. Directed by José María Elorrieta, Universitas
 Films, 1954.
Cuando los niños vienen de Marsella. Directed by José Luis Sáenz de
 Heredia, Arturo González Producciones Cinematográficas, 1974.
Las cuatro bodas de Marisol. Directed by Luis Lucia, Guión Producciones
 Cinematográficas, 1967.
Curro Jiménez. Performances by Sancho Gracia and José Sancho, Radio
 Televisión Española, 1976–9.
El diputado. Directed by Eloy de la Iglesia, Figaro Films, 1978.
Los económicamente débiles. Directed by Pedro Lazaga, Ágata Films SA,
 1960.
En tierra extraña. Directed by Icíar Bollaín, Tormenta Films, 2014.
Encrucijada para una monja. Directed by Julio Buchs, Ízaro Films, 1967.

Los energéticos. Directed by Mariano Ozores, Bermúdez de Castro, 1979.

Entre tinieblas. Directed by Pedro Almodóvar, Tesauro, 1983.

Esa mujer. Directed by Mario Camus, Cesáreo González Producciones Cinematográficas, 1969.

El escritor de un país sin librerías. Directed by Marc Serena, Toned Media, 2019.

Españistán. Directed by Aleix Saló. YouTube: Published on 25 May 2011).

Españolas en París. Directed by Roberto Bodegas, Ágata Films SA, 1971.

Eva Man. Directed by Antonio D'Agostino, Zodiac Produzioni,1980.

Flores de otro mundo. Directed by Icíar Bollaín, Producciones La Iguana SL, 1999.

Fray Escoba. Directed by Ramón Torrado, Copercines, 1961.

The Good, the Bad and the Ugly. Directed by Sergio Leone, Produzioni Europee Associate, 1966.

La gran familia. Directed by Fernando Palacios, Pedro Masó Producciones Cinematográficas, 1962.

Guess Who's Coming to Dinner. Directed by Stanley Kramer, Columbia Pictures, 1967.

Hijos de las nubes, la última colonia. Directed by Álvaro Longoria, Candescent Films, 2012.

Historia de nuestro cine. Directed by Francisco Quintanar, Javier Jado, and Elena S. Sánchez, Televisión Española, 2015–present.

Idrissa: Chronicle of an Ordinary Death. Directed by Xavier Artigas and Xapo Ortega, Metromuster, 2018.

Juana la loca … de vez en cuando. Directed by José Ramón Larraz, Constan Films, 1983.

Las que tienen que servir. Directed by José María Forqué, Ágata Films SA, 1967.

Lejos de África. Directed by Cecilia Bartolomé, Marea Films, 1996.

La ley de una raza. Directed by José Luis Gonçalvo, Alianza Cinematográfica Española, 1969.

Los liantes. Directed by Mariano Ozores, Ízaro Films, 1981.

Ligue Story. Directed by Alfonso Paso, Arturo González Producciones Cinematográficas, 1972.

Llenos de gracia. Directed by Roberto Bueso, Mod Producciones, 2022.

Lo nunca visto. Directed by Marina Seresesky, Tandem Films, 2019.

Lo verde empieza en los Pirineos. Directed by Vicente Escrivà, Filmayer, 1973.

Locura de amor. Directed by Juan de Orduña, CIFESA, 1948.

La Lola nos lleva al huerto. Directed by Mariano Ozores, Ízaro Films, 1984.

The Lord of the Rings: The Fellowship of the Ring. Directed by Peter Jackson, New Line Cinema, 2001.

El Lute: Camina o revienta. Directed by Vicente Aranda, MGC Producciones Cinematográficas y Audiovisuales, 1987.

El Lute II: Mañana seré libre. Directed by Vicente Aranda, Allumination Filmworks, 1988.

Macumba Sexual. Directed by Jess Franco, Golden Films Internacional,1983.

Madres paralelas. Directed by Pedro Almodóvar, El Deseo, 2021.

La manigua sin Dios. Directed by Arturo Ruiz-Castillo, Taurus Films, 1949.

Manolo, la nuit. Directed by Mariano Ozores, Filmayer, 1973.

La marcha verde. Directed by José Luis García Sánchez, Lolafilms, 2002.

Marisol rumbo a Río. Directed by Fernando Palacios, Cesáreo González Producciones Cinematográficas, 1963.

Me has hecho perder el juicio. Directed by Juan de Orduña, Arturo González Producciones Cinematográficas, 1973.

Me siento extraña. Directed by Enrique Martí Marqueda, Alborada PC, 1977.

Memorias de ultramar. Directed by Carmen Bellas and Alberto Berzosa, Filmoteca Española, 2021.

El mesón del gitano. Directed by Antonio Román, Cesáreo González Producciones Cinematográficas, 1969.

La mies es mucha. Directed by José Luis Saenz de Heredia, Chapalo Films SA, 1949.

Misión blanca. Directed by Juan de Orduña, Colonial AJE, 1946.

Molokai, la isla maldita. Directed by Luis Lucia, Europea de Cine SA, 1959.

Morena clara. Directed by Luis Lucia, CIFESA, 1954.

El negro que tenía el alma blanca. Directed by Benito Perojo, Goya Producciones Cinematográficas SA, 1928.

El negro que tenía el alma blanca. Directed by Benito Perojo, Balart y Simó, 1934.

El negro que tenía el alma blanca. Directed by Hugo del Carril, CIFESA, 1951.

La noche de los brujos. Directed by Armando de Ossorio, Hesperia Films SA, 1974.

The Nude Princess. Directed by Cesare Canevari, Andromeda Srl, 1976.

Ocaña: Retrat intermitent. Directed by Ventura Pons, Producciones Zeta, 1978.

Padre no hay más que dos. Directed by Mariano Ozores, Ízaro Films, 1982.

Padre no hay más que uno. Directed by Santiago Segura, Atresmedia, 2019.

Padre no hay más que uno 2: La llegada de la suegra. Directed by Santiago Segura, Atresmedia Cine, 2020.

Padre no hay más que uno 3. Directed by Santiago Segura, Atresmedia Cine, 2022.

Padre no hay más que uno 4. Directed by Santiago Segura, Sony Pictures España, 2024.

Pajares and CIA. Directed by Carlos Torres, Atresmedia Televisión, 2022.

Palmeras en la nieve. Directed by Fernando González Molina, Atresmedia, 2015.

The Parent Trap. Directed by David Swift, Walt Disney Productions, 1961.

París bien vale una moza. Directed by Pedro Lazaga, Estudios Roma, 1972.

Es peligroso casarse a los 60. Directed by Mariano Ozores, Filmayer, 1981.

Perdiendo el norte. Directed by Nacho Velilla, Producciones Aparte, 2015.

Peret: Jo soc la rumba. Directed by Paloma Zapata, La Fábrica Naranja, 2018.

Pero … ¿en qué país vivimos? Directed by José Luis Sáenz de Heredia, Arturo González Producciones Cinematográficas, 1967.

Perras callejeras. Directed by José Antonio de la Loma, Araba Films, 1985.

Perros callejeros. Directed by José Antonio de la Loma, Films Zodíaco, 1977.

Perros callejeros II: Busca y captura. Directed by José Antonio de la Loma, Films Zodíaco Prozesa, 1979.

Piedra de toque. Directed by Julio Buchs, Asturias Films, 1963.

La piel que habito. Directed by Pedro Almodóvar, El Deseo, 2011.

La piel quemada. Directed by Josep María Forn, Teide PC, 1967.

Placeres ocultos. Directed by Eloy de la Iglesia, Alborada PC, 1977.

Poltergeist. Directed by Tobe Hooper, Metro-Goldwyn-Mayer, 1982.

Préstame quince días. Directed by Fernando Merino, Atlántida Filma, 1972.

Proud Roma (2022). Directed by Pablo Vega, European Roma Institute for Arts and Culture, 2021.

Robin Hood: Men in Tights. Directed by Mel Brooks, Brooksfilms, 1993.

Rosa de Lima. Directed by José María Elorrieta, Unión Coop. Cinematográfica, 1962.

Selfie. Directed by Víctor García León, Apache Films, 2017.

Snow White and the Seven Dwarves. Directed by William Cottrell, David Hand, and Wilfred Jackson, Walt Disney Animation Studios, 1937.

Tacones lejanos. Directed by Pedro Almodóvar, El Deseo, 1991.

Tarajal. Directed by Xavier Artigas, Xapo Ortega and Marc Serra. Metromuster, 2016.

Los Tarantos. Directed by Francisco Rovira-Beleta, Mercurio Films, SA, 1963.

Taxi. Directed by Carlos Saura, Canal+ España, 1996.

Teresa de Jesús. Directed by Juan de Orduña, Agrupa Films, 1962.

Thi Mai, Rumbo a Vietnam. Directed by Patricia Ferreira, Atresmedia Cine, 2017.

Todos al suelo. Directed by Mariano Ozores, Bermúdez de Castro, 1982.

Tómbola. Directed by Luis Lucia, Guión Producciones Cinematográficas, 1962.

Torrente, el brazo tonto de la ley. Directed by Santiago Segura, CARTEL, 1998.

Torrente 2: Misión en Marbella. Directed by Santiago Segura, Amiguetes Entertainment, 2001.

Torrente 3: El protector. Directed by Santiago Segura, Amiguetes Entertainment, 2005.

Torrente 4: Crisis letal. Directed by Santiago Segura, Amiguetes Entertainment, 2011.

Torrente 5: Operación Eurovegas. Directed by Santiago Segura. Amiguetes Entertainment, 2014.

El tren de la memoria. Directed by Marta Arribas and Ana Pérez, Producciones La Iguana SL, 2005.

Los últimos golpes de El Torete. Directed by José Antonio de La Loma, CB Films, SA, 1980.

Vente a Alemania, Pepe. Directed by Pedro Lazaga, Filmayer, 1971.

Una vez al año ser hippy no hace daño. Directed by Javier Aguirre, Ágata Films SA, 1969.

Viaje a la explotación. Directed by Mercè Conesa, Joan Simó, Rosa Babí and Bartolomeu Vilà, Cooperativa de Cinema Alternatiu, 1974.

¡Vivan los novios! Directed by Luis García Berlanga, Suevia Films, 1970.

Yo, El Vaquilla. Directed by José Antonio de la Loma, Golden Sun, 1985.

Yo hice a Roque III. Directed by Mariano Ozores, Ízaro Films, 1980.

Yo quise hacer Los Bingueros 2. Directed by José Manuel Serrano Cueto, Creta Producciones, 2016.

Zorrita Martínez. Directed by Vicente Escrivà, Aspa Producciones Cinematográficas, 1975.

Works Cited

Abadía-Rexach, Bárbara. "(Re) pensando la negritud en la música popular puertorriqueña." *Revista de Ciencias Sociales*, vol. 21, Jan. 2009, pp. 8–43.

Abascal, Santiago [santi_abascal]. "En el pico #Tologorri #SierraSalvada #Alava #España. Estrando la camiseta de la #guardiacivil que me ha regalado un amigo." *Instagram*, 2 Sept. 2017, https://www.instagram. com/p/BYisq2shDT2/?hl=en.

Aguilar, Carlos and Anita Haas. *Flamenco y cine*. Cátedra, 2019.

Aixelà-Cabré, Yolanda. "Entre las dictaduras y el petróleo: Las migraciones trasnacionales de Guinea Ecuatorial." *Revista Andaluza de Antropología*, vol. 3, Jan. 2012, pp. 89–103.

Albert Sopale, Silvia. "No es país para negras." *Sillas en la frontera: Mujeres, teatro y migraciones*, edited by Concha Fernández Soto, Editorial Universidad de Almería, 2018, pp. 88–107.

Allan, Joanna. *Women, Dictatorships, and Genderwashing in Western Sahara and Equatorial Guinea*. U of Wisconsin P, 2021.

Aller, María. "Las 30 películas españolas más taquilleras de la historia." *Fotogramas*, 14 May 2022, https://www.fotogramas.es/noticias-cine /g39950716/peliculas-espanolas-taquilleras/.

Álvarez Chillida, Gonzalo. "El proceso de descolonización de Guinea Ecuatorial." *España frente a la independencia de Marruecos*, edited by Martín Corrales, Eloy, Edicions Bellaterra, 2017, pp. 71–92.

Álvarez Chillida, Gonzalo. "Palmeras en la nieve: El éxito de una visión de la colonización española en Guinea Ecuatorial." *Spagna contemporanea*, no. 50, 2016, pp. 251–63.

Añaños, Elena, Anna Valli, and Bárbara Gamero Huertas. "¿Cómo perciben los niños la Publicidad de Cola Cao?" Grupo de Investigación en Psicología, Comunicación y Publicidad, Universidad Autónoma de Barcelona, 2005.

Aranda, José Luis. "Dibujos para entender la crisis." *El País*, 21 June 2011, https://elpais.com/politica/2011/06/21/actualidad/1308688459_242294 .html.

"Arantxa Echevarría: 'Quiero seguir rodando con las tripas.'" *La Vanguardia*, 30 Sept. 2019, https://www.lavanguardia.com/vida/20190930/47732171322 /arantxa-echevarria-quiero-seguir-rodando-con-las-tripas.html.

Arenas, José Eduardo. "'Fui vetado por Pilar Miró,' dice Mariano Ozores en Las Palmas." *ABC.es*, 12 Mar. 2002, https://www.abc.es/play/cine /abci-vetado-pilar-miro-dice-mariano-ozores-palmas-200203120300-84528 _noticia.html.

Arondo, Maria. *Moi, la bonne.* Stock, 1975.

Ayanz, Miguel. "Mariano Ozores: 'Hay que hacer una película sobre Podemos.'" *El Español*, 19 Jan. 2016, https://www.elespanol.com/series /cine/20160119/95740448_0.html.

Ballesteros, Isolina. *Immigration Cinema in the New Europe.* Intellect, 2015.

Barbero, Iker, and Mariona Illamola-Dausà. "Deportations without the Right to Complaint: Cases from Spain." *Fundamental Rights Challenges in Border Controls and Expulsion of Irregular Immigrants in the European Union*, edited by Sergio Carrera and Marco Stefan, Routledge, 2020, pp. 43–63.

Barranco Nadal, Juan Carlos. "Avance para un estudio de los gitanos en la toponimia valenciana." *La linde*, no. 8, 2017, pp. 10–58.

Bela-Lobedde, Desirée. *Ser mujer negra en España.* Penguin Random House Grupo Editorial, 2019.

– *Minorías: Historias de desigualdad y valentía.* Penguin Random House Grupo Editorial, 2021.

Benítez, Jorge. "Fernando Esteso y los 40 años de 'Los Bingueros': 'Todo lo que tocábamos pajares y yo era un éxito.'" *El Mundo*, 16 July 2019, https://www. elmundo.es/papel/historias/2019/07/16/5d2c5761fc6c833c0b8b45e6.html.

Bermudez, Anastasia, and Elisa Brey. "Is Spain Becoming a Country of Emigration Again? Data Evidence and Public Responses." *South-North Migration of EU Citizens in Times of Crisis*, edited by Jean-Michel Lafleur and Miolaj Stanek, Springer Open, 2017, pp. 83–98.

Bermúdez, Rubén H. *And You, Why Are You Black?* Phree, 2019.

Bermúdez, Silvia. *Rocking the Boat: Migration and Race in Contemporary Spanish Music.* U of Toronto P, 2018.

Bermúdez, Silvia, Asunción Bernárdez Rodal, and Ana Paula Ferreira. "Panorama histórico en la Península Ibérica: de 1974/1975 a 1994/1996." *Una nueva historia de los feminismos ibéricos*, edited by Silvia Bermúdez and Roberta Johnson, *Tirant humanidades*, 2021, pp. 415–30.

Bizet, Georges, et al. *Bizet: Carmen.* 2005.

Bonilla-Silva, Eduardo. *Racism without Racists: Color-Blind Racism and the Persistence of Racial Inequality in America.* Rowman and Littlefield, 2022.

Bonnett, Alastair. "A White World? Whiteness and the Meaning of Modernity in Latin America and Japan." *Working through Whiteness: International Perspectives*, edited by Cynthia Levine-Rasky, SUNY Press, 2002, pp. 69–105.

Britland, Joanne. "La crisis, la risa y catarsis: The 2008 Financial Crash and Comedic Representations of Spanish Emigration." *Hispanic Studies Review*, vol. 4, no. 1, 2019, pp. 26–39.

– "El 'Selfie' de la España poscrisis: Una autorreflexión a través del mockumentary." *Crear entre mundos: Nuevas tendencias en la metaficción española*, edited by Iana Konstantinova and Sabrina S. Laroussi, Albatros, 2021, pp. 51–67.

Brodkin Sacks, Karen. *How Jews Became White Folks and What That Says about Race in America*. Rutgers UP, 2010.

Calvo Buezas, Tomás. *España racista?: Voces payas sobre los gitanos*. Editorial Anthropos, 1990.

"Carmen y Lola: Una película sobre el amor entre dos adolescentes gitanas que ha desatado la polémica." *La Vanguardia*, 31 Aug. 2018, https://www .lavanguardia.com/cultura/20180831/451543786863/carmen-y-lola -pelicula-amor-adolescentes-gitanas-polemica.html.

Camporesi, Valeria. *Para grandes y chicos: Un cine para los españoles, 1940–1990*. Turfan, 1994.

Campos Serrano, Alicia. "The Decolonization of Equatorial Guinea: The Relevance of the International Factor." *The Journal of African History*, vol. 44, Mar. 2003, pp. 95–116.

Canicio, Víctor. *Vida de un emigrante español: El testimonio auténtico de un obrero que emigró a Alemania*. Gedisa, 1979.

Castan Pinos, Jaume. "Building Fortress Europe? Schengen and the Cases of Ceuta and Melilla." *Centre for International Border Research*, 2009, pp. 1–29, https://www.researchgate.net/publication/251750668_Building_Fortress _Europe_Schengen_and_the_Cases_of_Ceuta_and_Melilla.

Castro de Paz, José Luis. "Ramón Torrado, un asalariado del cine bajo el régimen de Franco." 1993, *Cervantes Virtual*, http://www.cervantesvirtual.com/obra -visor/ramon-torrado-un-asalariado-del-cine-bajo-el-regimen-de-franco--0 /html/.

Cervantes Saavedra, Miguel de, and Harry Sieber. *La gitanilla*. Ed. Cátedra, 2015.

Chadderton, Charlotte. *Judith Butler, Race and Education*. Palgrave Macmillan, 2019.

Charnon-Deutsch, Lou. *The Spanish Gypsy: The History of a European Obsession*. Pennsylvania State UP, 2004.

Chen, Paloma. "Toda la vida." *Invocación a las mayorías silenciosas*, Letra Versal, 2022, pp. 91–2.

Coleman, Jeffrey K. *The Necropolitical Theater: Race and Immigration on the Contemporary Spanish Stage*. Northwestern UP, 2020.

Cornejo-Parriego, Rosalía. "Black Is Beautiful: Cuerpos negros en *Triunfo*." *Journal of Iberian and Latin American Studies*, vol. 3, no. 2, 2017, pp. 157–73.

Crumbaugh, Justin. *Destination Dictatorship: The Spectacle of Spain's Tourist Boom and the Reinvention of Difference*. SUNY P, 2010.

–. "'Spain Is Different': Touring Late Francoist Cinema with Manolo Escobar." *Hispanic Research Journal*, vol. 3, no. 3, pp. 261–76.

Cuesta, Mery. "Trenzar el mito: Volteretas estéticas, cine de urgencia y prensa sensacionalista." *Quinquis dels 80: cinema, premsa i carrer*, edited by Armanda Cuesta, Centre de Cultura Contemporánia de Barcelona, 2009, pp. 64–103.

Davis, Angela. "Rape, Racism and the Capitalist Setting." *The Black Scholar*, vol. 9, no. 7, 1978, pp. 24–30.

de León Hernández, Julia. "El antigitanismo y la Transición española: Un punto y seguido en un viaje secular a través de la construcción de una identidad cultural racializada." (Paper presented at ALCES XXI conference, 13–15 July 2020).

DeGuzmán, María. *Spain's Long Shadow: The Black Legend, Off-Whiteness, and Anglo-American Empire*. U of Minnesota P.

"Detención de banda de estafadores a la seguridad social francesa." *La Vanguardia Española*, 3 Mar. 1970.

Donovan, Mary Kate. *Chinese Spaniards: Race, Migration, and Representation in Contemporary Spain*. Book manuscript in progress.

– "Memory and Migrant Solidarity in Icíar Bollaín's *En tierra extraña*." *Journal of Spanish Cultural Studies*, vol. 21, no. 4, pp. 547–64.

– "'Se Ríen de La Crisis': Chinese Immigration as Economic Invasion in Spanish Film and Media." *Revista de Estudios Hispánicos*, vol. 51, no. 2, 2017, pp. 369–93.

Du Bois, W. E. B. *Black Reconstruction in America: Toward a History of the Part Which Black Folk Played in the Attempt to Reconstruct Democracy in America, 1860–1880*. Routledge, 2017.

– *The Philadelphia Negro*. Edited by Isabel Eaton, Cosimo, 2007.

– *The Souls of Black Folk*. Edited by Brent Hayes Edwards, Oxford UP, 2007.

– "The Souls of White Folk." *W.E.B. Du Bois: Writings*, Library of America, 1986, pp. 923–38.

Dyer, Richard. *Stars*, British Film Institute, 1998.

– *White*. Routledge, 2002.

El Hachmi, Najat. *L'últim patriarca*. Planeta, 2008.

Elena, Alberto. *La llamada de África: Estudios sobre el cine colonial español*. Edicions Bellaterra, 2010.

– "Representaciones de la inmigración en el cine español: La producción comercial y sus márgenes. *Archivos de la Filmoteca*, no. 49, 2005, pp. 55–65.

Epps, Brad. "Impressions of Africa: Desire, Sublimation and Looking 'Otherwise' in Three Spanish Colonial Films." *Spanish Erotic Cinema*, edited by Santiago Fouz-Hernández, Edinburgh UP, 2017, pp. 37–54.

Espinosa y Maribet, Silvia. "Análisis de un jingle icónico: ¿Por qué cuesta tanto crear otro 'Negrito del Cola-Cao?'" *Actas del II Congreso Publiradio,* Icono 14, 2012.

Estella, Iñaki. "The Collective Scene: Transvestite Cabaret during the End of Francoist Spain." *Transgender Studies Quarterly,* vol. 8., no. 4, 2021, pp. 498–515.

Evans, Peter. "Marisol: The Spanish Cinderella." *Spanish Popular Cinema,* edited by Antonio Lázaro Reboll and Andrew Willis, Manchester UP, 2004, pp. 129–51.

Faulkner, Sally. *A Cinema of Contradiction: Spanish Film in the 1960s.* Edinburgh UP, 2006.

Fernández, Iago. "Fui a ver 'Los bingueros' de Pajares y Esteso con las musas del destape." *Vice,* 10 Mar. 2016, https://www.vice.com/es/article/8gj8j5/los-bingueros-ozores-pajares-esteso-destape-cine-1003.

Fernández Asperilla, Ana Isabel. "El asociacionismo de los emigrantes españoles en Europa: Rupturas y continuidades." *Historia social,* no. 70, 2011, pp. 135–53.

– "La emigración como exportación de mano de obra: El fenómeno migratorio a Europa durante el franquismo." *Historia social,* no. 30, 1998, pp. 63–81.

Fernández de Alba, Francisco. *Sex, Drugs, and Fashion in 1970s Madrid.* U of Toronto P, 2020.

Flesler, Daniela. *The Return of the Moor: Spanish Responses to Contemporary Moroccan Immigration.* Purdue UP, 2008.

Florido Berrocal, Joaquín. "José Antonio de La Loma: Un conquistador en el universo indígena del quinqui." *Fuera de la ley: Asedios al fenómeno quinqui en la Transición española,* edited by Joaquín Florido Berrocal et al., Editorial Comares, 2015, pp. 131–49

Folch, Enric. "At the Crossroads of Flamenco, New Flamenco and Spanish Pop: The Case of Rumba." *Made in Spain: Studies in Popular Music,* edited by Sílvia Martínez and Héctor Fouce, Routledge, 2013. 17–27.

Fouz-Hernández, Santiago, and Alfredo Martínez Expósito. *Live Flesh: The Male Body in Contemporary Spanish Cinema.* I.B. Tauris, 2007.

Fra-Molinero, Baltasar. "The Suspect Whiteness of Spain." *At Home and Abroad Historicizing Twentieth-Century Whiteness in Literature and Performance,* edited by La Vinia Delois Jennings, U of Tennessee P, 2010, pp. 147–69.

Fraguas, Rafael. "Seis mil guineanos viven marginados en España." *El País,* 29 July 1978, https://elpais.com/diario/1978/07/29/ultima/270511201_850215.html.

Fuchs, Barbara. *Exotic Nation: Maurophilia and the Construction of Early Modern Spain.* U of Pennsylvania P, 2011.

García Añón, José, et al. *Identificación policial por perfil étnico en España: Informe sobre experiencias y actitudes en relación con las actuaciones policiales.* Tirant lo Blanch, 2013.

García de León, María Antonia. "El paleto, un estigma del mundo rural." *La ciudad contra el campo (sociedad rural y cambio social)*, edited by María Antonia García de León and José María Aguilar Idáñez, Diputación de Ciudad Real, 1992, pp. 41–55.

García Sanz, Carolina. "Presuntos culpables: Un estudio de casos sobre el estigma racial del 'gitano' en juzgados franquistas de vagos y maleantes." *Historia social*, no. 93, 2019, pp. 145–66.

García-Egocheaga, Javier. *Minorías malditas: La historia desconocida de otros pueblos de España*. Tikal, 2003.

Gerehou, Moha and José Manuel Maroto Blanco. "'Estamos en ese punto en el que no vale con no ser racistas.' Conversaciones con Moha Gerehou." *Migraciones y población africana en España: Historias, relatos y prácticas de resistencia*, edited by José Manuel Maroto Blanco and Rosalía López Fernández, Editorial U de Granada, 2019, pp. 209–28.

Gómez-Caminero, Rubio. "¡Marroquíes avizor!" *Blanco y negro*, 23 August 1976, pp. 22–3.

Gómez-Sierra, Esther. "'Palaces of Seeds': From an Experience of Local Cinemas in Post-War Madrid to a Suggested Approach to Film Audiences." *Spanish Popular Cinema*, edited by Antonio Lázaro-Reboll and Andrew Willis, Manchester UP, 2004, pp. 92–112.

González, David. "La nueva imagen fornida de Santiago Abascal, el líder de VOX convertido en un 'involuntario' icono LGTB." *El cierre digital*, 27 October 2019, https://elcierredigital.com/ventana-indiscreta/312131704/santiago-abascal-vox-icono-LGTB.html.

González-Allende, Iker. "The Migrant Family Man: Masculinity, Work, and Migration in Víctor Canicio's *Vida de un emigrante español*." *Iberoamericana*, vol. 16, no. 62, 2016, pp. 131–47.

González-Leonardo, Miguel, Niall Newsham, and Francisco Rowe. "Understanding Population Decline Trajectories in Spain Using Sequence Analysis." *Geographical Analysis*, 2023, pp. 1–23.

González del Pozo, Jorge. *"Quinqui" Film in Spain: Peripheries of Society and Myths on the Margins*. Anthem Press, 2020.

Goode, Joshua. *Impurity of Blood: Defining Race in Spain, 1870-1930*. Louisiana State UP, 2009.

Goytisolo, Juan. "Fantasmas en las Canarias." *España y sus ejidos*, Hijos de Muley-Rubio, 2003, pp. 103–6.

Grace, Pamela. *The Religious Film: Christianity and the Hagiopic*. Wiley-Blackwell, 2010.Guasch, Oscar. *La sociedad rosa*. Anagrama, 1991.

Guglielmo, Thomas A. *White on Arrival: Italians, Race, Color and Power in Chicago, 1890-1945*. Oxford UP, 2004.

"Guinea en el día de la Hispanidad." *ABC*, 12 Oct. 1968.

Harris, Cheryl I. "Whiteness as Property." *Harvard Law Review*, vol. 106, no. 8, 1993, pp. 1707–91.

Harrison, Joseph. "Economic Crisis and Democratic Consolidation in Spain, 1973–82." *Universidad Carlos III, Departamento de Historia Económica e Instituciones, Working Papers in Economic History*, vol. 610, Jan. 2006.

Hernández, José Cabanes, et al. "Gitanos: Historia de una migración." *Alternativas. Cuadernos de Trabajo Social*, no. 4, Dec. 1996, pp. 87–97. *alternativasts.ua.es*, https://doi.org/10.14198/ALTERN1996.4.6.

Hill, Mike. *After Whiteness: Unmaking an American Majority*. New York UP, 2004.

Hogan, Erin K. *The Two Cines Con Niño: Genre and the Child Protagonist in over Fifty Years of Spanish Film (1955–2010)*. Edinburgh UP, 2018.

Howard-Wagner, Deirdre, et al., editors. *Unveiling Whiteness in the Twenty-First Century: Global Manifestations, Transdisciplinary Interventions*. Lexington Books, 2015.

Huerta Floriano, Miguel Ángel, and Ernesto Pérez Morán. *El "Cine de barrio" tardofranquista: Reflejo de una sociedad*. E-book ed., Editorial Biblioteca Nueva, 2012.

– *El cine popular del tardofranquismo*. E-book ed., Editorial Los Barruecos, 2012.

– "La comedia subgenérica de la Transición española: Paradojas en la tormenta." *Historia y Comunicacion Social*, vol. 23, no. 2, U Complutense de Madrid, Jan. 2018, pp. 389–404.

– "Las comedias de Mariano Ozores, Andrés Pajares y Fernando Esteso: Cartografía cinematográfica de un país en transición." *Bulletin of Spanish Visual Studies*, vol. 1, no. 2, Routledge, July 2017, pp. 245–64.

Hunter, Shona, and Christi Van der Westhuizen. *Routledge Handbook of Critical Studies in Whiteness*. Routledge, 2022.

Iannone, Catalina. *Contested Cities: Race, Culture and Urban Development in Madrid and Lisbon*. Book manuscript in progress.

– "Visualizing Blackness in Contemporary Spain: Race and Representation in Juan Valbuena's *Salitre*." *Hispania*, vol. 103, no. 3, 2020, pp. 357–72.

Ikaz, Javier. *Disparate nacional: El cine de Mariano Ozores*. Applehead Team, 2018.

Insúa, Alberto. *El Negro que tenía el alma blanca: Novela*. Renacimiento, 1922.

Izquierdo Escribano, Antonio. *La inmigración en España: 1980–1990*. Ministerio de Trabajo y Seguridad Social, 1992.

Jacobson, Matthew Frye. *Whiteness of a Different Color: European Immigrants and the Alchemy of Race*. Harvard UP, 2003.

Jennings, La Vinia Delois, ed. *At Home and Abroad: Historicizing Twentieth-Century Whiteness in Literature and Performance*. U of Tennessee P, 2010.

Jordan, Barry. "Lethal Franchise: The Evolution of the Torrente Saga (1998–2011)." *Studies in Spanish and Latin-American Cinemas*, vol. 11, no. 3, Sept. 2014, pp. 289–306.

Kali, Rebe. "Las gitanas no achantamos la muí." *Asociación Gitanas Feministas por la Diversidad*, 13 May 2018, https://www.gitanasfeministas.org /intervenciones/las-gitanas-nos-achantamos-la-mui/.

Kennedy, Tammie M., et al. "Introduction: Oxymoronic Whiteness – from the White House to Ferguson." *Rhetorics of Whiteness: Postracial Hauntings in Popular Culture, Social Media, and Education*, edited by Tammie M. Kennedy et al., Southern Illinois UP, 2017, pp. 1–18.

Kitossa, Tamari. *Appealing Because He Is Appalling: Black Masculinities, Colonialism, and Erotic Racism*. U of Alberta P, 2021.

Labanyi, Jo. "Internalisations of Empire: Colonial Ambivalence and the Early Francoist Missionary Film." *Discourse*, vol. 23, no. 1, 2001, pp. 25–42.

– "Musical Battles: Populism and Hegemony in the Early Francoist Folkloric Musical." *Constructing Identity in Contemporary Spain: Theoretical Debates and Cultural Practice*, edited by Jo Labanyi, Oxford UP, 2002, pp. 206–21.

Laguna, Asela. "Mito y leyenda colombinos: En busca de Cristóbal Colón en el cine." *L'Atalante*, no. 12, 2011, pp. 100–7.

Lara, Fernando. "'La Batalla de Argel,' de Gillo Pontecorvo: El nacimiento de una nación." *Triunfo*, no. 780, Jan. 1978, pp. 36–7.

Lázaro-Reboll, Antonio. *Spanish Horror Film*. Edinburgh UP, 2012.

Lázaro-Reboll, Antonio, and Andrew Willis. *Spanish Popular Cinema*. Manchester UP, 2004.

Levine-Rasky, Cynthia, ed. *Working through Whiteness: International Perspectives*. SUNY P, 2002.

Lipsitz, George. *The Possessive Investment in Whiteness: How White People Profit from Identity Politics*, Revised and Expanded Edition. Temple UP, 2006.

Lomas Martínez, Santiago. "Reflexividad e ironía autoconsciente en el cine musical español de los años setenta." *Quintana: Revista de estudios do Departamento de Historia da Arte*, no. 20, 2021, pp. 1–14.

Loomba, Ania. *Colonialism/Postcolonialism*. Routledge, 2007.

López, Alfred J. "Introduction: Whiteness after Empire." *Postcolonial Whiteness: A Critical Reader on Race and Empire*, edited by Alfred J. Lopez, SUNY P, 2005, pp. 1–30.

–, ed. *Postcolonial Whiteness: A Critical Reader on Race and Empire*. State U of New York P, 2005.

López Frías, David. "El crowdfunding nos devuelve a 'Los Bingueros.'" *El Español*, 6 Mar. 2016, https://www.elespanol.com/reportajes/20160305/107239424_0.html.

López de Lera, Diego. "La inmigración a España a fines del siglo XX: Los que vienen a trabajar y los que vienen a descansar." *REIS: Revista Española de Investigaciones Sociológicas*, no. 71, Centro de Investigaciones Sociológicas (CIS), 1995, pp. 225–48.

López García, Bernabé. "El Sahara y las relaciones hispano-marroquíes." *RIPS: Revista de Investigaciones Políticas y Sociclógicas*, vol. 12, no. 2, 2013, *www.usc.es*, http://www.usc.es/revistas/index.php/rips/article/view/1576.

López Simón, Íñigo. "El chabolismo vertical: Los movimientos migratorios y la política de vivienda franquista [1955–1975]." *Huarte de San Juan. Geografía e historia*, no. 25, U Pública de Navarra, 2018, pp. 173–92.

Maghbouleh, Neda. *The Limits of Whiteness: Iranian Americans and the Everyday Politics of Race*. Stanford UP, 2017.

Manganas, Nicholas. "Iberian Swagger vs. Feminist Masculinity: Populist Narratives Of Masculinity in Contemporary Spain." *The Culture and Politics of Populist Masculinities*, edited by Outi Hakola et al., Lexington Books, 2021, pp. 3–28.

Marí, Jorge. "El umbral del destape." *Valoración de Francisco Umbral: Ensayos críticos entorno a su obra*, edited by Carlos X. Ardavín, Libros del Pexe, 2003, pp. 242–58.

Mariscal, George. "The Role of Spain in Contemporary Race Theory." *Arizona Journal of Hispanic Cultural Studies*, vol. 2, 1998, pp. 7–22.

Marsh, Steven. *Popular Spanish Film under Franco: Comedy and the Weakening of the State*. Palgrave Macmillan, 2006.

Martín, Annabel. "The *Desarrollismo* Years: The Failures of Sexualised Nationhood in 1960s Spain." *Spanish Erotic Cinema*, edited by Santiago Fouz-Hernández, Edinburgh UP, 2017, pp. 55–73.

Martín Cabrera, Luis. "Los quinquis nunca fueron blancos: Infrarrealismo, interseccionalidad y postsoberanía en el cine de José Antonio de La Loma." *Fuera de la ley: Asedios al fenómeno quinqui en la Transición española*, edited by Joaquín Florido Berrocal et al., Editorial Comares, 2015, pp. 109–27.

Martín Palomo, María Teresa. "Mujeres gitanas y el sistema penal." *Revista de estudios de género: La ventana*, vol. 2, no. 15, Universidad de Guadalajara, 2002, pp. 149–74.

Martín Sánchez, David. *Historia del pueblo gitano en España*. Catarata, 2018.

Martin-Márquez, Susan. "De Cristo negro a Cristo hueco: Formulaciones de raza y religión en la Guinea española." *Memoria colonial e inmigración: La negritud en la España posfranquista*, Ediciones Bellaterrra, 2007, pp. 53–80.

– *Disorientations: Spanish Colonialism in Africa and the Performance of Identity*. Yale UP, 2008.

Martín-Santos, Luis. *Tiempo de silencio*. Bibliotex, 2001.

Martínez Martínez, Manuel. *Los forzados de marina en el siglo xviii: El caso de los gitanos*. U de Almería, 2007, https://dialnet.unirioja.es/servlet/tesis?codigo=218806.

Martínez-Sáez, Celia. "La persistencia de la mirada imperial: Imaginando el colonialismo de la Guinea Española a través del filme 'Palmeras en la nieve' (2015)." *Afro-Hispanic Review*, vol. 35, no. 2, 2016, pp. 26–39.

Mathijs, Ernest and Xavier Mendik. "Editorial Introduction: What Is Cult Film?" *The Cult Film Reader*, edited by Ernest Mathis and Xavier Mendik, Open UP, 2008, pp. 1–12.

Mbomío Rubio, Lucía Asué. *Hija del camino*. Grijalbo, 2020.

– *Las que se atrevieron*. Sial, 2017.

Mejón, Ana and Rubén Romero Santos. "Perdiendo el norte: Una brújula para la crisis." *Discursos de la crisis: Respuestas de la cultura española ante nuevos desafíos*, edited by Jochen Mecke, Ralf Junkerjürgen, and Hubert Pöppel, Iberoamericana, 2017, pp. 123–137.

Melero, Alejandro. "Hormones and Silk: Gay Men in the Spanish Film Comedies of the Transition to Democracy (1976–1981)." *Journal of Homosexuality*, vol. 60, no. 10, 2013, pp. 1450–74.

– *Placeres ocultos: Gays y lesbianas en el cine español de la transición*. Notorious, 2010.

– "Representation and Excess: *Diferente* (Luis M. Delgado, 1961) and *Marisol rumbo a Río* (Fernando Palacios, 1963)." Instituto Cervantes, https://cvc .cervantes.es/artes/cine/parejas/melero.htm?es. Accessed 15 Apr. 2022.

Merimee, Prosper. *Carmen*. Gallimard, 2018.

Merkens, Anne-Maria. "Nun Tells of Savage Beatings by Rebels in Congo: Recalls Wishing for Death as She Was Forced to Parade Naked through Street." *The New York Times*, 27 Nov. 1964.

Miguel Trula, Esther. "'Carmen y Lola': La película de amor lésbico entre gitanas denunciada por las propias gitanas." *Magnet*, 6 June 2018, https://magnet.xataka.com/preguntas-no-tan-frecuentes/ carmen-lola-pelicula-amor-lesbico-gitanas-denunciada-propias-gitanas.

Mira Delli-Zotti, Guillermo. "Voces distantes, otras miradas examinan el círculo de hierro: Política, emigración y exilio en la declinación Argentina." *América Latina Hoy*, vol. 34, 2003, pp. 119–43.

Moral, Ignacio del. *La mirada del hombre oscuro*. Sociedad General de Autores de España, 1992.

Moreno, Luis, and Amparo Serrano. "Europeanization and Spanish Welfare: The Case of Employment Policy." *The Spanish Welfare State in European Context*, edited by Ana Marta Guillén and Margarita León, Routledge, 2011, pp. 39–58.

Morrison, Toni. *Playing in the Dark: Whiteness and the Literary Imagination*. Vintage Books, 2019.

Mortensen, Viggo. "La torpeza política y mediática de Vox." *El País*, 7 May 2019, https://elpais.com/elpais/2019/05/06/opinion/1557155162_532764. html.

Mudde, Cas. *The Far Right Today*. Polity Press, 2020.

Muñoz, René. "A San Martín de Porres yo le debo mucho." *TVyNovelas*. n.d. Accessed June 12, 2022. https://fraymartindeporres.wordpress.com/2012 /11/25/entrevista-a-renemunoz-a-san-martin-de-porres-yo-le-debo-mucho /entrevista-1/.

Muñoz Martínez, Celeste. "África en nuestros archivos: La historia que aún no puede ser contada." *La necesidad de conocer África*, Dykinson, 2017, pp. 129–40.

Muñoz Sánchez, Antonio. "Una introducción a la historia de la emigración española en la República Federal de Alemania (1960–1980)." *Iberoamericana (2001–)*, vol. 12, no. 46, 2012, pp. 23–42.

Murray, N. Michelle. *Home away from Home: Immigrant Narratives, Domesticity, and Coloniality in Contemporary Spanish Culture*. U of North Carolina P, 2018.

– *Unsettling Colonialism*. SUNY P, 2020.

Ndongo Bidyogo, Ndongo. "Una nueva realidad: Los afro-españoles." Asociación Gerard, 11 Jan. 2011, http://gerardenlablog.blogspot.com/2011/11/una-nueva-realidad-los-afro-espanoles-i.html.

Negrete Peña, Rocío. "María Arondo, ¿una voz representativa de las 'bonnes' españolas en París? Clase, género, raza y migración." *Kamchatka: Revista de análisis cultural*, no. 14, 2019, pp. 203–22.

Nerín, Gustau. *Guinea Ecuatorial, historia en blanco y negro: Hombres blancos y mujeres negras en Guinea Ecuatorial, 1843–1968*. Península, 1998.

Oliver, Federico, and Alberto Insúa. *El negro que tenía el alma blanca: Adaptación teatral en seis jornadas de la célebre novela del mismo título de don Alberlo Insúa*. La Farsa, 1930.

Olney, Ian. *Euro Horror: Classic European Horror Cinema in Contemporary American Culture*. Indiana UP, 2013.

Orgaz Alonso, Christian. "Origen y codificación social en prensa del encierro de extranjeros/as en Centros de Internamiento (1985–2005)." Paper presented at XI Congreso Español de Sociología, U Complutense de Madrid, 10–12 July 2013, pp. 1–23.

Ortega-Rivera, Enrique, Andreu Domingo i Valls, and Albert Sabater Coll. "La emigración española en tiempos de crisis y austeridad." *Scripta Nova*, vol. 20, no. 549(5), 2016, pp. 1–29.

Oyewumi, Oyeronke. "Ties That (Un)Bind: Feminism, Sisterhood and Other Foreign Relations." *JENdA: A Journal of Culture and African Women Studies*, vol. 1, no. 1, 2001.

Pajares, Andrés. *Mis memorias ... antes de que se me olviden*. Editorial Almuzara, 2020.

Palacio Arranz, Manuel. *El público cinematográfico en España*. Liceus, 2005.

Palardy, Diana. "The Evolution of Conguitos: Changing the Face of Race in Spanish Advertising." *Transmodernity* vol. 4, no. 2, 2014.

Pallister-Wilkins, Polly. "The Tensions of the Ceuta and Melilla Border Fences." *EurAfrican Borders and Migration Management: Political Cultures, Contested Spaces, and Ordinary Lives*, edited by Paolo Gaibazzi, Stephen Dünnwald, and Alice Bellagamba, Palgrave Macmillian, 2016, pp. 63–81.

Pavlovic, Tatjana, and Inc NetLibrary. *Despotic Bodies and Transgressive Bodies: Spanish Culture from Francisco Franco to Jesús Franco.* SUNY P, 2003.

Pardo Sanz, Rosa. "La décolonisation de l'Afrique espagnole: Maroc, Sahara occidental et Guinée Équatoriale." *L'Europe face à son passé colonial,* edited by Olivier Dard and Daniel Lefeuvre, Riveneuve éditions, 2008, pp. 169–96.

– "La política descolonizadora de Castiella." *Entre la historia y la memoria: Fernando María Castiella y la política exterior de España (1957–1969).* Real Academia de Ciencias Morales y Políticas, 2007, pp. 81–134.

Pavlović, Tatjana. *Despotic Bodies and Transgressive Bodies: Spanish Culture from Francisco Franco to Jesús Franco.* SUNY P, 2002.

Pérez, Jorge. *Confessional Cinema: Religion, Film, and Modernity in Spain's Development Years, 1960–1975.* U of Toronto P, 2017.

– *Fashioning Spanish Cinema.* U of Toronto P, 2021.

Pérez, Raúl. *The Souls of White Jokes: How Racist Humor Fuels White Supremacy.* Stanford UP, 2022.

Pérez-Rodríguez, Paula. "Historia conceptual del quinqui: Pluriempleo, policía, prensa y mito." *Kamchatka. Revista de Análisis Cultural,* vol. 16, 2020, p. 55–91.

Persánch, J.M. "Introduction to the Special Issue: Another Turn of the Screw toward Hispanic and Lusophone Whiteness Studies." *Transmodernity,* vol. 8, no. 2, 2018, pp. 1–10.

–, ed. "Special Issue on Hispanic and Lusophone Whiteness Studies: Another Turn of the Screw towards Hispanic and Lusophone Whiteness Studies." *Transmodernity,* vol. 8, no. 2, 2018.

Premios Goya. "Mariano Ozores recibe el Goya de Honor 2016." Youtube, 1 March 2016, https://www.youtube.com/watch?v=vie_II_6x18&ab_channel=PremiosGoya.

Preston, Paul. *El triunfo de la democracia en España: De Franco a Felipe González pasando por Juan Carlos.* E-book ed., translated by Manuel Vázquez, Debate, 2018.

Prieto Souto, Xose Antonio. *Prácticas fílmicas de transgresión en el estado español (tardofranquismo y transición democrática).* 2015. U Carlos III Madrid, Phd dissertation.

"El rap viral 'Superfacha' de Vox, protagonizado por el simpatizante camerunés Bertrand Ndongo." *Antena 3 Noticias,* 26 Apr. 2019, https://www.antena3.com/noticias/elecciones/elecciones-generales/rap-viral-superfacha-vox-protagonizado-simpatizante-camerunes-bertrand-ndongo_201904265cc2de650cf2f1f694a3d90e.html.

Repinecz, Martin. "Don Quijote in Africa: Fictionality as an Antidote to Racism." *Bulletin of Hispanic Studies,* vol. 94, no. 6, 2017, pp. 607–23.

– "'Salvaje primitiva, como vosotros': Race Camp in Almodóvar's Cinema." *Revista de Estudios Hispánicos,* vol. 51, no. 3, 2017, pp. 513–41.

– *Transmodernity* (Special issue: Theorizing and Decentering Luso/Hispanic Whiteness), vol. 8, no. 2, 2018, pp. 91–109.

Richardson, Matt. "Ajita Wilson: Blaxploitation, Sexploitation, and the Making of Black Womanhood." *TSQ: Transgender Studies Quarterly*, vol. 7, no. 2, May 2020, pp. 192–207.

Rincón, Sofía. "Superfacha" (with Bertrand N'dongo). *Youtube*, 29 May 2020, https://www.youtube.com/watch?v=cIFNCF98kwc&ab_channel=Sof%C3%ADaRinc%C3%B3n-Topic.

Río Ruiz, Manuel. "Políticas de realojo, comunidad gitana y conflictos urbanos en España. 1980–2000)." *Quid 16. Revista del Área de Estudios Urbanos*, no. 4, Nov. 2014, pp. 34–61.

Reybrouck, David Van. *Congo: The Epic History of a People*. Harper Collins, 2015.

Richardson, Nathan E. *Postmodern Paletos: Immigration, Democracy, and Globalization in Spanish Narrative and Film, 1950–2000*. Bucknell UP, 2002.

Riquer i Permanyer, Borja de. "Social and Economic Change in a Climate of Political Immobilism." *Spanish Cultural Studies: An Introduction*. Ed. Helen Graham and Jo Labanyi, Oxford UP, 1995, pp. 259–71.

Rodríguez Veiga, Diego. "Así se machaca el 'toro' Abascal en el gimnasio: Lo que esconde su chaqueta a punto de estallar." *El Español,* 16 Nov. 2019, https://www.elespanol.com/reportajes/20191116/machaca-abascal-gimnasio-esconde-chaqueta-punto-estallar/444706532_0.html.

Roediger, David R. *Wages of Whiteness: Race and the Making of the American Working Class*. Verso, 2022.

Romei, Valentina. "In Charts: Europe's Demographic Time-Bomb." *Financial Times*, 13 Jan. 2020, https://www.ft.com/content/49e1e106-0231-11ea-b7bc-f3fa4e77dd47.

Rosendorf, Neal Moses. "'Hollywood in Madrid': American Film Producers and the Franco Regime, 1950–1970." *Historical Journal of Film, Radio and Television*, vol. 27, no. 1, Routledge, Mar. 2007, pp. 77–109.

Rubiano Segovia, Sonia. "Melilla y la Ley de Extranjería de 1985. Trascendencia internacional de un conflicto local. Análisis de tres periódicos." *NORBA: Revista de historia*, vol. 33, 2020, pp. 245–74.

Ruiz Castillo, Marta. "Santiago Abascal, vuelve el hombre." *The Objective,* 29 Apr. 2019, https://theobjective.com/further/espana/2019-04-29/santiago-abascal-vuelve-el-hombre/.

Rumford, Chris. "Introduction: Theorizing Borders." *European Journal of Social Theory*, vol. 9, no. 2, 2006, pp. 155–69.

Saavedra, Rafa. "Procesos de realojo de población gitana en España. Consecuencias de prácticas basadas en antigitanismo." *Antigitanismo: Trece miradas*, Traficantes de Sueños, 2021, pp. 251–62.

Sainz de la Peña, José Antonio. "La política de inmigración en España." *Flujos migratorios norteafricanos hacia la Unión Europea: Asociación y diplomacia preventiva,* edited by Antonio Marquina Barrio, Agencia Española de Cooperación Internacional, 1997, pp. 123–88.

San Román, Teresa. *La diferència inquietant: Velles i noves estratègies culturals dels gitanos.* Fundació Serveis de Cultura Popular: Alta Fulla, 1998.

Santamaría Ibeas, J. J. "Los derechos fundamentales y el tribunal constitucional. Los infraderechos de los extranjeros en España. Reflexiones sobre la jurisprudencia constitucional." *Derechos y Libertades,* no. 2, 1993–1994, pp. 495–518.

Santaolalla, Isabel. *Los otros: Etnicidad y raza en el cine español contemporáneo.* PU de Zararagoza, 2005.

"Santi Abascal 'reconquista' Andalucía a caballo y las redes se llenan de memes." *El Mundo,* 12 Nov. 2018, https://www.elmundo.es/f5 /comparte/2018/11/12/5be9beeb468aeb8e558b45b4.html.

Schlumpf, Sandra. "Construcción del colectivo guineoecuatoriano en España a través de la prensa: El País y La Vanguardia (2010–2018)." *Discurso and Sociedad,* vol. 13, no. 2, 2019, pp. 287–324.

Smidakova, Bohumira. *El espectro de la figura gitana en el cine español.* 2016. Georgetown U., PhD dissertation.

"Spain and the European Union." *Ministerio de Asuntos Exteriores, Unión Europea, y Cooperación,* https://www.exteriores.gob.es/en/PoliticaExterior /Paginas/EspanaUE.aspx. Accessed 26 Apr. 2023.

St Louis, Brett. "Can Race Be Eradicated? The Post-Racial Problematic." *Theories of Race and Ethnicity: Contemporary Debates and Perspectives,* edited by John Solomos and Karim Murji, Cambridge UP, 2014, pp. 114–38.

Stallaert, Christiane. *Etnogénesis y etnicidad en España: Una aproximación histórico-antropológica al casticismo.* Proyecto A Ediciones, 1998.

Stoler, Ann Laura. "Colonial Aphasia: Race and Disabled Histories in France." *Public Culture,* vol. 23, no. 1, Jan. 2011, pp. 121–56.

Stone, Rob. *Spanish Cinema.* Routledge, 2016.

Stucki, Andreas. *Violence and Gender in Africa's Iberian Colonies: Feminizing the Portuguese and Spanish Empire, 1950s–1970s.* Palgrave Macmillan, 2019.

Surwillo, Lisa. *Monsters by Trade: Slave Traffickers in Modern Spanish Literature and Culture.* Stanford UP, 2020.

Thomas, Sarah. *Inhabiting the In-between: Childhood and Cinema in Spain's Long Transition.* U of Toronto P, 2019.

Tornos, Andrés. "La investigación sobre migraciones en España." Instituto Universitario de Estudios sobre Migraciones para el Observatorio Permanente de la Inmigración, U Pontificia Comillas, 2002, pp. 1–46.

Tur, Bruno. "'Et viva Conchita!' Le stéréotype de la 'bonne à tout faire' espagnole dans la chanson française (années 1960–1970)." *Volume!,* vol. 12, no. 1, pp. 71–83.

Triana-Toribio, Núria. "Santiago Segura: Just When You Thought That Spanish Masculinities Were Getting Better ..." *Hispanic Research Journal*, vol. 5, no. 2, June 2004, pp. 147–56.

– *Spanish National Cinema*. Routledge, 2003.

Ugarte, Michael. *Africans in Europe: The Culture of Exile and Emigration from Equatorial Guinea to Spain*. U of Illinois P, 2010.

Valencia-García, Louie Dean. *Antiauthoritarian Youth Culture in Francoist Spain: Clashing with Fascism*. Bloomsbury, 2020.

Vázquez Montalbán, Manuel. *Crónica sentimental de España*. DeBolsillo, 2003.

– "Los gitanos catalanes." *Triunfo*, vol. 21, no. 389, 1969, pp. 14–17.

Vega-Durán, Raquel. *Emigrant Dreams, Immigrant Borders: Migrants, Transnational Encounters, and Identity in Spain*. Bucknell UP, 2016.

Vegas, Valeria. *Libérate: La cultura LGBTQ que abrió camino en España*. Dos Bigotes, 2020.

"Vetadas Gitanas Feministas por la directora de «Carmen y Lola»." *Asociación Gitanas Feministas por la Diversidad*, 2 June 2018, https://www .gitanasfeministas.org/comunicados/vetadas-gitanas-feministas-por-la -directora-de-carmen-y-lola/.

Vieten, Ulrike M., and Scott Poynting. "Contemporary Far-Right Racist Populism in Europe." *Journal of Intercultural Studies*, vol. 37, no. 6, Nov. 2016, pp. 533–40.

Vox Noticias. "La reconquista comenzará en tierras andaluzas." *Twitter*, 12 Nov. 2018, 1:45 a.m., https://twitter.com/voxnoticias_es/status /1061917901031129088?lang=en.

Wheeler, Duncan. "The Future of Nostalgia: Reinvindicating Spanish Actors and Acting in and through Cine de Barrio." *Performance and Spanish Film*, edited by Dean Allbritton et al., 2016, pp. 142–58.

Whittaker, Tom. *The Spanish Quinqui Film: Delinquency, Sound, Sensation*. Manchester UP, 2020.

Wiegman, Robyn. "Whiteness Studies and the Paradox of Particularity." *Boundary 2*, vol. 26, no. 3, 1999, pp. 115–50.

Woods Peiró, Eva. *White Gypsies Race and Stardom in Spanish Musicals*. U of Minnesota P, 2012.

"Y el Goya de Honor es para ... Mariano Ozores." Premios Goya, 2016, https:// www.premiosgoya.com/los-goya/goyas-de-honor/mariano-ozores/.

Zamora Loboch, Francisco. *Cómo ser negro y no morir en Aravaca*. Ediciones B, 1994.

– "Estefanía." *Memoria De Laberintos*. Madrid: SIAL, 1999, pp. 49–50.

Permissions

Index

Toronto Iberic